Bobby Rich

My Life in Your Radio

by Pat Gaffey

Gleneealy Press

Book cover and interior design by Timothy W. Brittain

ISBN: 979-8-9934068-0-0 (paperback)
979-8-9934068-1-7 (hardback)
Also available as a Kindle book
Printed in the U.S.A.

Dedication

TO ANNIE, *who gave me the idea to write this book and the encouragement to complete it.*

Contents

Preface

I would have finished this book a whole lot sooner if only I hadn't started writing it so long ago.

The seed of an idea for a Bobby Rich book germinated in New England in 2013 and sprouted in Arizona when he heartily accepted my out-of-the-blue offer to write his authorized biography.

I figured Bobby was probably close to wrapping up his career because he'd been disc jockeying since the 1960s, for crying out loud. And Bobby probably figured I'd be prompt in turning out the book because of my availability (unemployed) and experience (former news reporter) writing on deadline.

To our mutual surprise, he decided to work another ten years before retiring from radio and I landed a new job that required full-time attention for another eight. The book got put on the back burner until my own retirement and relocation. Research and writing resumed in 2022.

I began the project while living in Connecticut, then moved to Mas sachusetts, and completed the manuscript in 2025 after moving back t California. A handful of chapters were composed in the Mojave Dese and south of the border in Jalisco, Mexico.

Bobby, in Arizona the entire time, made himself available for rec ring telephone interviews. We each took multiple road trips betw Tucson and San Diego for in-person reviews of the manuscript, phc and audio tapes.

As a reporter and corporate communications specialist for four decades, I wrote oodles of stories about people who led lives of great accomplishment and simple pleasure. People who witnessed and contributed to historic events, endured unthinkable tragedy, and experienced abundant joy.

It always fascinated me to encounter someone in a job that she or he totally enjoyed, individuals so perfectly suited for their chosen profession that it didn't even seem like work. Bobby is one of those people. The man was born to be a broadcaster. All he ever wanted to do is make great radio.

His guidance to DJs at the start of their shift was always simple. "Have fun," he instructed, "and sound like it." I adopted that same mindset at the start of this project.

Instinctively, I followed my journalistic training and methods in approaching the subject. Admittedly, it was not possible to be entirely objective about Bobby.

We are, after all, kind of like brothers. Not siblings who shared a bedroom as kids growing up, but broadcast brethren who shared a studio for five years in adulthood. Bobby chose me, Scott Kenyon, and Frank Anthony to be his Rich Brothers for a rise-and-shine radio show at B-100 FM in San Diego. With Bobby as ringmaster, the four of us had a blast doing our silly and serious *B Morning Zoo* from 1984 to 1989.

Having also worked with him at K-HITS in Los Angeles, I had first-hand knowledge of Bobby and two stations where he was my boss and colleague.

This created a dilemma decades later, when deciding how to appropriately acknowledge my own connection to Bobby's career. As author, I chose to write this book using the third-person point of view. Only in chapters 33 and 37 did I shift my narrative style to employ the first-person POV. This avoided the awkwardness of characterizing myself

as an outside observer when in fact I was an active participant in the events being described.

Some blurring of the lines between biography and autobiography occurred with Bobby's contribution of a set of personal reflections written in his first-person POV. The passages composed by Bobby are differentiated by the vinyl record symbols and distinctive shading of chapters 6, 14, 16, 20, 25, 31, 38, 43, 45, 47, and 48.

None of the writing of this book was generated by artificial intelligence (AI).

All my research was conducted by sifting through publicly available information and asking questions of individuals with personal memories and pertinent documents. Sixty years of Bobby's quasi-celebrityhood offered plenty of material for examination.

I took copious notes of my weekly interviews with him and my ad hoc interviews with more than fifty radio people representing a cross section of his coworkers, employees, bosses, and listeners.

My notes of these in-person and telephone conversations, conducted over a twelve-year period, were electronically cataloged for retrieval of accurate quotes and descriptions.

All participants were generous in sharing their stories and granting permission to use their names and comments.

Passages with attribution were excerpted from books, blog posts, emails, online comments, and station histories written by other jocks, programmers, and industry columnists.

Extensive digging through digitized back issues of industry magazines *Broadcasting* and *Billboard* and the trade paper *Radio & Records* yielded relevant articles, columns, profiles, blurbs, and ads. Online copies of *The Gavin Report* and *Cashbox* were additional sources for information and fact-checking. *Billboard*'s Hot 100 music charts provided historical data on the national performance of hit songs and albums.

In many of the fifteen cities where Bobby was an air personality, I was able to access archives of local newspapers that reported on him and his station's music, concerts, and contests.

Listening to stacks of old airchecks and cassette tape recordings of shows from nearly two dozen stations yielded verbatim accounts of DJ banter, commercials, and news reports from his past.

All the above primary and secondary sources were valuable in verifying names, dates, places, hirings, firings, promotions, ratings reports, and programming notes.

When two or three people who experienced the same event told me differing versions, every effort was made to include aspects of each account in a triangulated description.

It was not feasible to mention everyone who ever worked with Bobby from the 1960s to the 2020s. Any unintentional glaring omissions may be attributed to pre-internet data preservation methods, loss of garage and public storage spaces, and fading memory/memories.

In my first career, the demanding pace of broadcast journalism required news stories to be hammered out in minutes or hours. Same-day turnaround was the norm. I never had an assignment that took more than a decade to complete . . . until this one.

By trusting me to tell his life story, Bobby received my commitment to stick with it as long as necessary. I pushed that boundary to the limit and delivered the most thorough biography I could imagine.

His eagerness for me to hurry up and finish the manuscript was offset by an openness to add any "late-breaking" content that would advance the narrative. "We're only going to do this one book," Bobby insisted, "so let's get all the best stuff in there."

A prolonged timeline allowed the addition of several "must have" anecdotes that only surfaced in 2025. For a book twelve years in the making, we planned to celebrate its publication with appropriate song (Tom Petty's "The Waiting") and bourbon, well-aged.

My completion of the manuscript brought a shared sense of fulfillment that echoed Bobby's self-description of his life on the radio.

"Maybe not changing the world but making people happy seemed like a pretty good thing to do."

Chapter 1

Destined to Be on the Radio

Bobby Rich named himself for a life in show business.

At the age of ten, he knew exactly what he wanted to do in the world and proclaimed his intention to be a radio announcer. At fourteen, he had achieved that goal and for the next sixty-plus years he stayed true to the dream.

Landing his first professional disc jockey gig as a freshman in high school, he crafted an influential career in fifteen cities across eleven states. Along the way, he became a program director, general manager, and station co-owner.

Bobby's gift for blending hit music, local content, and relevant humor inspired hundreds of talented DJs and reached a collective audience of millions with a brand of personality radio he designed to make people smile.

Billboard magazine presented him with a Program Director of the Year award in 1987, based on nationwide voting by industry peers. He took B-100 FM to number one in the San Diego ratings and to Station of the Year honors in *Billboard's* Adult Contemporary (AC) medium market field.

Small-town start, big-city finish

He grew up in a town of five thousand people and was recruited by broadcast executives to work in three of the nation's top five media markets. "I never chose New York or Los Angeles or Philly," Bobby said. "They chose me.

"Until Paul Drew called to offer me a job offer at KHJ, it never crossed my mind that I'd be working in LA. It wasn't even on my wish list. I just wanted to be at great radio stations where I could keep learning and add to the excitement."

He did not chart a strategic career map or follow a blueprint for bouncing back after getting sacked in more than a half dozen cities. "I never really had a plan B, much less a plan A," Bobby said. "I suppose just being on the radio was my A, and B was to keep doing it."

His booming voice, contagious laugh, on-air excitement, and audience interaction were recognizable on KHJ, KFI, K-HITS, 99X, WWSH, B-100, KFMB, KMGI, KMXZ, KDRI, and a multitude of other stations.

Rock stars and heartthrobs

In New York, he helped make Meat Loaf into one of the best-selling musicians of all time, giving his *Bat Out of Hell* album steady airplay and arranging in-studio visits for the operatic rocker.

Bobby rode on a float with the Village People in the 1978 Macy's Thanksgiving Day parade, introduced the Beach Boys at stadium concerts in Southern California, and chauffeured Mickey Dolenz to a performance on the day that Monkees bandmate Peter Tork got punched in the face by a surly senior citizen.

Sponsoring a public appearance for teen idol Leif Garrett but forgetting to provide security guards, Bobby witnessed a throng of overexcited teenage girls initiate a near-riot in a San Diego pizza parlor.

He got away with an assortment of audacious radio pranks. University of Arizona basketball coach Lute Olson and Chicago Cubs third baseman Ron Cey were two targets of his on-air practical jokes.

Hired by twenty-four stations, Bobby was fired nine times. After every dismissal, he was welcomed back to another spot on the AM or FM dial.

In an era when getting high at work was overlooked by some employers in the radio and music industries, he never did illegal drugs but once quit a job because of others who did.

A magical life

Bobby's start as a broadcaster can be traced to his childhood bedroom in the 1950s, where a plastic microphone, hobby shop transmitter, and borrowed record player were all the equipment he needed to put on a nightly show for his sisters and parents. They listened in the dining room of their home in Ephrata, Washington.

He soon discovered a playground of magical toys in the town's only radio station and a Peter Pan recipe for endless childhood, fabulous adventures, and free passes to the theater of the mind. Peter could fly. Bobby lived on the air.

His entry into the world of make-believe was part romance, part fantasy.

A mysterious woman's voice emanating from a remote hilltop in Eastern Washington reached a nearby village via electromagnetic waves. A curious schoolboy followed the sound to its source. Arriving at a simple cement bungalow beside a transmission tower, he climbed up to the studio window and peeked inside.

Alone in her control room filled with electrified machines, meters, and dials, she released captivating stories and invisible music into the atmosphere. To Bobby's delight, she secretly imparted the power to make people listen, laugh, dance, and even skip school. The youngster was spellbound by the magic of it all.

Having seen behind the curtain, he became enchanted by radio.

There was no turning back. He followed his infatuation to faraway lands of amusement and showmanship.

The long and winding roadmap

As a seventeen-year-old, Bobby was confronted by his older sister, Jan, who had already earned a university degree. She tried to talk him out of becoming an announcer because she felt it was not a long-term or worthy profession.

"Oh man, that pissed me off," he said. "I got all puffed up and told her that I was put here to do something, and it was to be on the radio.

"And there will always be radio!"

Jan may have been the last to question her brother's determination. After several semesters of college broadcasting, he was hired at five stations in the Northwest before graduating to more prominent jobs in the Midwest, Northeast, Southeast, and ultimately Southwest.

Play and no play

The story of Bobby's nomadic and accomplished professional life celebrates the glory years of rock'n'roll, Top 40, and Hot AC. It's a greatest hits collection of his many radio friends. A mixtape of disc jockeys he emulated, hired, and coached. Homage to generations of AM and FM listeners who tuned in for favorite songs, likable personalities, and positive vibes. Credit to the precious few bosses who had his back. Commentary on many more who kicked his keister to the curb.

His philosophy was consistent in every era, city, and format. "I believe in having fun on the radio, appealing to the widest possible listening audience."

Known for selecting the hottest music with the broadest appeal, he also earned attention for choosing not to play certain popular songs and artists.

With the *Saturday Night Fever* soundtrack album dominating the airwaves in 1978, Bobby declared a "No Bee Gees Weekend" in New York. His trick to suspend the chart-topping "Night Fever" and every other title by the Bee Gees or Andy Gibb lasted forty-eight hours. "The record label didn't love it, but I knew people would talk about it," he said.

A year later, when Sister Sledge had the number one song, he imposed a "No Disco Weekend" with a tongue-in-cheek broadcast warning that any disco music played by one of his DJs would be considered grounds for immediate dismissal.

In Philadelphia, Bobby ran a "No Michael Jackson Weekend" during the King of Pop's heyday in 1984. Again, the publicity stunt achieved the desired effect of gaining media coverage and creating a buzz with listeners.

Give them something to smile about

"I don't have any high opinion of what I do or what I say. It's the fact that any little thing can make a difference to someone tuning in," Bobby said. "And if that's just being there to play the songs and say good morning and here's what time it is and here's what the weather's going to be, that's great.

"When I can add something informative or educational in any way to someone's life that gets them to say, 'Hey, that's interesting, I never knew that before,' or 'I'm gonna try that,' or 'I'm gonna look into that' or whatever, that's fantastic."

Pouring heart, soul, and life savings into a station that went bust in the early 1990s didn't dampen his passion. He continued well into the next century.

The broadcasting business underwent continuous transformation, the public's musical tastes shifted, and Bobby rolled with the changes. He played pop and rock songs at turntable speeds of 45 rpm, 78 rpm, and 33⅓ rpm until vinyl albums were replaced by tape machines, CDs, and digital files.

MTV, VH1, MP3s, Spotify, Apple, Google, YouTube, satellite, internet, and on-demand music streaming splintered the traditional radio audience. But the competition from next-generation media couldn't steal Bobby's voice or replace his personality on the airwaves.

Through it all, he kept adapting. Learning new tech and techniques, keeping current. Creating live and local content. Connecting with people through a microphone.

At age seventy-three, he started a new radio station with a music format and personalities appealing to baby boomers and pre-boomers.

A public love affair

Before the Beatles made their first American TV appearance on *The Ed Sullivan Show* in 1964, Bobby was a college DJ spinning their records on the radio. He was still on the air in 2023, the year that the Beatles' final single, "Now and Then," was released with state-of-the-art sound separation and machine learning.

At his induction into the Arizona Broadcasters Hall of Fame, Bobby said, "I do what I love. I love what I do. And I love my life."

The public romance lasted because people embraced his presence in the privacy of their daily routine. Waking to Bobby's familiar voice each morning, they made him an invisible breakfast guest at home and their director of entertainment on the road.

Accepting his award from the Arizona broadcasters in 2013, he celebrated his long-term affection for the listeners who welcomed him into their lives on AM, FM, and internet stations across America.

"If I can make them happy, that's the biggest key," Bobby said. "And not necessarily by telling jokes, but by just being a happy person myself, having a positive attitude, and translating that into the format of a radio show."

Chapter 2

This Thing That I Do

Wake up before the crack of dawn every morning. Make the day's first pot of coffee. Shower, trim beard, and drive to the station in darkness. Bring headphones, a show prep folder of topics, and mental notebook of fresh ideas to sustain four hours of on-air conversation.

Enter the studio, share the microphone with friendly broadcast partners and listeners. Entertain an unseen audience, countless thousands of people tuning in to start their morning with familiar radio voices, music, news and traffic reports, smiles and laughter.

"This thing that I do," Bobby said, "is a boyhood dream come true. The magic of radio made real.

"I think often about my fifth-grade teacher, Roger Holman, who produced a yearbook for our class. There were like twenty-three of us and he took all the pictures and went down to the drug store and had copies made. Then he put together a little booklet, and we all pasted the pictures in and created our mini-biographies. One of the topics was 'What do you want to be when you grow up?'

"And I didn't answer disc jockey because I didn't really know the term back then. But I put down radio announcer. And Mr. Holman changed it to entertainer because he didn't think that radio announcer was a valid or good enough career. It really angered me that he did that, and I didn't find out until he handed us our yearbooks at the end of the school year."

Bobby gave his teacher high marks as an educator, if not an editor. "He was a really cool teacher, and I liked him," Bobby said. "Years later, my family took me to visit him. He had moved to Seattle, and we went over to his place and sat and talked. I asked him why he did that, changing my yearbook entry. And he said, 'Well, you have a lot of abilities, and I see you as being more than just a radio announcer.' And I said, 'Yeah, but that's what I want to be.'"

Mr. Holman, it turns out, was right about how much more Bobby would achieve.

Chapter 3

Shoeshines and Bowling Balls

On the way to radio stardom, Bobby paid his dues shining shoes. And deodorizing them.

"I had various businesses that I ran out of my bedroom as a child," he said. "They included a sign company, which is pretty funny because I have no artistic talent whatsoever. My only client was the Ephrata Bowling Center, operated by Howard A. Nessen, my father.

"I remember when our grandparents came to visit, I had my sign company sign on my bedroom door and I tried to explain to them what that meant and they didn't get it. I got embarrassed and soon made an exit sign for myself.

"Next, I did shoeshines at the barber shop in our town," Bobby reminisced. "My motivation was to save up for a summer camping trip. I made enough money to pay my half so that my dad would send me to the Boy Scout Jamboree in Colorado Springs."

"For twenty-five cents, I'd shine the businessmen's shoes while they were having their hair cut. Which meant that I couldn't jiggle the customers. So, I learned to be a nonjiggler," he said.

The importance of steady hands carried over into Bobby's later employment in the bowling and broadcasting industries.

"Of course, I worked for my dad at the bowling center back in the days before automatic pinsetters. As the kid in the pit, after every break of the pins I'd jump down and pick 'em up, put 'em in the overhead rack thing. Then I'd grab the bowling ball and put it in the return rack. So that was really exciting," he joked.

"I was also an expert at spraying shoes, the rental bowling shoes, with that bad-smelling foot spray stuff. That was kind of my claim to fame," Bobby humbly recalled.

His next employment opportunity came with the advent of bowling balls made of colored plastic. The Columbia 300, invented in Ephrata, provided an unbreakable alternative to the plain black Ebonite balls that had dominated the sport.

Once again, Bobby chased a dream job. When not setting pins and disinfecting shoes, he accompanied his father on bowling ball sales trips throughout the Northwest.

"My dad had a Chrysler Imperial, desert rose color. Everyone called it pink, and he hated that. 'No, it's not pink. It's desert rose,' he'd insist. We'd fill the trunk of his car with the latest product and head out to call on all the bowling centers in the region. This was 1962 and '63. He was just getting the ball rolling."

The father-son duo enjoyed their time together on the road, listening to the car radio to help pass the time. But Bobby decided against a career in the family bowling business. He didn't see a great future in plastics.

His brief stint going door-to-door for the Fuller Brush company also helped to steer the young entrepreneur away from a career as a traveling salesman.

Ultimately, Bobby chose broadcasting over brushes, bowling balls, and barber shops.

Chapter 4

Story Lady Lures Local Boy into Life of Radio

Bobby's inspiration to be on the radio began with the enchanting Story Lady of Ephrata.

"When I was about ten years old, my best friend Warren Olson and I went hiking up Beezley Hill one Saturday morning. About halfway up the hill, we stopped at the transmitter site of KULE, the only radio station in our town," Bobby said.

"It was a daytime-only AM, still doing live programming out of the transmitter building because they didn't have a studio built in downtown Ephrata yet. I remember peeking through the window and catching a glimpse of the KULE Story Lady reading a children's book into the microphone.

"She looked like a librarian, with little spectacles and her hair in a bun. Wearing a gingham peasant dress, she somehow resembled a mature Natalie Wood. At least, that's how I remember it.

"But it was all the equipment surrounding her that really grabbed my attention. Microphones, reel-to-reel tape decks, consoles with buttons and lights flashing, and a wall of 45 rpm records in individual green cardboard sleeves, which I later learned were known as shucks.

"There was something magical about seeing her on that Saturday morning, and I just thought that was really cool."

One glance at the Story Lady and Bobby had fallen under the spell of radio.

He didn't knock on the door that day, but soon returned, stepping through the KULE portal into a life of broadcasting.

Front-row seat in small-town radio

"By the time I was a fifth grader, I was ready to make some contacts at the station. So, I walked in one day and told them I was doing a story for the school newspaper," Bobby said. "We didn't have a school paper. But I always figured they let me in because my dad owned the bowling center in town and was an advertiser, so they probably thought, 'Oh, it's Howard's kid. We'll be nice to him.'

"Jerry Robinson was chief engineer and midday announcer on KULE. He was a great guy and taught me a lot about the business. For hours and hours, every Saturday morning and during the summer when I wasn't in school, Jerry let me sit on the floor in the back of the room and just watch him work."

With access to the production booth, Bobby learned to play records and tape record himself. Eventually, he was ready to take on the awesome responsibilities of a radio gofer.

"I went around to all the remote broadcasts and station appearances. At the county fair they let me run wires across the dirt from the electrical outlet to where we set up our broadcast table."

The kid who loved to hang around the station was given free rein of the building and its basement. There he found treasure.

"My favorite part," said Bobby, "was emptying the trash cans next to the teletype machine because I'd dig out all the thrown-away news copy and commercials.

"The National Association of Broadcasters used to send out sample ad copy so local salespeople could take it and just plug in, you know, John's Auto Repair Shop offers this and that. I collected those commercials and issues of *Broadcasting Telecasting* that had not only articles, but pictures of equipment."

Fascinated with radio studio setups, he cut out pictures of turntables, mics, and consoles from the discarded trade magazines and pinned them to a corkboard at home.

Dinner and a show

Home was where Bobby established a primitive but functional broadcast system. "Initially it was a battery-powered microphone with a long cord attached to a little rinky-dink plastic speaker designed for a model train setup to announce the arrival of the trains," he explained.

"By running extra wire, I could be back in my bedroom and the speaker could be out in the dining room. And every night I'd do a radio show from my room, eating dinner off a TV tray that my mom would bring in to me.

"While my parents and sisters sat at the dining room table, I provided the nightly entertainment. It was quite a challenge because the microphone had a press-to-talk button, so I had to figure out some way, probably with rubber bands, to keep the mic open when I played 45s on my sister's record player.

"I would talk, read a commercial for my dad's bowling center, and do a couple news stories pulled from the trash can at KULE. Then I'd put on a song, lay the microphone down next to the speaker, and have a few bites of dinner while the record played. That was my first radio station."

It wasn't long before Bobby invested in more powerful equipment to reach an even bigger audience. "For under twelve dollars you could buy from Radio Shack, and I still have it, an actual transmitter that was tunable and you could set it to broadcast on an AM radio.

"My friend Jerry the engineer did a little hot wiring for me. He tinkered with some wires wrapped around a coil inside of this little transmitter and extended my antenna up to the roof of our house. That gave me a broadcast coverage of about one square mile. Nobody ever listened outside of me and my friend Warren, but still, I had a radio station of my own."

In his early teens, having logged countless hours of amateur announcing practice and preparation, Bobby was about to turn pro.

Chapter 5

Pussyface and His Orchestra

For someone who would make a career of talking on the radio, it's only fitting that Bobby talked his way into his first paid job as an announcer.

Ephrata's only licensed station was KULE AM 730, airing a middle of the road (MOR) format that featured mostly pop hits by singers such as Doris Day and Robert Goulet.

The KULE call letters were pronounced "Coo-lee," like the Grand Coulee Dam on the nearby Columbia River. DJs referred to their broadcast territory as "Coulee Land," gave temperature readings from the "Coulee-ometer," and did their own "rip 'n' read" news reports using headlines from the UPI and AP wire services.

Having listened to the station for his entire boyhood, Bobby at age fourteen pitched a bold idea that would mark his transition from radio listener to programmer. He suggested a new show on KULE and convinced station management that he should host it.

"I went in and said, you know what would be interesting to a lot of people would be high school news. And they said okay. So, they gave me a weekly time slot to do the news for the one high school in Ephrata," Bobby recalled.

Coulee Land teen time

"Our town had a population of about five thousand. The nearby towns were Quincy, Moses Lake, and Soap Lake. All the high schools put out a newspaper, usually once a week, some of them once a month. So, I got on their mailing list, and they'd send me their papers. From that I would assemble the *KULE High School News Report*, which aired Fridays at 3:55 p.m.

"After doing that for a few months, the station manager asked me if I would come in and work on a Saturday afternoon. I thought that meant either cleaning the basement or dragging a bunch of dusty wires to a remote broadcast. I said, 'Sure, what do you want me to do?' And he replied, 'Well, we want you to go on the air!' So, that was my first time being a real DJ.

"Secret Love" by Doris Day was the first record he played at KULE.

"I remember that I had to write down every title and artist so that when I opened the microphone at the end of the song, I'd know what to say. Word for word, I was reading cue cards.

"That was 'Smoke Gets in Your Eyes' by the Platters on KULE . . . and here's another song," the young DJ announced.

"I had no idea, really, and for a minute there, I thought this is never going to work," Bobby said. "The difference between practicing in a production room or my bedroom to suddenly being on a legit radio station of 1,000 watts, broadcasting to a real live audience was unbelievable. It just freaked me out totally."

By his second show, he had gotten past the nervousness. "After that, I remember that everything just came easily and naturally. And nobody was critiquing me or telling me what not to do or what to do," Bobby recalled. "They just kind of let me go.

"I figure it's because I was doing the right things, so they must have thought, well, he's doing fine, we don't need to tell him anything in particular."

Jock on a bike

He had a full-time DJ shift at KULE during summer vacation but worked part time during his junior and senior years at Ephrata High.

"My show started when I could get there on my bicycle, depending on if I had to stay after school, which I occasionally did," Bobby admitted.

Because the station was a daytimer, programming had to end at local sunset, which in December could be as early as 4:15 p.m. "That meant I might not even get a full hour's pay," he added, "but I was proud to promote my show as 'All the Hits that Fits . . . in Less than Sixty Minutes.'"

Between records, it was Bobby's job to announce "It's Coulee music time . . ." but the songs were most definitely not cool for a fifteen-year-old in the 1960s. "Here I am a high school kid playing Perry Como, Patti Page, Dean Martin, and Lawrence Welk records."

"When I had a record by the Percy Faith Orchestra and Chorus, sometimes I would casually introduce it as 'Pussyface and His Orchestra'—just to see if anybody was actually listening."

After graduating in the class of '63, Bobby set out for college and enrolled in broadcasting classes at Eastern Washington State. That experience enabled him to return to Ephrata after his freshman year and assume the responsibilities of news director at KULE.

The following semester, Bobby left his hometown station and landed his first DJ job in Top 40 radio.

1961 KULE high school news and more audio at bobbyrichradio.com.

Chapter 6

I'd Do Anything for Love (But I Won't Do That)

One hundred percent love. That's how I describe my mother.

As we age, we realize the significance of how we were raised into the real world. Mom was a woman of great faith, and although she never had a job or a driver's license, she was very social and dedicated to her family and church. She and my two older sisters had beautiful soprano singing voices. Mom played the piano like a pro and served in every volunteer way at the church. My sisters had many of those same qualities. I got what was left over.

I learned early on that I could be more popular with girls by telling them that I loved them. That may have gotten a little out of hand a few times in my life, but at least it was in that positive vein.

Okay, so the truth is, when I started on the radio at age fifteen it made me more popular in school. Before that, I didn't have a great time at school and was definitely in the bullied group. Older kids who worked for my dad at the bowling center took out their job dissatisfaction on me.

There were days I had to pretend to be sick to stay home from school because I was afraid I was going to get beat up. I especially hated P.E., and when it came to "shirts and skins" activities, I had to get out of it unless I could be a "shirt."

But once I got on the air some of the kids suddenly knew who I was and were nicer to me. In particular the girls. I had a very low opinion of myself, and even though I tried to be friendly, I was extremely shy, especially with the female population.

My first real girlfriend was a classmate in high school. I was crazy about her, and we actually dated and everything! Well, not everything . . . I didn't cross that bridge until college when I dated the lovely Laura. Bless her sweet soul.

My biggest love lesson came when I eventually understood that there is a big difference between loving someone and being IN love with them.

So, I'm a lover, not a fighter. Music, radio, funny and intelligent people, I love all of them.

But when it comes to riding a circus elephant while wearing shorts or going in a dunk tank without a shirt (yes, I've done both in radio station stunts), as my friend Meat Loaf famously sang, "I'd Do Anything for Love (But I Won't Do THAT)" again.

—Bobby Rich, September 2023

Chapter 7

The Beatles and Bobby

Before the Beatles made their first trip to the U.S. in 1964, Bobby was already playing their hit single "I Want to Hold Your Hand" on the radio.

He kept spinning Beatles records for the next six decades, and commercial airplay helped them reach the top ten of *Billboard* magazine's music chart thirty-five times.

Bobby's broadcast connection with the Beatles began at Eastern Washington State College (later renamed Eastern Washington State University) in the town of Cheney. He adopted a new name for his debut on the campus radio station.

"KEWC is where I started being a Top 40 DJ and called myself Buddy 'Beatle' Rich. I brought in my own copy of *Meet the Beatles* to play on the air because our little college station didn't get any freebie albums from the labels.

"Because I was the Beatles guy, I bought everything I could find, including imports and singles, at the record stores in Cheney or Spokane," he said. "I also wrote a music column for the school newspaper and was a promoter of teen dances, so I was all about the Beatles. The night they first appeared on *The Ed Sullivan Show*, I was sitting on the floor of the student union with a bunch of other college kids, watching on a big, clunky, black-and-white TV."

Mohair and Moptop

Even his sense of fashion was influenced by the Fab Four in their mohair suits and moptop haircuts. "I wore tight pants and ankle-high Beatles boots and started styling my hair like Paul, John, George, and Ringo," Bobby admitted.

Leaving college for a disc jockey job in Corvallis and then Spokane, he played "A Hard Day's Night," "Eight Days a Week," and other Beatles chart climbers as the Lads from Liverpool claimed the number one spot on *Billboard's* Hot 100 a record twenty times by 1970.

"Anything new by the Beatles was automatically added to the playlist, including international releases. Most stations had a guy with a friend in England who could get you pirated copies of songs on vinyl or reel-to-reel tape," Bobby said. That led to dubious claims of exclusivity on new Beatles music.

"Over a song intro and sometimes even over the lyrics, you'd hear a DJ's voice announcing: 'A KFLY exclusive!' I don't know how much listeners appreciated hearing a talkover in the middle of a song, but they were so thrilled to hear the latest hit.

"The jocks were excited too and highly competitive with the other stations in town. Turning on the mic every day was like being a cheerleader in the studio," he recalled. "Breaking a new album by the Beatles was the ultimate high for a DJ because of the craziness, just a frenetic reaction to anything they put out."

In August of 1966, returning from a vacation on the Oregon coast, Bobby and his first wife Judy drove through Seattle and heard on the radio that seats were still available for one of two Beatles concerts later that day.

"We went to a Bon Marche department store and got decent tickets to the afternoon show at Seattle Coliseum for about four bucks a seat. It was unbelievable. The Beatles played ten or eleven songs, including

"Day Tripper," "Nowhere Man," and "Yesterday." Pat O'Day and Lan Roberts of KJR introduced them on stage," Bobby recalled.

"Eleanor Rigby" debuted at number sixty-five on the *Billboard* Hot 100 chart that week, and "Yellow Submarine" was in the number eight spot. "Paperback Writer" had already hit number one twice that summer.

Opening acts for the Beatles in Seattle were Bobby Hebb, the Ronettes, the Remains, and the Cyrkle. Hebb's song "Sunny" was the second-most popular song in the U.S., while the Cyrkle had just cracked the Top 40 with "Turn Down Day," a follow-up to their smash hit "Red Rubber Ball."

After the two arena shows in Seattle, the Beatles performed at Dodger Stadium in Los Angeles and at Candlestick Park in San Francisco to end the final concert tour of their career.

Jungle and Bobby and Sgt. Pepper

The groundbreaking album *Sgt. Pepper's Lonely Hearts Club Band* released in May of 1967 marked a new chapter in Beatlemania. At the time, Bobby was in Toledo with his friend Michael O'Shea doing their nightly *Jungle and Bobby* show on WOHO.

"When *Sgt. Pepper* came out it took a while for many fans to adapt to the new musical direction the Beatles were taking. It was psychedelic, electronic, orchestral, avant-garde, much deeper, and more experimental than their earlier rock'n'roll, pop, and simple love songs," Bobby reminisced.

"We played the new singles and the album cuts on our show, but Michael and I also put together a six-hour special called 'Jungle and Bobby Remember the Good Old Beatles,' featuring all the well-known favorites that people loved from their previous albums."

Fans quickly embraced the new sound, as radio airplay and record sales pushed *Sgt. Pepper* to a fifteen-week run at number one on the album chart. It won four Grammy awards including album of the year.

In 1968, "Lady Madonna," "Revolution," and "Hey Jude" were radio hits, and by the time the *White Album* came out, Bobby had moved to Davenport, Iowa, as program director and afternoon DJ on KSTT. There he produced "Beatlemania Revisited," another special. "I had gathered tons of research and clippings from newspapers and music magazines over the years," he said, "to weave interesting stories into the program."

McCartney conspiracy theory

Before the release of *Abbey Road* in 1969, a student newspaper at Drake University in Des Moines published an article with the headline "Is Beatle Paul McCartney Dead?" A macabre McCartney conspiracy theory that had circulated for several years gained new attention on radio and TV after the report in the collegiate *Times-Delphic.*[1]

"I mentioned it on the air at KSTT and got quoted in the *Quad City Times* or the Rock Island paper," Bobby remembered. "They interviewed me and ran a story saying local Beatles expert has heard all the rumors but seen no proof of McCartney's death."

Let It Be, the band's final studio album, was released in 1970, and Bobby did a handful of additional Beatles specials before leaving Iowa in 1972.

He continued to play their music for the next fifty years on AM, FM, and internet stations in California, New York, Pennsylvania, Washington, and Arizona.

Love songs

In 2018, when Bobby and his second wife, Debbie, married each other

[1]The *Times-Delphic*, Apr 24, 2013, https://timesdelphic.com/2013/04/pop-stars-death-rumor-begins-at-drake/

for the third time, their wedding singer was friend Tony Kishman, who has performed professionally as Paul McCartney in the Broadway musical *Beatlemania* and tribute concerts around the world.

Kishman serenaded the couple with a pair of McCartney's love songs, "The Long and Winding Road" and "My Love."

Bookends on the Beatles

Bobby's start as a DJ in the 1960s preceded the Beatles' arrival in America and his retirement from radio occurred in 2023, the same year that their final song was released, the AI-assisted "Now and Then."

"They had a huge influence on my career and maybe I had a small part in helping to popularize their music," he said.

KSTT Good Guys John Novak and Bobby hosted concert by Sonny and Cher at Davenport Masonic Temple, Feb. 22, 1968. (Photo from Bobby Rich Radio collection)

Hanging out with Wolfman Jack at station promotional event, Hotel Circle, San Diego, c. 1975. (Photo from Bobby Rich Radio collection)

Chapter 8

Bwana Johnny Punks Buddy Bobby

If KULE was the launching pad for his career as a radio star, KFLY was the booster rocket that propelled Bobby into a whole new galaxy. For starters, his pay soared to a whopping $325 per month. He also found himself on the receiving end of a world-class radio prank.

"Right before I would have returned for my sophomore year of college in 1964, I got an opportunity for what I would call my first 'real' station away from my hometown. It was KFLY in Corvallis, Oregon. I actually got hired to be a DJ there at age eighteen," Bobby proudly recounted.

Once again, he used the air name Buddy Rich, borrowed from the famed jazz drummer and bandleader.

Everything about KFLY was a step up for the young broadcaster. Located in the city's business district, the studio had giant windows overlooking downtown Corvallis. People driving by could look up and see the DJ talking into the microphone while they listened to his voice coming out of their car radio.

Hoping to look even cooler for fans watching him at work, he smoked cigarettes in the studio and danced to the music.

Buddy Rich meets his match

KFLY's Top 40 playlist featured songs by the Beatles such as "I'll Follow the Sun" and other new releases by British Invasion bands including the Animals, the Dave Clark Five, Gerry and the Pacemakers, Herman's Hermits, and Chad and Jeremy.

Shortly after Bobby's arrival in Corvallis, competing AM station KLOO hired an up-and-coming jock named Dick Johnson for their 6-10 p.m. show. Johnson, who later changed his name to Bwana Johnny, immediately earned Bobby's respect.

"KLOO played chicken rock—what we considered milquetoast Top 40," Bobby recalled. "Dick was from Vancouver, Washington, and about the same age as me. As soon as I heard him on the air with his many character voices and drop-ins, I thought wow, this guy is a real pro. I've got to study his show and find out why he's so good."

The two ambitious DJs first spoke by phone and agreed to meet at a time when their six-day work schedules did not conflict. Bobby had Sundays off, and Johnson said, "Why don't you come over to KLOO on Sunday while I'm on the air and we can hang out and then go get pie?"

"When I showed up to meet him," Bobby said, "I was surprised to see there were seven or eight cars in the parking lot and a receptionist working on a Sunday afternoon. 'May I tell Mr. Johnson who is calling?' she asked, and I replied 'Buddy Rich'. After letting the on-air studio know that Mr. B. Rich was waiting in the lobby, the receptionist turned to me and said, 'Take a seat, they'll send someone for you.'

"A few minutes later, a guy comes out to the lobby and says, 'Please follow me. Mr. Johnson will see you now.' He leads me past three production rooms and a news booth, all filled with people doing stuff and red lights to signal that recordings were in progress. All this activity on a Sunday afternoon in Corvallis, Oregon!

"When we finally reach the control room, there's Dick in the announcer booth with a producer working across the glass, doing a weekend air shift! I'm blown away by how big-time it is.

"Dick then turns to greet me in one of his many character voices: 'So you're Buddy Rich! Is that your real name?'"

Bobby, in amazement, could only respond, "How are you doing all of this with so many employees on a Sunday? We don't even have half this many people at KFLY working on a weekday!"

Johnson then confessed, "Hey man, this is all a stunt. These are my friends from Vancouver. I just wanted to screw with you."

Pie and bye bye KFLY

Bobby had been punked big-time, but his new friend's elaborate prank was the start of a mutual appreciation club for the two late-night jocks. "He liked me on the air, and I was a big fan of his show. I even told him he belonged on my station, KFLY, doing real Top 40 instead of working at KLOO," Bobby reminisced.

"A couple times a week after our shifts we'd drive out to the T&R truck stop restaurant on Interstate 5 in Albany, Oregon, and have pie and coffee at midnight and talk about radio."

A hot topic of discussion that summer was the mysterious destruction of two signboards advertising KLOO. The first sign alongside Highway 99 was chopped down with an axe, and the second sign was vandalized with a saw. While the Benton County sheriff's department investigated, the DJs speculated that a higher-up at KFLY brought down the rival station's billboards.

"About six months after we met," Bobby said, "Dick told me, 'You know how you always said I should be on KFLY, Buddy? Well, your general manager called me today and offered me a job! But I can't take it.'"

Bobby's immediate response was, "Oh my gosh, that's great. Finally, you'll be on the right station. I'm so happy for you!"

Johnson replied, "But Buddy, don't you understand? If they hire me, they're going to fire you!"

After pausing a moment to think about it, Bobby told his friend, "That's all right, you belong on our station, I'll be okay."

Johnson called the GM to accept the job with one condition. He insisted that KFLY had to keep Buddy. It remains a gesture of kindness unheard of in the radio business.

Remarkably, station bosses agreed to the unusual demand. They reassigned Buddy Rich to the midnight to 6 a.m. air shift and built a new studio at the truck stop in Albany.

The favor of keeping Bobby employed didn't last long. Two months later, KFLY fired both DJs.

The prankster Johnson, rebranding himself as Bwana Johnny, moved on to become a top air personality in San Diego, Miami, New York, and Seattle.

After gaining experience in Corvallis, Bobby also had a major market career working in those same cities. He and Bwana remained lifelong friends.

Chapter 9

Night Jock Leads Double Life in Luxury Hotel

On the rebound after getting blown out for the first time in his career, nineteen-year-old Bobby landed a DJ job in Spokane, the second-biggest city in Washington state.

"At that point I was trying to be a hip guy, letting my hair grow so I could have a Beatles haircut and buying some fashionable hipster clothes to wear," Bobby said. But his next station was not exactly hip.

"KDNC 1440 AM played background music. This was the mid-'60s, FM hadn't caught on yet. The call letters were pronounced like 'Cadence,' and our easy listening format was known as companion radio."

"They brought me in to do the night shift. It was instrumental music or orchestras accompanied by a chorus. Composers and conductors like Hugo Winterhalter and the Mantovani Orchestra."

Outside work, he listened to Beatles albums, danced to "Hang on Sloopy" by the McCoys, and went to college concerts and parties with popular Northwest rock and roll bands like the Wailers, the Sonics, and Merrilee Rush and the Turnabouts.

"Those were all wild, crazy, loud rock bands," Bobby said. "And then I'd go to KDNC and be playing these big fat tapes with twenty-five minutes of music by 101 Strings, Henry Mancini, and Percy Faith. So, I was really being two different people.

"But if you listened on the radio, you wouldn't know. I had to be professional on the air," he added.

Having returned to college on a part-time basis, Bobby took broadcast classes during the day and drove between Cheney and Spokane for his nightly shift at KDNC.

The station's studio and offices were in the historic Davenport Hotel in downtown Spokane. Opened in 1914, the luxury hotel over the years had hosted celebrity guests including Babe Ruth, Amelia Earhart, Charles Lindbergh, and Benny Goodman. Broadcasting from the first floor of the Davenport, KDNC announcers worked in a glassed-in corner of the main lobby.

"This allowed people on the street, as well as street people, people with street smarts and people with no smarts who shouldn't have even been allowed on the street, to congregate outside and watch me work," Bobby recalled with a hint of lingering trepidation.

"Lookie-loos with nothing better to do stood in front of the window and stared at the disc jockey. And I only talked twice per hour because all the music was on those big twelve-inch reels of tape."

To pass the time while keeping the live audience and spectators entertained, he added some tricks to his nightly on-air performance. Learning the moves to a popular 1964 dance hit, he bopped around the studio and lip-synched the lyrics to Bobby Freeman's "C'mon and Swim."

"I also made up things to do, like pretending to take meter readings in the control room. Every once in a while, I'd pretend to answer the phone and have a fake conversation. Whatever I could invent, so it looked like I was busy during my shift."

Ever the showman, Bobby made a habit of putting on the best possible program for his listeners.

The gig at KDNC was short-lived. After about three months, it was time to check out of the hotel studio and move down the dial to another station across town.

KDNC studio, Davenport Hotel lobby (behind window, center right), Spokane.
(Credit: Photo by Charles A. Libby, with permission of Washington State Historical Society)

Yes, DJs wore neckties in the 1960s and radio control rooms had ashtrays. (Photo from Bobby Rich Radio collection)

Chapter 10

Twangy and Hokey Show

The shortest chapter in Bobby's professional biography was a country music stint that was over before he could even break in his first pair of cowboy boots.

"The only job I could get at the time was doing the overnight shift at KSPO in Spokane," he said. "They expected me to also go out and sell advertising during the day. I said I don't do that, but I'd be glad to do the DJ shift.

"It was a very traditional country and western station. I remember playing 'Tiger by the Tail' by Buck Owens, 'King of the Road' by Roger Miller, and lots of twangy music from the '40s and '50s.

"I also remember saying some hokey things on the air, like 'I sure got a hankering to stick around and play some of this here music for you.'"

Bobby didn't get to stick around long, lasting less than three months at KSPO. The boss called one day to tell him, "Well, we found someone to do both jobs—DJ and sales. So, you don't need to come in anymore."

Chapter 11

Canned and Spokane'd

Spinning records at easy listening and country/western stations is not how Bobby found his groove in Spokane. For a young DJ with Top 40 ambitions, the music was too stodgy on KDNC and too twangy on KSPO.

Turning the dial to 920 AM, he gladly accepted an offer to play the pop hits at KXLY, a well-established outlet with studios near the campus of Gonzaga University.

"The Mighty 92" was Spokane's second-most popular music station, with a playlist that included the Byrds, the Beach Boys, and Sonny and Cher. Its Top 40 menu expanded with the British Invasion and a wave of new singles from the Beatles, the Animals, and the Dave Clark Five.

"KXLY was a distant second in the ratings, but it was still a big deal, and I had a lot of fun, again doing nights as Buddy Rich," Bobby mused.

"It's where I first used one of my favorite DJ jokes stolen from Bwana Johnny. After playing a tune like 'You Turn Me On' by Ian Whitcomb, I liked to say, 'We get a lot of calls about that song, but we play it anyway.'"

AM still ruled

Bobby's college friend Larry Davis was already working at the station and suggested his classmate when the midday shift opened. Returning the favor, Bobby later helped Davis get a job in Lansing and then hired him to do mornings in Davenport.

The jocks at KXLY-AM were also responsible for "babysitting" the company's semi-automated FM station. That meant stacking eight or nine albums on an automatic record changer and moving the tonearm into position to play the first disc.

"As each LP dropped down, the needle on the arm would be lowered onto the first cut of the record and it would play through all the songs until the next album dropped onto the turntable," Bobby explained.

"My job, while working nights on the AM, was to go into our FM station every couple of hours and turn the albums over. That was the rotation," he recalled with amusement.

"At the time, FM stations were almost a joke. Hardly anybody had FM radio, and if they did, it was like classical or background music. No one was spending any money promoting or marketing it."

The big letdown

Much to his delight, moving to KXLY boosted Bobby's self-esteem and confidence as a jock. "I was getting more attention from listeners, including rivals," he said. "Even the program director of our biggest competitor used to drive around listening to my show and admitted that we were killing his station."

A teenage fan just as quickly dashed Bobby's ego. "A cheerleader whose mother dropped her off at KXLY stood outside my studio one night for about an hour, just hanging around," he remembered.

"I must have said my name, Buddy Rich, on the air about seven times and there was a speaker right above the door, so she heard everything I said before and after each song. But when I walked out of the studio and asked, 'So what do you think?' she replied, 'Where's Buddy?!'

"Obviously, my appearance did not match her image of the Top 40

DJ she was hoping to meet. I asked my friend Mark Majors, waiting to do his overnight shift, to please inform the girl that I was Buddy."

Refusing to believe it, the young listener insisted, "That can't be Buddy because Buddy's cool!" To make matters worse, she said the experience was such a bummer that she could never listen to her favorite DJ again.

The uncool insult dealt a major blow to Bobby's self-confidence. "I can still feel it now," he revealed, more than fifty years later.

Three strikes and out

The radio fun stopped abruptly when KXLY's newly hired disc jockey got in trouble for multiple violations of local broadcast standards.

Bobby's first offense was a comment to a nervous listener who called in to answer a music trivia question and score a pair of tickets to see Paul Revere and the Raiders perform at the Spokane Coliseum.

"The caller was having trouble coming up with three song titles to win the contest. Time was running out, and she'd only gotten two. Just in the nick of time, she named the third song and started screaming. I got animated and blurted out on the air, 'Boy, you're really excited, Maryann Fernley . . . you almost wet your panties there!'

"The next day I was called in to the program director's office and scolded by Tom Conners. He told me, 'You can't say wet your panties on the radio! That's just like saying you pissed yourself!'"

Conners's feathers were ruffled again when he read a "Rich on Radio" column that Bobby wrote for the Eastern Washington college newspaper. Critiquing the local broadcast market, the student journalist showed no favoritism to his employer.

"I mentioned that our big competitor, KJRB, had good jocks and they were kicking our ass," Bobby said. "Plus, they had a brand-new jingle package that sounded great while our jingles on KXLY were so old they must have been made shortly before recording tape was invented.

The column included a lot of positive observations about KJRB and not very many compliments about my own station.

"Well, the boss got ahold of the newspaper and was visibly upset. That was strike two against me."

The final straw leading to Bobby's exit was a nighttime joyride through downtown Spokane in a brand-new Pontiac Tiger GTO. The eye-catching muscle car had just been introduced, and a local auto dealer loaned one to KXLY.

All the DJs got to drive the tiger-striped speedster around town and announce on the air who was out showing it off on Division Street. Bobby was miffed that he missed his turn behind the wheel.

"I was the night jock and the only one who didn't get to take the Tiger GTO for a spin. So, when the weekend guy came back from driving it at 10 p.m., I said, 'Gimme the keys, I'm gonna take it out.'

"And by golly, if I didn't get in some drag racing down there on Division Street after midnight. Apparently, the police called the Pontiac dealer at home and told him, 'One of those DJs is hot-rodding that GTO of yours.' So, the next day I was fired."

Bobby and Der Bingle Worked Here

Legendary singer and movie star Bing Crosby was a part owner of KXLY in the 1940s. An Oscar and Grammy Award winner, Crosby attended Gonzaga University in Spokane and bought a share of the station some years after performing there.

While Bing and Bobby never met, the two entertainers share several remarkable personal and professional similarities. They both grew up in Washington state, left college before graduating, gained fame in Spokane, achieved national broadcast stardom, and acquired memorable nicknames.

Der Bingle and Dr. Boogie frequented the Del Mar Racetrack and Del Mar Fair and are forever linked to radio airplay of "The Teddy Bears' Picnic" song.

Chapter 12

Crème de la KREM

Newlywed, newly fired, and newly expectant father. Not necessarily in that order, and not exactly persuasive talking points in Bobby's search for a new gig playing records on the radio.

Having quit college to pursue the dream of disc jockeying, he quickly learned a harsh reality. Job security was not a defining attribute of his chosen profession.

"I was canned by three stations in my first three years as a professional DJ," Bobby said of his early-career firings in Oregon and Washington. "I had burned my bridges in Spokane but needed to stick around town because I was about to become a father."

Bobby's next gig came in 1965 with an assist from his friend Bob Adkins at KREM. Known on the air as Addy Bobkins, he had previously hosted a TV show for children and a radio show at KNEW where he was one of The Five Bobs.

"Bob was one of those really cool guys who told me if you ever need anything, I'll help you out," Bobby remembered. "So, I called him and said, 'Hey man, I just got blown out.'"

Adkins hired Bobby at middle of the road (MOR) station KREM in Spokane and put him on nights, spinning records by Jack Jones, Frank Sinatra, Nat King Cole, Patti Page, and other adult artists of the era.

Starting the job just a few days after his son was born, Bobby hit the airwaves with a new identity to go with his new station. "I named myself Bryan Richards because those were my son's first and middle names," he said.

"I knew I wasn't going be there too long," Bobby emphasized. Yearning to play younger music and be a Top 40 DJ, he started scanning the dial for opportunities beyond Spokane.

The job at KREM and the air name of Bryan Richards lasted about four months, until it was time to leave his home state and move east to a bigger radio market.

More than two decades later, Bobby would be lured back to Washington as morning show host and boss of two stations in the biggest city in the Northwest.

Chapter 13

Last Train to Jimsville

Imagine going on a blind date to an improv club where you are required to get onstage and do a completely extemporaneous performance to entertain an audience watching and judging you through a soundproof window.

In radio, that's called a "naked audition," and it was certainly the strangest thing Bobby ever did to get a job as a DJ.

"In 1966, I saw a help wanted ad in *Broadcasting* or *Billboard* magazine, which was the primary way of finding radio jobs in those days. I desperately wanted to leave Spokane and was looking for anything really, but something about this ad just appealed to me," Bobby recalled.

He sent an aircheck tape and application to WJIM in Lansing, Michigan. The program director requested an in-person interview and offered to pay travel expenses.

Working at WJIM would be a huge career advancement if Bobby could pass the odd audition. "Big Jim Radio" was part of an AM/FM/TV broadcast group whose proximity to Detroit and the Motown scene made it an important Top 40 music station.

Go in there and do a show

Bobby left Spokane on an afternoon train, arrived in Michigan's capital the next morning, and walked to a nearby Howard Johnson's motel, hoping to catch a few hours of sleep before his job interview.

After a nearly two-thousand-mile rail journey and a quick nap at HoJo's, he met his future boss in downtown Lansing. The program director didn't exactly match the young DJ's expectation of what a Top 40 programmer should look like.

"Bryan Halter was this very buttoned up, professorial guy in glasses with his hair combed back, and he wore an ascot," Bobby said.

The PD's style of auditioning talent was equally unorthodox. Halter invited Bobby to prove he could generate excitement and make people smile, using little more than his voice and creativity.

"He handed me a stack of advertising copy and station announcements," Bobby recalled. "Then he swung open the door to a fully equipped studio and told me, 'Okay, go in there and do a show.'"

To his astonishment, Bobby was given no music to play. A disc jockey tryout without a single song on record or tape available. Just a handful of commercials and station promos to read.

The PD and three of his staff sat in an adjoining production room and watched through the glass. Bobby thought it was the most ridiculous scenario but decided to have fun and do his best to impress.

"So, I would say something like, 'Hey, it's Big Jim Radio and here's The Supremes,' to introduce a make-believe record. Then I'd sing some lyrics about heartbreak and the name of love, before changing back to my announcer voice for the backsell, 'WJIM, that was The Supremes. It's 10:18 on Big Jim Radio … ' And then I'd read a commercial.

"Here I was intro'ing records that weren't there, singing bits of imaginary songs, and improvising my own make-believe jingles! It was so bizarre. Meanwhile, over in the production room, they loved it. Every one of them, including Halter, thought it was hysterical."

Every jock is Jim

"He hired me on the spot for the noon to 3 p.m. shift," Bobby proudly recalled. After passing the naked audition with flying colors, there was one more quirky condition of employment. "I had to change my name from Bobby Rich to Jim Rich because all the DJs on Big Jim Radio were named Jim."

A lifelong friendship began at WJIM with Michael O'Shea, who was on the air from 7-to-midnight using the name Jungle Jim Williams. "Our morning guy was Jim Shaw," O'Shea remembered, "and Big Jim Lyons did afternoons."

Bobby's ability to create theater of the mind and ad-lib with self-confidence and spontaneity impressed his friend and coworker. "They handed him pieces of copy, and he sang the Sears jingle," remarked O'Shea. "I always thought that Bobby just exuded a great vibe, and he was cool. That's why I enjoyed hanging out with him."

Tearful farewell

The number one song on WJIM's music survey in late December of 1966 was "We Can Work It Out/Day Tripper" by the Beatles. The Supremes topped the station's chart in November with "I Hear a Symphony." The Temptations, the Miracles, and Marvin Gaye were among the other most popular artists on Big Jim Radio that year.

Resigning in 1967 for a job in a bigger market, Bobby made a dramatic exit from WJIM. He played "Softly as I Leave You" by Matt Monro as his last song. The tender ballad brought tears to his eyes as he said farewell. A final encounter with the program director was almost as awkward as his first.

"I had my DJ stuff loaded in a cardboard box and was headed for the door," Bobby remembered, "when Halter stops me to see what's in the box. He pulls out a couple of tape cartridges and says, 'These look like some of ours.'"

Bobby responded, "No, I brought them with me to Lansing."

"While not directly accusing me of stealing, he still wanted to take the tapes," Bobby recalled. "I had to tell him, 'Sorry, Bryan, but I swiped these carts from my stations in Spokane and Corvallis!'"

At that, Bobby said, the PD let him leave the building and offered these parting words: "Well, you did a good job while you were here."

Chapter 14

Making People Happy Seemed Like a Pretty Good Thing

Moving to Toledo in 1967 and working at WOHO was the first time that I was bottom man on the pole. All the other DJs there were more experienced than I was, and I learned a lot in that year.

Just being around guys who were way ahead of me in terms of professionalism and knowledge of broadcasting was way more valuable than studying the business in college.

Surrounded by talent like that, I got a deeper understanding of personality radio, music programming and production, how to deal with management, and how to relate to the listeners.

Toledo is where I hung out with my friends Michael O'Shea and Jim Davis after our night shifts, talking about what we would do if we ruled the world of radio. For young and ambitious jocks like us, it was the perfect place to refine our skills, learn some tricks of the trade, and gain the confidence to move up to bigger markets as DJs and program directors.

Toledo in 1967 wasn't just me having fun. It became me making a living from what I already loved. And I would have done it for free because making great radio was euphoria, the coolest thing I could imagine.

Little by little, I found that having fun on the air also meant the listeners were having fun. I began to realize that I really was doing something meaningful. Maybe not changing the world but making people happy seemed like a pretty good thing to do.

I never stopped feeling that way, thrilled that I was spreading joy on the radio . . . which somehow might be helping others.

—Bobby Rich, September 2023

Chapter 15

Three Men and a Cougar

As the Summer of Love blossomed in 1967, Bobby was in the garden of WOHO, tending Toledo's flower power rotation of hit songs "San Francisco (Be Sure to Wear Flowers in Your Hair)" by Scott McKenzie, "All You Need is Love" by the Beatles, and "I Was Made to Love Her" by Stevie Wonder.

"When I did 9 p.m. to 1 a.m. on WOHO, my last hour was called the Bobby Rich Love-In. I played all the romantic singles and the psychedelic hits 'White Rabbit' by Jefferson Airplane and 'A Whiter Shade of Pale' by Procol Harum," he said.

Bobby and his late-night show followed his good friend Michael O'Shea, who did the 6-9 p.m. shift as Jungle Jim, a name he acquired at WJIM in Lansing. Shortly after moving to Toledo, O'Shea recommended Bobby when WOHO AM 1470 needed another jock. They soon paired up on a crossover show, sharing a fun-filled hour at eight o'clock.

"I used to describe it as a morning show at night," O'Shea said. "Our program director told us you guys are really entertaining."

PD Sam Holman then put them together on a four-hour nightly program called *Jungle and Bobby*. The two-man show was an instant hit, soon becoming Toledo's highest rated evening program.[2]

[2]*Broadcasting*, Sep 1, 1980, pg 28 https://www.worldradiohistory.com/hd2/IDX-Business/Magazines/Archive-BC-IDX/80-OCR/1980-09-01-BC-OCR-Page-0028.pdf#search=%22bobby%20rich%20woho%22

The Purple Palace on Pickle Road

"As a twenty-one-year-old rookie trying to sound more mature on the air, I got one of the best coaching tips ever from Sam," Bobby said. "Think thirty-five, he told me. "If I could imagine being ten or fifteen years older, without losing my screaming high energy and goofiness, I'd be more relatable and comfortable, he said. It's a technique I used throughout my career, adjusting my mindset to connect with people older and younger than me."

The Mojo Man and Frank "Swingin" Sweeney were well-known personalities who welcomed Bobby to the air staff collectively known as the WOHO Good Guys. They worked in a building affectionately known as the Purple Palace on Pickle Road.

"It was a dump," Bobby admitted, "the only thing on Pickle Road, in the middle of nothing but open fields and weeds." Despite their less-than-luxurious studios and a signal of only 1,000 watts, WOHO managed to compete against bigger stations in Detroit and 50,000-watt blowtorch CKLW in Windsor, Ontario.

Tom Dean was one of several WOHO jocks who made the jump from Toledo to Detroit.

Working in Ohio gave O'Shea and Bobby the confidence to believe they would someday be program directors of their own stations. "We knew we could be successful without being pricks like so many of the PDs we'd each encountered before getting to WOHO," Bobby said.

Happy jalopy

Jungle and Bobby acquired a beat-up pickup truck they named the WOHO Happy Machine and drove it to high schools and businesses to attract attention for their show. "A listener or somebody came down to the station with this old jalopy," O'Shea remembered. "And we retrofitted it with an acetylene torch and help from a welder who again was one of our listeners or advertisers."

"The Happy Machine was a collection of junk items—old bicycle frames, mattress springs, even the mast of a sailboat—welded to the frame of the flatbed," Bobby recalled. "Assembled in an artistic way, it became like a pop culture sculpture."

On a visit to Woodward High School, the DJs passed out WOHO buttons and pens, and the senior class donated a school flag to fly from the roof of the Happy Machine.

According to an article in the school newspaper, the *Woodward Tattler,* about one hundred teens surrounded Jungle and Bobby on campus. "Before they left," the report added, "several loud explosions split the air. It was the Happy Machine starting up!"

The *Tattler's* coverage included a comment from a female student who gushed, "Both DJs were wonderful, and handsome, too! I wonder if they're married?"

The funky truck, O'Shea pointed out, "was our way of getting out there and making a statement, being funny, live, and local."

"We were kind of a big deal," Bobby said of their public appearances. "We volunteered to promote our show and the station. It was just us out in the community having fun and doing things that made people happy."

Toledo was also where Bobby first met Scott Kenyon (Benjamin Gall), who started as his phone screener at WOHO while still in high school.

"We hung out together and sounded so much alike that people would ask if Benjie was my brother," Bobby reminisced. He and Kenyon developed an instant friendship and eventually became brothers on the radio at stations in Davenport and San Diego.

Dress code for disc jockeys

"WOHO was the place that we learned the kind of radio that we loved and still do love," Bobby said in a 2013 interview, with O'Shea nodding in agreement. They credited station owner Lew Dickey Sr. for establishing a creative environment but questioned his insistence on a dress code for all DJs.

"We were just trying to be rock'n'roll stars and be cool with girls and the younger crowd," Bobby said with a chuckle, "and the guy who owns the place wants everybody on air in a shirt and tie and maybe a jacket. We just didn't really go for that."

One day, Bobby arrived several hours before the start of his show and Dickey scolded him for violating the disc jockey wardrobe rules. Noticing that the big boss had come straight to work after playing golf, Bobby commented, "But, Lew, you're wearing Bermuda shorts." With a stern look and a cutting smile, Dickey replied, "Well, Bobby, what's good for the goose is not always good for the gander."

Low-stakes poker and DJ espionage

The young DJs enjoyed a friendly game of cards once a week to supplement their meager paychecks and help pay for their nightlife in Toledo. "We'd play penny poker at Bobby's house," O'Shea recalled. "Each of us brought a can of Campbell's soup and a bag of pennies. At the end of the night, whoever won would give their tomato or chicken soup to the guy who lost his money."

Jungle and Bobby's chief competitor at the time was James K. Davis, whose evening show on WTTO originated from the downtown Commodore Perry Motor Inn. "Our goal is to beat these guys and do it any way we know how," Davis remembered his program director, Don Kelly, telling the WTTO staff.

That challenge prompted Davis and fellow DJ Rick Snyder to hatch a clandestine plan to infiltrate WOHO. Posing as college students writing a paper on local radio, they were able to gain access to their crosstown rival's studio.

"Here we were inside their control room," Davis said, "and saw how WOHO ran everything. We came back to WTTO with more information than we knew what to do with and immediately made a strategy to kick the livin' daylights out of the competition."

That insider information, however, did not give WTTO a winning hand. WOHO continued to dominate in Toledo's Top 40 ratings battle.

Secret Cougar rendezvous

Davis, O'Shea, and Bobby let professional competitiveness take a back seat to their mutual love for radio. The trio became fast friends, occasionally socializing on weekends.

"We didn't even drink," Bobby explained. "We just enjoyed hanging out, listening to radio, and talking about radio."

"Had our stations found out we were chumming together, we'd all have been fired," said O'Shea. Sitting in his '67 Mercury Cougar in a Kmart parking lot one night, they had a deep discussion about their friendship and career prospects. They agreed to stay put in the city where they were enjoying professional success and camaraderie.

"Our handshake on that night was we were going to anchor in Toledo as our base to be big fish in a little sea," Davis remembered.

Their deal to stick around long-term lasted only a short time. Within a few months, they all received better job offers and went their separate ways. Davis left to work for Paul Drew at the legendary CKLW and O'Shea joined Gordon McLendon's KLIF in Dallas. Bobby departed for Davenport after placing an ad in *Broadcasting* magazine.

"I announced that I was ready for my first programming job and got hired at KSTT," he said. Bobby worked his final shift at WOHO on December 31, 1967.

Nearly sixty years after meeting up for the first time, the three amigos still held onto their personal and professional connections, sharing ideas and celebrating each other's achievements as prominent radio personalities, programmers, general managers, and station owners.

Davis in 2024 described Bobby's attributes and influence on their industry. "Inspirational and obviously creative. He set the mark for being consistently good and always had a cheery, upbeat personality to inspire a team through contagious enthusiasm," said Davis.

Pictured above in their Happy Machine are WOHO's favorite disk jockies, "Jungle" Jim Williams and Bobby B. Rich.

WOHO DJ's Visit Woodward

Radio Station WOHO recently declared Woodward, "High School of the Day."

Last Thursday WOHO sent its "Happy Machine", complete with its two most popular Disk Jockies, "Jungle" Jim Williams and Bobby B. Rich, to the Stricker Street Seat of Learning. While here, the DJ's commented on the "fantastic reception" given them by the students of Woodward. They also passed out "good guy" buttons and WOHO ball point pens.

A crowd of about 100 teens assembled around the "Happy Machine" which in reality was an old blue pick-up truck decorated with silver letters, a car fender and wheel hub soddered to the side, and a combination see-saw flag mast attached to the roof. The Senior Class presented a multi-colored flag for this mast.

Before they left, several loud explosions split the air. It was the "Happy Machine" starting up! Bobby B. Rich promised the flag would fly atop the mast when the machine visited other area schools. On his show that evening, "Jungle" Jim stated that if all Toledo teens were like Woodward's there would be no delinquency! The Tattler thanks them for their compliments!

One female by-stander said, "Both DJ's were wonderful, and handsome, too! I wonder if they're married?"

Jungle Jim and Bobby, with WOHO Happy Machine. [c. 1967, *The Tattler,* Woodward High School newspaper, Toledo, Ohio.]

Hear a 1967 WOHO aircheck at bobbyrichradio.com.

Chapter 16

The Name Game

Bobby, Bobby, bo-obby
Banana fana fo-fobby
Fee fie mo-mobby
Bobby!

Yes, Bobby Rich is my real name. But I didn't come into the world as Bobby. My parents, Marge and Howard Nessen, named me Richard. My mom, dad, and sisters called me Richie as a boy, and until I graduated from high school in Ephrata, Washington, I was Rich Nessen.

By age ten, I knew I was going to be a radio announcer. Then I found out that in show business you could give yourself a stage name. So I did!

When I was about fifteen, I went to visit my sister who was living in New York City. One afternoon I went for a walk in Times Square and passed this jazz club that had a poster advertising "Battle of the Drummers—Gene Krupa and Buddy Rich." I knew their names because I loved the drums, bought jazz records, listened to the George Shearing Quintet, and was a fan of rock drummer Sandy Nelson.

The door of the jazz lounge was propped open so you could hear the drumming and catch a glimpse of the musicians inside.

Too young to get into the club, I watched from the sidewalk with a crowd of people who stopped for a peek at Krupa and Rich playing furiously on a stage behind the bar. Two of the greatest jazz drummers, composers, and bandleaders of their time. Unquestionably cool cats.

That experience in New York made a huge impression on me. Right then and there I knew I had found my radio name. I was going to be Buddy Rich.

My debut hosting the *Buddy Rich Show* was on KEWC, the campus radio station at Eastern Washington State College in Cheney, Washington. As a seventeen-year-old freshman, I was Buddy "Beatle" Rich, spinning as many Beatles songs as possible. The DJs played our own records on the college station, and I went out and bought my copy of *Meet the Beatles* as soon as it came out in 1964.

Later that year, I was hired at KFLY in Corvallis, Oregon, where I did the night shift as Buddy Rich. After that in Spokane, Washington, I was Buddy Rich at KDNC and KXLY.

I changed my air name to Bryan Richards in 1966 for a short-term gig at KREM in Spokane. That was homage to my newborn son Bryan Richard Nessen.

My next move was to WJIM in Lansing, Michigan, where I became Jim Rich and my friend Michael O'Shea was Jungle Jim because all the jocks on Big Jim Radio had to be named Jim.

In 1967, I followed Michael to WOHO in Toledo, Ohio. He was still Jungle Jim on the air, and Program Director Frank "Swingin" Sweeney asked me, "Are you really attached to the name Jim Rich? Because I don't like it at all." "Nah," I told him, "It wasn't my choice." Sweeney replied, "Good. I was thinking you could be

Jimmy Rich or Bobby Rich." I said, "I'll take Bobby." And that's been my name ever since.

At times I've also called myself Bobby B. Rich. To this day, my friend Charley Steiner, who worked with me at WAVZ in New Haven before he became the radio voice of the LA Dodgers, calls me Bobby "B for Boogie" Rich.

In 1984, I changed my legal name to Bobby Rich, and that's what is on my driver's license and other government records.

So, you could say I've been Bobby Rich professionally and personally for nearly sixty years and legally for over forty years.

There was another Bobby Rich, who appeared as a character in the TV show *M*A*S*H* in 1978. An episode entitled "Point of View" conveyed the horrors of war through the eyes of a soldier gravely wounded on the battlefield and treated in the mobile army surgical hospital. The soldier's name was Private Bobby Rich.

That episode of *M*A*S*H* was co-written by my Emmy-winning friend Ken Levine, whose career as a TV writer in Hollywood took off after we worked together at B-100 in San Diego. It makes me really proud knowing Ken gave my name to that character as a tribute to me.

By the way, before Ken became famous writing TV scripts for *M*A*S*H* and *Cheers*, his radio name was Beaver Cleaver.

—Bobby Rich, June 2023

Chapter 17

All the World's a Stage

"...And one man in his time plays many parts."
—William Shakespeare, from *As You Like It*

At the heart of Bobby's career as an entertainer was his love of musical theater. As longtime listeners and coworkers can attest, he enjoyed regaling the audience with spontaneous outbursts of songs and accompanying theatrics from *The Music Man*. "Gary, Indiana" and "Marian the Librarian" were two favorite show tunes whose lyrics he knew word for word.

A mere mention of the state of Oklahoma in a radio newscast or sports report could trigger Bobby's involuntary "Rodgers and Hammerstein response." He livened up many local weather forecasts with his stirring rendition of "Oh, What a Beautiful Mornin'" delivered in full Gordon MacRae baritone.

This fondness for American musical theater was inherited from his mother, Marge. "My mom loved show tunes and always had the radio on in the kitchen. If nobody was around, she'd turn it up and sing out loud," Bobby said.

"On a family trip to New York in the early '60s, we went to two Broadway shows. One was *Camelot* with Richard Burton, Julie Andrews, and Robert Goulet. The other was *West Side Story*. It didn't hit me until years later how much those performances influenced my fascination with putting on a show and entertaining people."

Bobby's crowning moment as a teenage performer was in the Ephrata High School production of *Ask Any Girl*. He was cast in the romantic comedy as supporting character Alvin. The 1962 class play followed the film release of *Ask Any Girl* with Shirley MacLaine, David Niven, and Gig Young co-starring in the farcical love triangle.

As a disc jockey and program director in Iowa, Bobby found new meaning in songs composed by Meredith Willson for *The Music Man*. KSTT's listening area included "Rock Island" and Bobby encountered his own "Trouble in River City" when he challenged the station owner's programming ideas.

Chapter 18

First-Time PD in Four, Almost Five Cities

At the ripe age of twenty-two, Bobby scored his first program director job at KSTT, a top station in Davenport, Iowa, with a Top 40 format. Thrilled to accept a $10,000 starting salary, about twice what he was paid in Toledo, he took an afternoon DJ shift and learned on the job how to be a boss.

"In Davenport I found out that managing people and programming the station was fun and personally as rewarding as performing," Bobby said.

"It was a place almost perfect for someone like me who knew what he was doing as a programmer but hadn't had a chance to prove it yet. I was fortunate to inherit a staff of talented jocks known collectively as the KSTT Good Guys."

News Director Morry Alter was impressed with the new PD because Bobby had produced his own vinyl record with Toledo's nighttime skyline on the album cover. "To me that was bringing in a guy from the big city," Alter recalled. "He seemed like a heavy hitter."

Bobby's enthusiasm as a jock also struck a positive chord. "He was very organized, bright, and fun to listen to," Alter added. "I sometimes wondered how the hell does he do that, how is he so happy on the air?"

Fine-tuning a Top 40 lineup

Joining KSTT on January 1, 1968, Bobby encountered an eclectic program lineup. "A real strong DJ in morning drive, Lee Shannon, was followed by a one-hour version of *Don McNeil's Breakfast Club* from ABC Radio in Chicago. A variety show in the style of Arthur Godfrey, it featured comedy, but I thought it was oriented to old folks," he said.

The *Breakfast Club* led into an hourlong local talk show hosted by the station's owners, Fred and Ruth Epstein. After their call-in program, the station returned to music with longtime KSTT announcer Lou Gutenberger.

Establishing a more contemporary sound was Bobby's initial focus. "I realized I had a lot to learn about being a PD, but by gradually earning the trust of management I was able to make a lot of improvements.

"KSTT was already so successful that I didn't want to mess with it too much," he said.

Keeping its mainstream Top 40 format, Bobby targeted the programming to match peak listening patterns of teens and adults.

"We appealed to all demographics, playing the biggest hits in the mornings and the softer music in middays when the teenagers were in school. The tempo picked up in afternoon drive, and then it was high energy at night."

One month after his arrival, Bobby told *Billboard* magazine that DJs chose their own music from the playlist "because each guy has a different audience to aim for . . . this town is very industrial. There's a large John Deere factory here, as well as an Alcoa factory. We have to plan our programming around the changing of the shifts to some extent."[3]

---

[3]*Billboard,* Feb. 24, 1968, pg 22 https://www.worldradiohistory.com/hd2/IDX-Business/Music/Billboard-Index/IDX/1968/Billboard%201968-02-24-OCR-Page-0018.pdf#search=%22wjim%20lansing%22

KSTT boasted on air of its place in the nation's eighty-sixth largest radio market. Formally known as the Quad Cities, the region encompassed Davenport and the bordering communities of Moline, East Moline, and Rock Island in Illinois.

The rapid development of neighboring Bettendorf, Iowa, prompted KSTT to rebrand the Quad Cities "the Quint Cities." Bobby ordered a "Quint Cities USA" singing jingles package for the station as the combined metropolitan population of KSTT's listening area grew to more than 350,000 by 1969.

The renaming initiative lasted more than ten years, but the region eventually reclaimed its identity as the Quad Cities.

Talent management for Good Guys

When Shannon left Davenport for a country station in Indianapolis, Bobby brought in Johnny Novak as the new morning man. They were college classmates at Eastern Washington State and had previously worked together at KXLY in Spokane and at WJIM in Lansing.

"This was my first time getting to hire jocks to fit the sound I wanted to create for a station. Being in a smaller market, I had to go with younger people just getting started or with only a couple years of experience," he said.

For an opening in middays, Bobby turned to J.P. Lamont, whom he knew from WOHO. Roger Monday was another Toledo jock recruited to Davenport.

Bill Vancil, who had resigned as PD of KSTT in late 1967, returned the following year when Bobby hired him to host the midday show. Clark Anthony, already established in the DJ lineup, became a lifelong friend and later helped Bobby get hired in San Diego.

The roster of KSTT Good Guys from 1968-1972 also included Dennis Allen, Mark Mathew, Don Williams, Don Steele, Chuck Hamilton,

Barry James, Rex Miller, Charley O'Dey, Tim West, Lee Michaels, Mike McCartney, David Bradley, Steve "Ain't No Other Brother" Bridges, and Brad Scott.

Scott left radio for medical school and pursued a second career as an oncologist. Bridges stayed in broadcasting and became a radio station owner in Iowa City. McCartney went on to run a group of TV stations in Maine. Bradley later joined Bobby in Philadelphia.

Dale "the Voiceman" Reeves, arriving with Top 40 experience from two stations in Louisville, had to change his name to Brian Christie because Bobby thought "Dale Reeves" sounded too much like a country DJ. But Reeves appreciated that his boss at KSTT allowed him the creative freedom to do an evening show filled with his humorous characters.

"Bobby pretty much let me do what I wanted, never really criticized me or told me to tighten up," the Voiceman said.

In managing the jocks, Bobby explained, "My favorite part was hearing something fun in what they did on air and telling them they've got it, even if they didn't know themselves. I just encouraged them to do more of the same and reminded them what not to do.

"It wasn't leading by the hand, but more of saying, 'What you do is so cool.' I've always told my staff, 'You need to do more of that.' It's the best way I know to coach and handle people.

"I grew into the business when being program director was central to the character of a radio station. We used to say that the PD was the overall personality of the station. KSTT was already great, with big personalities on the air, and I helped them become greater," Bobby said.

He branded it "The Full Time Fun Station" and continued to place a heavy emphasis on fun at every subsequent stop throughout his career.

F-bomb on the FCC

"He had the guts to try things," Reeves noted, recalling a show on which

Bobby asked listeners, "You know how to pronounce the FCC?" and then voiced several alternative pronunciations of the regulatory agency's acronym. "He did this whole improvised bit," Reeves remembered, "and it came out 'fuck' on the air!"

Reminded of the FCC F-bomb incident, Bobby stated, "I remember the bit, and I don't think I clearly said 'fuck' on the air, but you would have heard that in your head. It might have been more like 'fick' or 'fook' or 'fukeekee.' At any rate, I didn't get any complaints or fines from the Federal Communications Commission."

In the summer of 1968, the *KSTT Psychedelic Circus* appeared in Davenport. It was Bobby's idea for refreshing the station's long-running *Good Guys A-Go-Go* dance party for teenagers. He held auditions and hired a new house band for KSTT's live broadcasts from the downtown Col Ballroom. The *Psychedelic Circus* continued to draw hundreds of teens to the weekly dance party.

Jimi Hendrix rocked the same Col Ballroom that same psychedelic summer. Station owner Epstein was a concert promoter and booked the legendary rock guitarist's band for the one and only performance in Iowa by the Jimi Hendrix Experience.

Eager to keep growing the station's sizable teen and young adult audience, Bobby introduced album tracks and broadened the weekly Top 30 Survey into a Super 40 Survey of most popular songs. "I actually expanded it a couple of times," he said, "creating the 1170 Hit List that featured a Top Eleven plus other chart-topping tunes from our current, recurrent, and oldies categories."

The Beatles were a consistent favorite on KSTT, and a series of "All Beatles Weekends" featuring their newest releases and previous singles was hosted by Bobby "Beatle" Rich.

In the last week of December 1969, he and the other DJs presented a countdown of the decade's most popular songs. At midnight on New Year's Eve, KSTT aired its number one hit of the '60s: "Hey Jude."

Make way for Thing Ray

Looking for a gimmick to entice listeners and grab local media attention, Bobby found an old flatbed truck and had it painted bright red, emblazoned with the station's call letters and decorated with random metal objects welded to the frame. He named it Thing Ray and unleashed the exotic contraption into the community.

DJs on the KSTT Summer Fun Patrol drove Thing Ray to local high schools, parks, pools, parties, and other public appearances, passing out contest prizes and promotional freebies from the oddly festooned truck.

"KSTT was a place where I got to have the most bizarre and most original ideas and pulled them off. Many times, I would hear about other stations doing an on-air contest and think of a different way to do it in Davenport.

"One of my favorites was called 'The Big Switch.' All our promos were made to sound like the station was going to be switching over to something completely different—like a new format or new DJs or something. We got a lot of buzz teasing that for days until it was revealed that the big switch was actually giving away appliances like a washer or dryer because they had an on/off switch."

Fans often stopped by the station to watch the DJs playing records in the KSTT showcase studio on River Drive. A large picture window allowed listeners in the parking lot and on the street below to look up at their favorite jock behind the microphone.

"It was like going to a drive-in movie, but without the movie," Bobby quipped. "Sometimes the kids would get out of their car, sit on the hood, and hold up their transistor radios. We'd see them through the glass and wave hello."

Bridge closures and poor-boy sandwiches

Multiple highway and railroad bridges over the Mississippi River connected the Quint Cities and gave Bobby a revenue generation idea. He floated a plan to monetize traffic reports on the Government Bridge, a double-decker linking Davenport and Rock Island.

To allow large boats and barges to pass, the steel truss swing bridge was routinely closed to vehicles and trains. KSTT broadcast the temporary closures whenever government authorities notified the station via an automated phone line that activated a flashing light in the studio.

Bobby arranged for his friend Jim Davis, a.k.a. Big Jim Edwards from "The Big 8" CKLW in Windsor, Ontario, to record the official radio announcement: "This is KSTT's Direct Line Bridge Control. The Government Bridge is now closed to traffic. We will inform you when it reopens."

Adding electronic reverberation (reverb) to the recording made Big Jim's deep voice sound even deeper, and a foghorn sound effect was inserted in each report. The station's sales team then offered advertisers the opportunity to sponsor the bridge closures.

This resulted in Davis stretching an eight-word announcement into a half-minute spot: "Bridge Control is a service of the Chef's Hat, Bettendorf, the home of real Italian beef sandwiches, and the mouth-watering meal in one poor-boy sandwich. Call the Chef's Hat, 355-4755 for pickup or delivery. This is Bridge Control."

A few minutes later, listeners heard another announcement on resumption of vehicle movement over the Mississippi: "This is KSTT Bridge Control . . . the Government Bridge is again open."

Dramatizing routine traffic advisories was one example of Bobby turning something relatively minor into a big deal and keeping the fun in full-service radio.

Trouble in River City

As he was finding his comfort zone as a first-time PD, Bobby had a major conflict with station owner Fred Epstein, who ordered the DJs to "backsell" every song. Bobby insisted it was not necessary or important to identify the name of each record and artist after every tune.

"We'd been playing 'This Diamond Ring' by Gary Lewis & the Playboys for a couple of years, so it was very familiar, and I was working with my jocks to break bad habits like redundant backselling on well-known records," Bobby said.

He told his boss he would quit rather than follow the backsell directive. Epstein didn't believe it, but Bobby insisted, "No, I'm serious—and I'm prepared for any eventuality."

Epstein backed down, and Bobby stayed for another two years.

Station calls out injustice

KSTT put a heavy emphasis on news, stopping the music at fifty-five and twenty-five minutes past each hour and using the slogan "News Five Minutes Sooner" to beat competitor stations airing their newscasts at the top and bottom of every hour.

Morry Alter led a six-person team that covered politics, peace marches, and the assassinations of Martin Luther King Jr. and Robert F. Kennedy. He called in reports from the 1968 Democratic National Convention in Chicago, where Vietnam War protests and street violence erupted before the presidential nomination of Hubert Humphrey.

KSTT newsman Wes Sidney, one of the first black reporters hired in Davenport, partnered with Alter on an investigation that exposed racial discrimination by landlords in violation of the recently passed Fair Housing Act. When Sidney inquired about renting at an upscale apartment complex in the city, the manager told him there were no vacancies. Alter then visited the same apartment building and was shown several units available for immediate rental.

Upset about KSTT's reporting that revealed the discriminatory behavior, a local savings and loan association canceled its $15,000 advertising contract, according to a history of the station written by Dave Coopman. His book *Someplace Special - KSTT* described Epstein defending the news team and encouraging his station manager, Jim Watt, to confront the S&L executives.

In Coopman's account of the incident, Esptein praised Watt for shaming the ultra-conservative bankers and added, "To show the strength of the station, the savings and loan was back on the air in three weeks."[4]

Larry Cooper, Jeff Blake, Dan Hibbs, Don Sanford, and Peter Buckley were among the reporters who covered local and national events that year, including the Charles City, Iowa, tornado that caused thirteen deaths and injured more than 450 people.

Jerry Reid succeeded Alter as news director, and the KSTT news staff in the late '60s and '70s also included John Hunter, Roger Lewis, Steve Shay, Peter Buckley, Bob Huber, Bill Adams, Dave Burkett, Rob McCann, David Morgan, Bill Longman, Don Wilson, Paulee Lipsman, Mike Eauclair, Gary Hummell, Wydell Boyd, and sportscaster Charley Steiner.

After leaving KSTT, Steiner was hired by Bobby at 99X in New York before joining ESPN and then the Los Angeles Dodgers.

Recognition, resignation, reinvention

Coopman's history of the station included former sales manager Dan Olson's comment, "During Bobby's tenure at KSTT, ratings were

[4]*Someplace Special—KSTT Radio* by Dave Coopman, Chapter 16
https://ksttgoodguysdotnet.wordpress.com/history-of-kstt/

incredible. Listeners really appreciated his talent, the talent he brought to the station, and what he did on the air."

Looking back on his time in Iowa, Bobby remarked, "I made plenty of mistakes there, but when I left after four and a half years, I had a dominant share of the audience."

"Dan was one of my biggest supporters," he recalled, "always open to creative promotions that we knew would generate revenue and be better than some of the ideas pitched by sales reps that didn't fit our station image."

Ready to prove himself on a larger stage, Bobby announced his resignation at the end of 1972. "I realized I might not ever make it to a major market if I waited any longer," he said. "A lot of the jocks in big markets were in their twenties and thirties, and I was twenty-seven. If I didn't quit, I might have stayed there in Davenport forever. So, I gave three months' notice."

With high expectations but no job prospects in sight, Bobby planned to sell all his belongings, buy an RV, and hit the road with his wife, Judy, and their sons Bryan and Jeff, in search of prominent Top 40 stations beyond Iowa. His plan to hand-deliver an audition tape to potential employers changed, however, when the phone rang during one of his last shows at KSTT.

"Two weeks before my final day, I got a call from a well-known Chicago jock who had just taken a new job as a first-time program director in Miami. He said, 'I think I have a place for you if you're interested in making a move.'"

Jumping at the opportunity, Bobby made his next segue south to Florida for his first FM gig.

Bobby at the mic with bicycle horn, KSTT, Davenport, Iowa. (Photo from Bobby Rich Radio collection)

For KSTT airchecks and more audio go to bobbyrichradio.com.

Chapter 19

Sharing the Microphone with Dick Clark

Dick Clark was the DJ who introduced America to rock'n'roll on television, and Bobby Rich was the DJ who introduced the Quint Cities to Dick Clark on KSTT radio.

The star of *American Bandstand* and host of the Miss Teenage America pageant came to Davenport in November of 1968 to promote his newly released movie, *Killers Three*, and graciously accepted an invitation to appear on Bobby's afternoon show.

"KSTT was the sponsor of the Miss Teenage Quint Cities pageant, and when Dick Clark's PR people told us he was coming to town, I arranged for him to join me on the air," Bobby said. "He was great, very playful, and I got him to record some promos mentioning all the jocks on our station."

Clark and Bobby traded one-liners for a full hour, took calls from listeners, and played hits including "Goody Goody Gumdrops" by the 1910 Fruitgum Company and "Not Enough Indians" by Dean Martin. A song by Vanilla Fudge got the guest DJ talking about other bands with strange names, most notably Stark Naked & the Car Thieves.

Clark aced a set of "cold reads" (unrehearsed live commercials) for Quint Cities Petroleum, the Hullabaloo teenage dance club, and Parker's department store. He sprinkled some '60s slang into his weather forecast ("These are the temperatures, man") and a pep talk with a caller recovering from a fractured tailbone ("How do you dig the crutches?").

Somebody is listening to you!

Fascinated with KSTT's studio window that allowed passing motorists on River Street to see into the station, the media mogul kidded the local DJ.

"It's wild, you got people driving by waving. Somebody, Bobby, is listening to you! I wouldn't have believed it myself," Clark joked.

Their good-natured teasing continued with a snappy critique of the *Bandstand* host's latest theatrical release. "I saw a preview of your movie," Bobby said. "It had a good beat, hard to dance to. I'd give it an 85."

Clark laughed and downplayed his character's homicidal tendencies in the low-budget crime drama, telling Bobby, "In this motion picture, I play a drunken stumblebum . . . a rather unusual cat." He wrote, produced, and starred in the film, whose cast and soundtrack included country music legend Merle Haggard.

"Even if you don't want to see the movie, go see the theater," suggested Clark, hugely impressed with the brand-new Sierra cinema that was screening *Killers Three* in downtown Moline.

At the end of their hour on the air, Bobby persuaded "America's oldest teenager" to make a surprise appearance at a house party for a local Miss Teenage America finalist. After a stop at the Coronet Theater in Davenport to plug his new movie that night, Clark met Bobby outside the home of a Moline High School student celebrating with her friends and family.

"It was a big surprise, no one told her that he had arrived," Bobby recalled, "so when Dick Clark walked into the party, the girl and all her guests just flipped out. Dick was terrific to do that, signing autographs and posing for pictures."

Clark emceed *American Bandstand* from 1957 to 1989 and was inducted into the Rock & Roll Hall of Fame with the notation, "He curated the soundtrack of the American teenager's life."

On his brief visit to Davenport, Clark created lifetime memories for a seventeen-year-old beauty pageant contestant and a twenty-three-year-old DJ who would go on to establish his own long-running career in the music business.

Dick Clark and Bobby strike a pose, Davenport Fashion Week, 1968. (Photo from Bobby Rich Radio collection)

Chapter 20

Bad Bobby—Things I Shouldn't Have Said

"But I was going to pay for them before I left."

- What I said when I was caught shoplifting two stupid little toy trucks from the Sprouse-Reitz store in Ephrata at age eight.

"What's wrong with being average? That means there are many others worse than me!"

- Response to my dad, who questioned why he was still paying for me to be in college for another semester when I was only pulling a 2.3 grade point average.

"Piss, I love you!"

- How I introduced the Beatles song "P.S. I Love You" on KFLY Corvallis during a New Year's Eve remote broadcast at the T & R Restaurant.

"No problem, officer, I'm Bobby Rich!"

- What I said to the cop who pulled me over for circling the KSTT building in Davenport while my passengers went inside to pee. It was the last night of Daylight-Saving Time, and we took that extra hour to go drinking.

"No problem, Bobby Rich, turn off your vehicle and step out of the car."

- What the Davenport police officer said to me. Luckily, he knew I worked at the station.

"We'll just say on the air that we give away more money than anyone in town, with a guarantee to double any other station's contest prize money."

- My brilliant recommendation to Gene Chenault, owner of KYNO in Fresno whose competitor was running a "Bank Vault" contest promising one lucky winner all the cash they could take out of the vault in ninety-five seconds. To our great surprise, their winner grabbed more than $50,000. We had to fork over more than $100,000 to our contest winner!

"We're fucked!"

- What I once shouted in exasperation (off the air) to my San Diego morning show partners Scott, Frank, and Pat the day they had no content for our next set with just fifteen seconds before a song ended.

"I am prepared for any eventuality."

- What I told at least three different general managers when they threatened to fire me if I didn't stop doing whatever it was that they didn't like. None of those GMs carried through on their threats, but several others fired me when I didn't say it!

Bobby Rich, November 2023

Chapter 21

Miami Beach Showdown: Bobby vs. the Dopers

Four years in the same job was such a surprisingly long stretch of time that when Bobby announced in 1972 that he was leaving KSTT Davenport for a larger market, *Billboard* magazine radio columnist Claude Hall commented, "He'd been program director of the station a ton of years."[5]

His next gig in Miami lasted less than six months, ending with a letter of resignation published in *Billboard* in which Bobby cited a "moral decision" to leave the major market station.

"Miami was never on my radar until Kris Erik Stevens called, offering me the 9-to-midnight shift at WMYQ," he recalled.

Stevens, a self-described "fast-talkin', finger poppin' jock" from WLS in Chicago, was the new PD at the high-energy FM in South Florida owned by the Bartell Broadcasters group.

"I liked what I'd heard of Bobby on the air," Stevens said, "and I was glad to be able to hire him."

Keep on truckin'

One of the first FM Top 40 stations, WMYQ debuted in 1971. Like KCBQ in San Diego and WDRQ in Detroit, it achieved early success

[5]Billboard, Apr 22, 1972, pg 16; https://www.worldradiohistory.com/Archive-All-Music/Billboard/70s/1972/BB-1972-04-22.pdf

under the direction of programming guru Buzz Bennett. Pioneer rock radio consultant Lee Abrams was one of Bennett's first hires at WMYQ and got his start as a programmer there.

"All of Bartell's Q stations played the same Q format," Bobby said. "Buzz started a lot of stuff like establishing their identity in one simple shotgun jingle with the call letters sung a cappella after a high-speed electric drum sound."

The cartoon image and phrase "Keep on Truckin'" were prominent in WMYQ's logo and branding in 1972. "Alone Again (Naturally)" by Gilbert O'Sullivan was number one on the station's Top 96 singles chart that year, and "American Pie" by Don McLean finished second.

"WMYQ had several really strong jocks," Bobby said, "including Steve Mitchell, who later worked for me briefly in Los Angeles, and Phil Flowers, who I hired in San Diego. Dave Thomson was another of those guys who had a natural warmth on the air, sounded very hip and youthful, but it was hard to pin down how old they were."

The lineup of personalities on 'MYQ also included Chuck Bennett, Johnny Dark, Robert W. Walker, J. Michael Stone, Jim Kelly, and Fast Eddie.

Rolling Stones and Carpenters

DJs took requests from WMYQ listeners on separate phone lines for Dade County and Broward County. Their summer playlist was a blend of hard rock anthems, soft rock ballads, and sugary pop hits, ranging from "Layla" (Derek and the Dominoes) and "Bang a Gong" (T. Rex) to "Rocket Man" (Elton John) and "Candy Man" (Sammy Davis Jr.).

"Take it Easy" (The Eagles), "Tumbling Dice" (The Rolling Stones), and "School's Out" (Alice Cooper), could be heard on WMYQ along with "Puppy Love" (Donny Osmond) and "Goodbye to Love" (Carpenters).

The entire playlist of songs was transferred from vinyl albums to carts (tape cartridges) and numerically cataloged for easy access by the DJs. The shift from turntables to cart machines allowed them to activate every musical selection with the push of a single button.

Florida morning man finds Electric Weenie

After a month and a half on late-nights, Bobby was offered a prime-time air shift when WMYQ fired morning man Roby Yonge. Miami's "Big Kahuna," Yonge previously worked in New York until he was let go by WABC for spreading the "Paul is dead" rumor about the Beatles' Paul McCartney.

"I had never done mornings before, except for some fill-ins," Bobby said, "but I jumped at the chance. Waking up for that 6 a.m. shift was a big adjustment. I'd gotten used to working till midnight and then staying up late to watch Johnny Carson on TV.

"Our general manager, Russ Wittberger, told me I was the only jock who didn't follow the rules," Bobby remembered, "but he realized that mornings is a breakout shift, and he liked that I understood how to be fun and entertaining."

"At first, I didn't really know what it was like to get up so early, let alone be funny on the radio at that hour. I was fortunate to have a natural level of high energy and enthusiasm to match the up-tempo music. I wrote a lot of material and found a couple of joke services like the Electric Weenie."

Advertised as "Radio's Most Popular DJ Personality Gag Sheet," the Electric Weenie provided jocks with humorous one-liners for a modest subscription fee.

"By using professionally written jokes, I started to figure out how they were structured, with a setup and payoff, always delivering the funny part last," Bobby said. "The early comics like Jack Benny and Bob Hope had brought this to radio."

"In the morning show, we had all the hot songs—nine or ten of them repeating every hour and fifteen minutes. I hated having to play 'My Ding-A-Ling' by Chuck Berry several times a day," he admitted, "but the double entendre lyrics made it a hit in Miami and nationwide."

WMYQ's song selection, Wittberger told *Billboard*, was based on "jukebox surveillance," local record sales, calls to the station's request line, and outreach to listeners in the target demographic. "Because if you only judge by sales and requests, you end up playing strictly music for teenagers," he said.[6]

"Through research, we find out what teens want to hear, but also what the 18- to 34-year-old listener wants to hear. These people don't telephone you asking to hear a record, and they don't ordinarily buy singles at all," the GM explained.

"So, we go into the shopping centers at midday and talk to housewives. Often, they'll tell you that they like such and such a record, even though they never considered buying it. Jukeboxes are also very valuable in determining what people want to hear that they don't buy."

Dolphins, donkeys, and elephants

WMYQ presented concerts by Creedence Clearwater Revival and Rod Stewart at the Hollywood Sportatorium in the suburb of Pembroke Pines. Jethro Tull performed at Convention Hall Miami.

Street celebrations broke out as the Miami Dolphins played their perfect NFL season in '72. Led by quarterback Bob Griese and running backs Mercury Morris and Larry Csonka, the city's pro football team was undefeated in seventeen games and won Super Bowl VII.

Miami Beach was also a political hot spot that summer, hosting the Democratic National Convention, where George McGovern accepted

[6]*Billboard Apr 1, 1972, pg 24;* https://www.worldradiohistory.com/Archive-All-Music/Billboard/70s/1972/BB-1972-04-01.pdf

his party's presidential nomination, and the Republican National Convention, at which Richard Nixon was nominated for reelection. Tens of thousands of demonstrators converged to protest the Vietnam War.

'These are not my people'

Located on the Miami Beach strip, the station experienced a high rate of talent and management turnover. "Bartell stations were a bit of a swinging door," noted Stevens, who left WMYQ after six months as PD and returned to Chicago in September to do nights at WCFL.

Bobby made his exit a few weeks after that.

What soured him on Miami, he revealed more than fifty years later, was feeling ostracized because he shunned the pervasive drug use surrounding the radio station and local music scene.

"The druggies had their own clique, and I felt like an outcast because I wasn't into that lifestyle," he said. "Doing my own thing on the air, I had a really good time but never felt accepted and knew it wasn't going to be a long-term gig at the Q."

Fed up with the situation, Bobby informed his GM that he was resigning for strictly personal reasons. "These are not my people," he wrote in a letter referencing "the dopers" faction without identifying any of them.

Billboard obtained his resignation letter and published it in October after the magazine's editor deleted the station's call letters and the names of Bobby and his bosses.

By the time the anonymous letter appeared in print, Bobby was gone from WMYQ. He had proven himself in a major market and enjoyed his debut as a morning man, but never warmed to Miami Beach or its party atmosphere.[7]

[7] *Billboard, Oct 14, 1972, pg 32;* https://www.worldradiohistory.com/Archive-All-Music/Billboard/70s/1972/BB-1972-10-14.pdf

A Letter of Resignation

EDITOR'S NOTE: This is an actual letter of resignation by an air personality in a major market. Names have been deleted to protect the innocent. But I'm apologizing for also having to protect the guilty, including, evidently, the radio station. The letter was to the general manager.

Dear ____________________,

Enclosed is a copy of my resignation. In it, I have stated "strictly personal reasons" for leaving XXXX. This was a difficult decision to make.

When _____ __________ hired me, I was impressed and excited to become a part of one of the country's most talked about, as well as listened to, stations. When you and ______ let me take a crack at the morning show, I was flattered and proud.

When _______ was let go, I was confused.

I can see now how the station was getting farther and farther away from the original concept. At the same time, ______ was doing at least *some* good. Perhaps, like _____ ________ and _____ ________, he just wasn't given a real chance to prove he could do the job.

But this fifth-quarter quarterbacking does not really say anything about my reasons for leaving. If in fact anyone really cares, since disk jockeys come and go at will. But I like to be remembered and I like people to know where I stand.

Whether or not the choice of the new program director was sound remains to be seen (or heard, as the case may be). I will not deny him his well-deserved chance to prove he can do the job. And he very well may do just that. At any rate he will conquer with or without _____ ________ or __ _____ ______.

Professionalism aside, this could really be described as a moral decision. These are not my people. Undoubtedly, I am just as cliqueish as the dopers when it comes to lack of acceptance of the opposite faction. In this regard, I concur with your recent memo completely . . . but I can't seem to "live" with the situation on a day-to-day basis.

Finally, I want to again thank you for our talk last Thursday. It made the decision even harder. I was very much reassured once your policy was stated, but again, it is different on a person-to-person level (me vs. the dopers).

I genuinely enjoyed my experiences here. I will retain a massive respect for XXXX, ________, and _____ ________. Thank you very much for everything.

Sincerely,

____

Anonymous letter of resignation, *Billboard* magazine, Oct. 14, 1972.

Chapter 22

Serious Drug Problem

Miami's drug scene in 1972 made Bobby so uncomfortable that he quit his first morning DJ job to get away from it. He took another antidrug stance on his San Diego morning show in 1986.

A day after Super Bowl XX, in which the Chicago Bears humiliated the New England Patriots by a score of 46-10, Patriots coach Raymond Berry revealed that five or more of his players had a serious drug problem. The team took a vote and agreed to institute a voluntary drug testing program, the first of its kind in the NFL.

Reacting to a B-100 morning news report about the scandal, Bobby took issue with the phrase "serious drug problem."

"I'd just like to point out, every time a news story like that comes up, that particular terminology is used. In my way of thinking, there is no such thing as a drug problem that's not serious," Bobby said on the air.

"If you've got a drug problem, it's serious," he emphasized.

Chapter 23

Screaming Jocks on The Lucky 13

Determined to escape South Florida, Bobby was beyond thrilled when his friend John Long threw him a lifeline from Connecticut, more than 1,300 miles away.

"I had stayed in touch with John since the late '60s when we worked for competing stations in Iowa. He knew I was unhappy down in Miami," Bobby said, "and the offer to join him as assistant PD and afternoon personality at WAVZ in New Haven was a real boost to my career.

"Even though it was a smaller market, working with John and doing the kind of radio I loved eventually led me to Los Angeles. I was in my screaming DJ phase, and he liked that," Bobby said of his time at the high-energy station located near the downtown campus of Yale University.

"All these years later, it's almost embarrassing for me to listen to, but that style was hugely popular at the time. I wanted to outdo my competitors by giving the most energetic and upbeat performance to win the biggest audience of teens and young adults."

Hired as operations manager and PD to breathe new life into the formerly "chicken rock" station, Long turned it into a more youthful Top 40, rebranded as The New WAVZ 13 (pronounced "Waves").

"John loved making charts and figuring how to rotate a three-hundred-song music library," Bobby recalled. "It was cool being his assistant because we shared a lot of philosophies, and I got to be involved in programming decisions that were new to me."

Yelling into the mic

This was an era when jocks were encouraged to crank up their vocal intensity to match the up-tempo hit music. "I would introduce songs like 'Love Train' by the O'Jays, give the weather, and promote our contests and events by yelling into the microphone," Bobby said.

Also known as The Lucky 13 to emphasize its 1300 AM dial position, WAVZ rewarded listeners with more than the usual giveaways of cash, concert tickets, and albums. The prize list included Polaroid cameras, color TVs, five hundred gallons of gas, a trip to Acapulco, a minibike, a Suzuki 250 Savage motorcycle, and a 1973 Corvette Stingray.

Besides Long, the air personalities on WAVZ included Cash Sunshine, Mason Dixon, Tom Britton, Kris Edwards, Brian Phoenix, Buzzy Hart, Smokin' Joe Hager, Al Perkins, Paul Robins, Jim Ryan, and Paul "the Morning" Mayer. Charley Steiner led the WAVZ Eyewitness News department.

Five years later in New York, Bobby would hire Britton and Steiner to join his staff at 99X.

"Neither One of Us (Wants to Be the First to Say Goodbye)" by Gladys Knight & The Pips was the most popular song on WAVZ in early April of 1973, as Bobby's time in New Haven was ending.

He had enjoyed good fortune at The Lucky 13, with the encouragement of a boss and a renowned Top 40 consultant who valued his highly animated on-air delivery, production skills, and station imaging work.

Earning their respect led to the opportunity of a lifetime.

Next up on Bobby's career path: Hollywood.

"I always wanted to be a rock jock!"

Chapter 24

Welcome to LA, Epicenter of Boss Radio

As the afternoon jock at WAVZ in New Haven, Bobby was unaware that higher-ups were considering him for a much bigger job on the other side of the country.

Waking up one morning to an unexpected call from program director John Long, Bobby recalled, "I picked up the phone and was blown away by what happened next."

Long told him, "There are only two reasons why I'd call you this early in the morning. One is somebody just won our thousand-dollar contest, and we need you to come in to record a new promo with the winner. And the other reason is Paul Drew wants you to come work at KHJ in Los Angeles."

Thinking a gig in Hollywood was too far-fetched to be true, Bobby responded, "Okay, I'll be right in to record the promo." But his boss replied, "No, it's the other reason. Paul is going to call you in twenty minutes."

Drew, the Top 40 pioneer at CKLW and KFRC in the Detroit and San Francisco markets before taking the helm at KHJ and becoming vice president of programming for the RKO General Broadcasting chain, was a consultant to WAVZ. He had received tapes of Bobby's air shifts and production work from Long.

"I saw Paul in our lobby in New Haven once, chatting with John. He always wore a suit and a pork pie hat with a wire in his ear connected to a transistor radio to constantly monitor his client stations," Bobby said.

"I knew the two of them talked almost daily, but it never occurred to me that Paul would want to bring me to KHJ."

Moving to Los Angeles, sight unseen

Drew called and offered a job in LA with a salary of $25,000, more money than Bobby had ever earned. He quickly accepted, and after packing a U-Haul and driving his family three thousand miles from Connecticut to California, he started at KHJ in June of 1973.

No strategic career map or professional development plan led him to Los Angeles. "I was offered a job I never asked for in a city I'd never been to or considered. I didn't even like LA or what I imagined it to be," Bobby admitted. But the twenty-seven-year-old DJ was confident that he could help continue the iconic station's greatness.

KHJ had been a consistent ratings powerhouse since the mid-'60s, thanks to renowned Boss Radio programmers Bill Drake and Ron Jacobs and legendary DJs including the Real Don Steele, Robert W. Morgan, and Humble Harve. They established 93 KHJ as a dominant force with teenage and young adult listeners, competing against rival AM music stations KFWB, KRLA, and KMPC.

No pressure at all

Bobby's arrival followed the departure of the program directors and boss jocks who reigned supreme during the golden age of KHJ. Drew had succeeded Drake as PD, and Morgan would soon join Steele in exiting for a new competitor, K-100 (KIQQ-FM), owned by Drake and his business partner, Gene Chenault.

"In rebuilding the air staff, Drew brought in a bunch of young bucks like me, in our mid- to late-twenties, and encouraged us to be high energy and not sound like the old guys."

The famous PD offered Bobby some advice on handling the pressure of working in LA. "He sat me down and said, 'I know how intimidating it is to be in a top-three market, and it's Hollywood, but just think of it as a bunch of New Havens,'" Bobby remembered.

"I didn't feel that way when I got there, I wasn't nervous or overwhelmed. There were a lot of things to get used to, like working with a board operator for the first time, an engineer who controlled the equipment that played our songs and commercials."

Zap, you're Morganized!

In his first week at KHJ, Bobby was required to do three supervised overnight shows to get acquainted with the studio, equipment, and format. During one of these break-in shifts, he met longtime morning man Robert W. Morgan, whose show was billed as "Robert W. in the Morgan."

"Near the end of my shift, around 5:40 a.m., Robert W. came into the studio to check his mailbox and prep the music for his show that started at six o'clock," Bobby recalled. "I reached out to shake his hand and said, 'Good Morgan!' because that was his signature catchphrase.

"And Robert W. Morgan snarled back at me, 'How the fuck would you know?!'

"I was shocked. Those were the first words he ever spoke to me. I just looked away, he grumbled something, got his stuff from his cubby, and left to go prep for his show.

"Fifteen minutes later, he was back in the studio and even more pissed off because I played 'Good Day Sunshine' by the Beatles for my last record. Morgan said, 'Thanks a lot for ruining my first set, you stole the power gold song that I scheduled for 6:10.'

"I saw him make a fist and raise his arm, and I'm pretty sure he would have hit me if Johnny Williams hadn't intervened. Johnny was the all-night jock supervising my first air shifts. He got Robert W. calmed down, and I grabbed my papers and got out of there.

"I figured he resented me because I was one of the young and less experienced jocks that Paul Drew brought to KHJ," Bobby said. Shortly after the incident, Bobby was moved into the 9-to-midnight shift and had no further encounters with Morgan.

Captain John, Barry Kaye, and Danny Martinez were added to the lineup in 1973, joining KHJ veterans Bill Wade and peacemaker Williams.

In July, Bobby made his first appearance on the KHJ Thirty music survey, a weekly flyer that ranked the station's most popular songs and featured a photo of one of the DJs. Topping the hit list was "One Tin Soldier" by Coven, followed by "Natural High" by Bloodstone, "Smoke on the Water" by Deep Purple, and "Shambala" by Three Dog Night.

A few weeks later, Morgan announced he was leaving the station. The news was reported in the Vox Jox column of *Billboard* magazine, which included his acerbic comment, "I no longer feel it is beneficial to my career to be associated with the level of professionalism now existent at KHJ." [8]

Jim Carson from KFRC in San Francisco was brought in to host the morning show until August, when Charlie Van Dyke returned from WLS in Chicago to take over as KHJ morning man.

In other news that summer, KHJ's B.R. Bradbury was honored in August as *Billboard's* Radio Newsman of the Year.

---

[8]*Billboard* July 28, 1973, pg 32 https://www.worldradiohistory.com/hd2/IDX-Business/Music/Billboard-Index/IDX/1972/1972-01-01-Billboard-Page-0066.pdf#search=%22charlie%20van%20dyke%20khj%22

Life in the fast lane

The KHJ studios were on the same block of Melrose Avenue as Paramount Pictures and the TV production company Desilu, founded by Desi Arnaz and Lucille Ball. The neighborhood was also home to Nickodell, a favorite restaurant and watering hole for stars of the radio, movie, and TV industries.

Bobby didn't feel comfortable in the atmosphere of old-timers, martinis, and cigarette smoke at Nickodell's bar and dining room, a place that was suitably darkened for Hollywood dealmakers. But he took a liking to the margaritas served across the street at Lucy's El Adobe.

Jackson Brown and Don Henley were among the music and show business regulars at the Mexican café on Melrose. Lucy's was where Linda Ronstadt and Jerry Brown met in the 1970s, still early in their respective Grammy and gubernatorial careers.

After a year in LA, Bobby said, "I got to learn where Top 40 was going, and it's what I would eventually bring when given the chance to be a PD again."

That opportunity would come in 1974, in California's second-biggest city.

Bobby on KHJ, 1973, and more audio at bobbyrichradio.com.

Bobby's first time on the KHJ Weekly Survey, July 3, 1973.

Chapter 25

Radio Inspiration

I am often asked what caused me to choose radio broadcasting for my career. It is assumed that there is some big story about a cosmic realization, or a dream I had, or an influence from a specific person or whatever. Spoiler alert: None of these things happened.

What drew me into the entertainment arena? I didn't come from a showbiz family although my mother and my older sisters were proficient in music. Specifically, vocals, piano, and the love that comes from performing. Marcia and Jan collected records and sheet music of hits of the day. Our mother, Margaret, when she was not rehearsing for her weekly solo at church, always had the radio turned on to the local station.

My father applied his talents in government work and in the private sector. A businessman, community leader, public speaker, and semiprofessional duplicate bridge player, he was active in the Kiwanis Club and received the Silver Beaver Award from the Boy Scouts of America for distinguished service to youth. Dad worked for the U.S. Department of Agriculture in Washington, DC, (where I was born) before being transferred to the West for an administrator's job when the Bureau of Reclamation was building hydropower dams that turned the not-yet-fertile land of eastern and central Washington state into growing fields.

Dad became quite the entrepreneur after resigning from his federal government job to build the first bowling center in Ephrata, Washington. This risky venture was a success for many years and led to his next career as a bowling ball tycoon. Working with the inventor, he started a company that manufactured the first non-Ebonite bowling ball, the Columbia 300. Made from a plastic solution, this manufacturing innovation changed modern bowling and launched a champion brand.

As a kid, I was always starting a new business. For instance, I had a sign company. I put up a sign on my bedroom door announcing that you could have your signs made here. When Mom and Dad's friends would come over to the house, they would always ask me, "What does this mean?" And I would explain that if you have a business and you need to put up a sign to advertise it, I will make one for you.

It was all they could do to keep from laughing, although many of them thought it was so cute. I made and sold signs to my grandparents and anybody else who would give me a nickel.

All that at age eight.

My entrepreneurial spirit included the usual kid jobs like mowing lawns, shoveling snow, and stacking lumber. When I was about twelve, I assembled my own radio station capable of broadcasting to a one-mile radius! By that time, I had made friends at the only radio station in our town, and they helped me. The station engineer taught me how to modify the transmitter kit that I purchased by mail order. By taking some of the wire off the coil and running a copper wire from my bedroom window up to the roof of our house, I was able to increase the coverage of my signal.

Between the ages of seven and fourteen, I worked for my dad at the bowling center. He hated it when anybody called it a bowling "alley." I also shined shoes at a barbershop, delivered the hometown newspaper (which had about three pages once a week), and gave free lovelorn advice to some of the girls in high school. Yes, I had ulterior motives for that one, but honestly, it didn't help a lot.

Having already determined my career would be in radio, I pursued that all the time. I went to the radio station every Saturday and Sunday and a couple of times during the week. Sitting on the floor in the corner of the studio, I would ask the DJs a gazillion questions. Eventually, they set me up in the recording studio, and I figured out the rest.

In my senior year of high school, I became a promoter for teenage dances at the recreation center in Ephrata. To persuade my parents to let me risk my savings on such a questionable gig, I convinced my friend Jerry to join me as a silent partner. Well, Jerry didn't have any money.

Luckily "our" Jericho Productions made a few dollars hiring bands from Spokane, Bellingham, and Seattle. I cut a deal with the local police department, hiring all their off-duty officers (both of them) for sock hop security and making a donation to their foundation. That allowed me to get public service announcements (PSAs) on the radio station.

I wrote and produced those PSAs and spent most of my marketing budget to get posters printed professionally. Then I hit the road in my dad's car, driving to businesses in a thirty-five-mile radius and asking to post my dance signs in their windows.

A few years later in Iowa, my side gig was managing local bands. Doing business as Super Bee Productions, I was the emcee and backstage coordinator for some big-name shows in Davenport, including Sonny & Cher, Paul Revere & the Raiders, The Association, Bobby Sherman, Blood, Sweat & Tears, and the 5th Dimension.

Only now do I fully appreciate how my family provided the early exposure to music and a competitive and entrepreneurial spirit that inspired me to perform, entertain, and explore creativity.

—Bobby Rich, November 2023

Chapter 26

One of America's Three Great Stations

A weekend getaway to San Diego was Bobby's introduction to the city where he would experience his most enduring and enjoyable career success. Twice. In two decades. At the same station.

Clark Anthony, his friend from KSTT in Davenport, Iowa, extended the invitation to visit.

"Clark is the one responsible for getting me to San Diego," Bobby explained, "because he knew I was eager to get back into programming and recommended me to his general manager when KFMB had an opening."

Anthony, hosting an afternoon show on the station, scored a hit with his job referral in 1974.

Hired at the hibachi grill

Paul Palmer, the GM of KFMB, was impressed with Bobby's on-air work at KHJ and arranged for them to meet at his favorite restaurant in Los Angeles. It was a memorable meal.

"Paul flew up to Burbank and I picked him up at the airport in my Buick Riviera. He scheduled my job interview at Benihana on La Cienega Boulevard," Bobby remembered. "He was bragging that all the stars went there.

"We got a first-time chef doing his chop-chop knife tricks with the seafood and flaming onions, and a flying shrimp landed in Paul's bouffant hairdo."

Despite the embarrassing hibachi flub, Palmer convinced Bobby to leave LA and join his AM station in San Diego.

'He'll fit right in'

"KFMB was big-time, with great ratings and strong professionals who knew what they were doing," Bobby said. Originally hired as afternoon DJ, he later moved to the 6-9 p.m. shift and was operations manager under Program Director Jack Woods.

Palmer reminisced at a 2015 radio reunion about hiring Bobby from Los Angeles. "People told me he's high maintenance and an asshole," Palmer quipped. "And I said, 'Well, I can handle the high maintenance part. And about the asshole part, I think he'll fit right in.'"

The station's top-rated morning show, Charlie and Harrigan, featured Woods as Charlie Brown and Paul Menard as Irv Harrigan. Perry Allen held the afternoon shift before and after Bobby's arrival.

The jock lineup also included Skip Conover, Dave Love, and Lenny Mitchell, while Fred Stemen and Danuta were among the reporters led by news director Phil Stewart and later Tony LaMonica. Sportscaster Mike Wolfe called the action on San Diego State University games before Ron Reina joined as sports director and play-by-play man for Aztecs football and basketball broadcasts.

Turkeys on the turntable

The fun zone of KFMB programming included a weekly show of big DJ energy and novelty records called the *Bobby Rich Turkey Hour*.

A typical turkey song was "Troglodyte (Cave Man)" by the Jimmy Castor Bunch, a novelty funk record from 1972 about Bertha Butt. The song helped set the stage for the band's 1975 release "The Bertha Butt Boogie."

Pigmeat Markham's "Here Comes the Judge" was another so-called gobbler that Bobby played when his friend and fellow record collector Jerry Peterson appeared as a "guest turkey" on the show. Peterson was better known as Gene Knight, the popular DJ and music director hired three times by Bobby at radio stations in San Diego and Los Angeles.

Liking the laidback vibe

"I kind of knew early on that my stay in San Diego was going to be a longer-term gig than most of my prior jobs," Bobby said. "I got a good feeling from being a part of the community and worked really hard on researching and exploring the city."

After years of entertaining mostly teenagers, he turned his attention to the interests and activities of an older audience. Grownups were the target demographic of KFMB, with programming focused on adults ages 25–49.

To create a big-time image, Bobby said, "We made up a slogan and got Charlie Van Dyke to record the liner."

Their baritone announcer proclaimed the tongue-in-cheek catchphrase, "KFMB . . . one of America's three great radio stations!"

"We never did name the other two," Bobby said with a chuckle.

Enjoying his work environment as well as the desirable weather and relaxed lifestyle, he felt at home in San Diego. "Compared to LA, the population wasn't so massive and there was a laidback beach vibe in the '70s. People used to call it mellow because chill hadn't been invented yet," Bobby observed.

While at KFMB, he befriended future programmer Rob Sisco, who got his start in radio as an intern on Allen's show and went on to become a research analyst, marketing consultant, and broadcast industry executive. Bobby chose him to be assistant program director at 99X in New York and PD and operations manager of KMGI in Seattle. Sisco was later chief operating officer of entertainment and president of music at the Nielsen Company.

As their professional association grew, Bobby became friends with Sisco's family in San Diego. Ten years later, after four other radio stations, three other cities, and one divorce, Bobby would marry Rob's twin sister, Debbie.

Waiting in the wings

Palmer had another job in mind for Bobby but didn't tip his hand during the first year they worked together.

"Paul had built a successful full-service station, brought in jocks with big personality, a serious news team, lots of community involvement, and music geared to young adults. KFMB reflected his leadership, fun-loving style, and commitment to San Diego," Bobby recalled.

Midwest Television Inc. had owned KFMB-AM 760 and its sister stations KFMB-FM 100.7 and KFMB-TV Channel 8 since the company's entry into the San Diego market in the 1960s. The FM station, airing an automated beautiful music format, had yet to generate significant revenue by 1974. It ranked twenty-third in the local ratings.

"I didn't know how unimportant our FM was to ownership until I saw the budget for all three stations," Bobby said. As AM operations manager, he reviewed a statement listing the company's income sources as TV, radio, and other. The asset of least importance designated "other" was the underperforming FM, he realized.

If the owners did not yet realize its potential, Bobby and his boss did.

By 1975 Palmer was ready to entrust Bobby with the keys to the company's "other" station. Together they would hatch a plan to breathe new life into the stagnant FM and reach number one in the San Diego ratings.

KFMB billboard, c. 1974. From left: Charlie & Harrigan, Clark Anthony, Bobby Rich, Ron Reina, Skip Conover, Perry Allen. (Photo by L. Rosen)

KFMB airchecks of Bobby and the Turkey Hour, 1975, at bobbyrichradio.com.

Chapter 27

Hour of Turkey

Comedian Stan Freberg's schtick was Bobby's introduction to the world of novelty records.

"In Cub Scouts, I put together a group of friends to do skits from Freberg's albums," Bobby said, "like his parody of the TV cop show *Dragnet.* We made costumes and memorized his 'St. George and the Dragonet' sketch. Then we'd take a record player to parents' night and act out our favorite Freberg comedy routine."

Bobby named his Cub Scout den the Tailbone Patrol, but their stage name was "The Singin' 63" when performing Freberg's spoofs of "Rock Island Line" and "Ya Got Trouble."

Having decided early in life to be a novelty music devotee, Bobby kept a personal stash of unconventional songs on LP records and 45s. With every move to another job in radio, his vinyl medley was boxed up and relocated to the next city.

Occasionally he plucked a ditty from the eccentric collection to play on the air for a special occasion. That all changed with his creation of a weekly show specifically designed to showcase quirky and often gimmicky songs that didn't fit the format of any traditional station.

Not necessarily bad songs

The Bobby Rich Turkey Hour was hatched on July 26, 1975, at KFMB-AM in San Diego.

"That was the day I was cleaning up the closet in my den in my very own home, and I came across a whole box of dumb, dusty old records," he explained on the air.

"And I said to myself: 'Self, these are songs which you don't hardly ever hear anymore . . . anyhow, no how, nowhere, anywhere, anyway, anyhow, no how, nowhere, no way, no place, no how, anyway, no kidding, and like that.'

"So, I thought, well, why not bring 'em to the radio station so people can hear 'em on their electric radios. And I did. And the rest is history," Bobby exclaimed to his audience of offbeat music listeners.

"Right before your startled earlobes," the screaming host of the fast-paced Monday night show revealed that the "gobblers" composing his *Turkey Hour* set list had been carefully transported in a paper bag from Ralphs supermarket.

As grand poobah of the program, he accepted song requests and awarded honorary guest turkey status to several listeners who appeared in studio and shared their own novelty record rarities.

In one episode, His Turkeyness highlighted the great moments in 1975 poultry programming:

- August 12: First airing of a Nervous Norvus record, "Transfusion." Music by guest turkey Al Lopez
- September 23: First time playing records by Anita Bryant and Fabian back-to-back
- October 7: First appearance of Turkey News, later renamed the 20/20 Turkey Report
- October 14: First country-western gobbler played, "Tennessee Bird Walk" by Jack Blanchard and Misty Morgan
- October 21: Salute to Annette Funicello. Photo of Funicello and unedited Lou Christie's "Rhapsody in the Rain" from Steve Bailey

- November 4: The last legitimate commercial aired on the show, an ad for Di-Gel
- November 11: Lloyd Thaxton's first appearance. Music by guest turkey Jim Bartels
- November 18: Played "Kookie, Kookie (Lend Me Your Comb)" by Connie Francis in Japanese and Yiddish
- November 25: Entered "Let It All Hang Out" by the Hombres in the Turkey Hall of Famine. Music by guest turkey Bruce McCandless

A show favorite was Warren Smith's rockabilly song "Ubangi Stomp," which inevitably prompted Bobby to ask the question "Ubangi?" and answer with a resounding "You betchy!"

Other gobblers included "Black Slacks" by Joe Bennett and the Sparkletones, "Big Boy Pete" by the Olympics, "Angel Baby" by Rosie & the Originals, and "A Sweet Old-Fashioned Girl" by Teresa Brewer.

The all-time most-requested song on the *Bobby Rich Turkey Hour* was a country-western record called "Radio Heaven," about a place in the sky where disc jockeys go when they die. In a commercial-free afterlife with diamond microphones and golden records, every DJ gets to play the hits on an eternal turntable at a celestial station without any dead air.

In early November of 1976, a real, live turkey appeared on the *Turkey Hour*. Radio pranksters Shotgun Tom Kelly and JR Rogers surprised Bobby by bringing the large bird into the KFMB studio while he was on the air.

Turned loose in the announcer booth, the fully grown turkey ignored Bobby's command, "Give me a damn gobble!"

When verbal and other prodding at the microphone failed to produce any animal chatter, Bobby resorted to a Thanksgiving threat. "It's all over for you in another two weeks!" he howled at the bird.

KFMB's newly hired Mark Larson, host of the late-night show that followed Bobby's, described a hilarious lead-in but a "godawful mess" left behind by the turkey.

"It crapped all over the studio, and Bobby just left after his show. I had to do my newscast in the turkey coop."

This chaotic episode of the *Bobby Rich Turkey Hour* was captured on a Super 8 movie camera and later appeared as an online video.

CONGRATULATIONS!

YOU ARE NOW AN HONORARY TURKEY. YOU MAY LISTEN TO, PLAY, AND EVEN GOBBLE ALONG WITH: SONGS YOU DON'T HARDLY EVER HEAR NO MORE, NO WHERE, NO HOW, ANY-MORE, ANYHOW, ANYWHERE, ANYWAY, NO WAY.

BOBBY RICH, "HIS TURKEYNESS"

Turkey Club membership card, KFMB San Diego, 1974.

Chapter 28

Doctor Boogie and the Most Fun Ever

About a year into his run at the thriving KFMB-AM in San Diego, Bobby was unexpectedly approached by his boss with a question about the company's lackluster sister station. Paul Palmer, general manager of the KFMB radio combo, put it bluntly: "What would you do with the FM if you had your hands on it?"

Without hesitation, Bobby responded, "I'd rock that sucker!" and the GM told him, "Good, that's what I've been thinking too."

Palmer had found his next program director. They agreed to a deal in late 1974, and Bobby got to work on transforming the station. "This place is gonna boogie!" the new PD declared.

Their goal was to go head-to-head with market leader KCBQ-AM, widely known as "the Q." Bobby presented a two-page plan to blow up KFMB-FM's syndicated beautiful music format and replace it with "Better Boogie" Top 40 hits—the likes of which San Diegans had never heard on the FM band before.

"It was a wonderful feeling of satisfaction to build the programming of a station from scratch," he said. "Paul gave me that opportunity."

In addition to his on-air and operations manager responsibilities for the AM station, Bobby began assembling a music library and recruiting young, dynamic DJs for KFMB-FM. He envisioned a high-energy station unique to San Diego, blending some innovative Top 40 features from his prior stations WMYQ in Miami, WAVZ in New Haven, and KHJ in Los Angeles.

"I got some good ideas from John Long and Bwana Johnny," Bobby said, crediting two friends who offered their advice for the startup.

The launch timing was accelerated when KSEA, San Diego's only FM playing Top 40, ditched its format the week before Christmas, raising fears that another competitor might swoop in to capture their teenaged and young adult listeners.

Palmer approved Bobby's transformation strategy, but the station's owner, Midwest Television Inc., denied his request to adopt new call letters and rebrand as "Q-FM."

Ownership insisted on keeping the KFMB designation for their FM property to retain group identity with sister stations KFMB-AM 760 and KFMB-TV Channel 8.

"If they wouldn't let me change the call letters, I had to figure out another way to differentiate us," Bobby said. He devised a technique that would preserve the station's heritage and create a fresh identity by instructing the jocks to add a dramatic pause when voicing the station's legal ID at the top of each hour. The result was "KFM … BFM … San Diego's B-100."

"It was a just a little extra flair that created a memorable feeling," Bobby said. "And it caught on with listeners, who started repeating this new way of saying our call letters."

Gold record haul

As the B-100 "go live" date approached, Bobby assembled a team of lively jocks that he believed would project the perfect sound for the cool new station.

"I found talent where they were," Bobby said. "For instance, Rob 'Wingding Wisenheimer' Landree was in Bakersfield at KERN. So, I drove up there to hire Rob as our original morning man." On the two-day road trip, Bobby listened to Landree's show on a motel room clock radio to verify that he was as good on the air as he sounded on his audition tape. Bobby chose Teri Lynn as B-100's first newscaster and paired her with Landree in morning drive.

To dethrone the dominant Top 40 station in San Diego, Bobby pursued several of KCBQ's top personalities, signing Dave Conley for B-100's midday show, Jimi Fox ("The Fox That Rocks") for late-nights, and Billy Martin for weekends.

Fox, who doubled as music director and assistant program director, said of B-100's early years, "We probably got more gold records during that period than any other station in the country."

Producers of Bruce Springsteen's *Born to Run* and Electric Light Orchestra's *Face the Music* gave framed copies of the albums to B-100 in appreciation of airplay that helped them achieve gold record sales status.

"Rikki Don't Lose That Number" by Steely Dan, "Diamonds and Rust" by Joan Baez, "Peace Train" by Cat Stevens, and "I Will Survive" by Gloria Gaynor were among the many top-selling singles that earned recognition for the station from the record labels.

Fox credited Bobby for formulating an "absolutely spectacular" oldies rotation and establishing "camaraderie with the talent that was exceptional."

Rounding out the original lineup were Rocket Man on evenings and Willie B. Goode on afternoons. Rocket Man was previously Jeff "Mother" Robbins at U100 in Minneapolis. He went on to work in LA as Shadow Steele at Pirate Radio and in New York as Shadow Stevens at Z-100.

Willie B. Goode was just out of high school and working at KELP in El Paso when Bobby invited him to leave West Texas for Southern

California. On his drive to San Diego, the eighteen-year-old DJ tuned in KCBQ and heard Shotgun Tom Kelly, who would be his competition in afternoon drive.

"I was intimidated," Willie B admitted. "Bobby asked if I had listened to Shotgun. I said yep. Then he told me, 'Well, you're going to have to beat him, or you'll be out on your ass!'"

Pure adrenaline with laughing gas

B-100 was introduced in March of 1975 with a wild party. The nonstop "100 Hours of No Commercial Boogie" broadcast featured Bobby signing on for the first time as "Doctor Boogie," a nickname that has lasted throughout his career.

"The debut of B-100 was magical," he said, "like a reunion of something that hadn't even happened yet." Newly hired "Boogiemasters" were frantically spinning records and announcing giveaways of "B-100 Dollar Bills Every 100 Minutes," with the help of guest DJs Johnny Driscoll from WCFL in Chicago, KCBQ alums Rich Brother Robbin and Phil Flowers, and ex-KSEA jock Beaver Cleaver (Ken Levine).

Levine turned down Bobby's offer of a full-time job at B-100 to pursue his dream of writing television comedy in Los Angeles but agreed to work weekends in exchange for roundtrip flights to San Diego and motel accommodations near the station. Once or twice a month for two years, he flew down to do a Saturday and Sunday air shift as Beaver Cleaver. His move to TV led to even greater acclaim as a writer on *M*A*S*H*, *Cheers*, and *Frasier*.

After playing the hits at more than half a dozen stations in California, Levine called the B-100 launch his single most fun experience in radio and Bobby the best boss and program director ever. "He understood that you hire really talented people, give them all the support elements they need to succeed, and then just let them do their thing,"

Levine said. "The result was a cooking radio station that sounded like pure adrenaline mixed with laughing gas."[9]

Patience and compliments

"What I learned from Bobby," said Willie B, "was just be real, be yourself on the air. But you have to be an engaging and gregarious yet caring and empathetic personality. I think people have a sixth sense and pick up on a genuine good person."

Still a teenager, Willie B struggled to find his authentic voice for the first few months at B-100. Trying to copy the sound of more experienced jocks, he feared getting sacked, but his boss was patient with him. "One afternoon Bobby came in the studio and told me, 'Man, you're sounding damn good today,'" Willie B remembered.

"That compliment meant more than my mother saying I love you. I got a bit of self-confidence back." The rocky start, he said, "turned into a lifelong friendship, and Bobby has meant more to me than any other radio person in the world times ten." Continuing his career in Los Angeles, Boston, and Baltimore, Willie B was still a morning personality and program director nearly fifty years after leaving San Diego.

Another ex-KCBQ jock who joined the "Boogie Brothers" went by the air name Just Kevin. From KMBY in Monterey, Bobby recruited B-100's first female DJ and "Boogie Sister" who also used only her first name, Cherie.

Native San Diegan Christopher Lance joined from KRIZ in Phoenix and described his time in Bobby's lineup as "the fun, electric days of B-100. All the other stations were pretty much in fear of him in 1975-76. He was a winner, and B-100 was magical from the get-go."

Lance did weekends and vacation relief for nearly all the full-time

---

[9]Ken Levine blog, April 20, 2011
https://kenlevine.blogspot.com/2011/04/most-fun-i-ever-had-in-radio.html

jocks. "Bobby was the first guy I worked for who was upper management but was also just one of the guys. He did a lot for my career," added Lance, who went on to KYA and KFRC in San Francisco and KRTH and KKHR in Los Angeles.

Phil Flowers joined the weekend lineup and by the summer of 1975, Glen McCartney from KPOI in Honolulu arrived to do overnights.

Better Boogie and faster turntables

"From the beginning, B-100 was very high energy, and all the jocks sounded like they were coming out of their skin they were so excited to be there," Bobby said. "All of us were pretty much screaming to match the music, which was almost always up-tempo. We were shooting for a target audience of 12 to 24-year-olds, teenagers plus the next older demo of young adults who didn't want to admit it."

Palmer credited Bobby with defining B-100 as "a Top 40 all-hit radio station with music in stereo on FM and with fewer commercials. The big difference is the amount of fun and involvement we have."

"Better Boogie" also meant that listeners got the first chance to hear album versions of songs instead of the shorter recordings edited for AM stations. "For example, the live album version of Peter Frampton's 'Do You Feel Like We Do' was almost seven minutes long," Bobby said. "Playing that one gave us an edge over any station with a restriction of three minutes per song. It was Jimi Fox who convinced me we should go with the longer records."

For competitive advantage B-100 also employed a Top 40 trick that Fox called "tempo enhancement"—increasing the speed of certain songs to add some sparkle to the audio.

"When all the songs were on vinyl or dubbed from vinyl to cartridges," Bobby explained, "to make us sound a tiny bit different than KCBQ, we made our turntables spin just a couple percent faster than normal by wrapping a thin strip of editing tape to the capstans. If both stations were playing the same song at the same time, we figured listeners would like our 'brighter' audio, and that would be reflected in the ratings."

Engineers at B-100 discovered the gimmick, and KFMB Chief Engineer Charlie Abel reprimanded Bobby for tampering with broadcast equipment. Thus began a ritual in which all traces of turntable tinkering were removed on Sunday night before weekly maintenance by the engineering department, only to be reinstalled by the programming department each Monday morning.

Boogie Balls and Lady Stroke

B-100's first major promotional event was the Boogie Ball contest, awarding cash to a thousand winners in one weekend. Station staffers fanned out across San Diego to find people with Boogie Ball stickers displayed on their vehicles and reward them with a "B-100 dollar bill" or prize of fifty, twenty, ten, five, or two dollars.

Another of Bobby's big ideas was the Stroke It and Win contest, featuring a mysterious character named Lady Stroke who gave on-air hints about what park, beach, or shopping center she would be visiting to hand out cash. Lured by Lady Stroke's sexy voice and prize money, listeners followed her clues to show their "Stroke It" stickers and scribbled lists of songs recently played on B-100.

In a month when Arbitron enlisted a random sample of San Diegans to keep daily diaries of their time listening to the radio, "We encouraged everyone to just write down B-100 on a piece of paper," Bobby explained. "Or in other words, to stroke it when listening to B-100."

In a not-so-subtle message to the ratings diary keepers, the station aired a promo reminding listeners, "It only takes six strokes to write down B-100."

With its sexually suggestive theme, the contest grabbed widespread attention, especially among teenagers. "High school guys were putting Stroke It stickers on their zippers," recalled Dave Sniff, a local kid who eventually joined the B-100 air staff.

"A stroke of genius and idiocy" is how Bobby later described the contest.

Talent turnover

To celebrate the station's first anniversary, he threw another hundred-hour "Better Boogie" broadcast party in April of 1976 with past, present, and future B-100 jocks plus guest DJs including Chuck Browning, Billy Pearl, Doc Holliday, Rich Brother Robbin, Johnny Toot, and Beaver Cleaver.

For four days and nights, they were free to have fun and boogie to their heart's delight in a commercial-free hit music extravaganza and disc jockey screamfest.

In July of that year, Jimi Fox surprised Bobby by quitting B-100 to program a new Top 40 station in Los Angeles and taking Dave Conley and Willie B with him to KTNQ ("Ten-Q").

As a result of the split, Bobby and Fox didn't speak to each other for more than forty years. They reconnected and mended their friendship at a B-100 reunion in 2017.

"I know he was upset because I stole Conley and Willie," Fox acknowledged in a 2024 interview. Giving credit to Bobby for a fun and electrifying station, he added, "Our time at B-100 and all the promotions and energy and community involvement were absolutely exceptional."

The departures left Bobby feeling betrayed but gave him an opportunity to reinvigorate B-100 with a second wave of top talent that would further drive the station's success in San Diego.

He put Gene Knight, "The Greener," already popular with listeners at KCBQ, in the evening shift. "The Greener I think just has the perfect warm and energetic sound," Bobby said, "fun and youthful but not immature. Those were the types of voices I wanted on B-100."

Gary Kelley was another native San Diegan and ex-KCBQ jock whose vocal warmth and personality matched that description. Kelley landed the night shift at B-100, with McCartney transferring to middays.

For afternoon drive, Bobby went back to El Paso and recruited Danny Wilde to San Diego. Wilde described the B-100 air staff as "crazed, hyper-caffeinated jocks" who matched the up-tempo playlist, received "loads of freedom and encouragement" from Bobby, and were inspired by their boss to have fun on the air every day.

Shotgun Tom signs on

In October of 1976, Bobby further strengthened the station by hiring Shotgun Tom Kelly away from KCBQ to be the next morning man at B-100. "That was a big get for us," Bobby said. "Shotgun was doing afternoons at the Q and had a lot of fans and exposure from his years on local radio and the TV game show he hosted, *Words-A-Poppin'*. It was a turning point when we hired Tom, telling advertisers and the business community that B-100 was for real."

At sister station KFMB-AM, new afternoon personality Mark Larson was in an adjoining studio when he found out about B-100's big hire for morning drive. "I got on the intercom and said, 'Hey Bobby, that's great, getting Shotgun Tom!'" Larson recalled. "I could see Bobby lean into the intercom in his studio, and he responded, 'It's not just great, it's a fucking coup!'"

Signing a higher-profile local talent for the morning show meant that Bobby had to let Landree go after a year and a half in the prime-time slot. He broke the bad news in the parking lot as Landree arrived at work.

"That was a hard one," Bobby admitted. Shotgun Tom, already inside the building, took his place at the mic just minutes later and was immediately welcomed with radio promos and TV spots featuring the hit song "Get Up and Boogie" by Silver Convention. Shotgun did mornings on B-100 until 1980, before moving to Los Angeles and hosting afternoons at KRTH for eighteen years.

Landree, who remained friends with Bobby after his dismissal, moved to Memphis for a job at WHBQ. The lineup changes at B-100 brought another fresh voice to mornings, with newsman Uncle Fred Stemen moving over from KFMB-AM where his reporting duties had included updates on the weekly *Bobby Rich Turkey Hour*.

By 1977 the station had moved out of "World Boogie Headquarters" at Fifth Avenue and Ash Street in downtown San Diego and into new studios on Engineer Road in Kearny Mesa.

Owner's daughter, money problems

Jimmy "JR" Rogers came to B-100 to work on Shotgun Tom's show and coordinate the station's live broadcasts from beaches, ballgames, concerts, the San Diego Zoo, Del Mar Fair, SeaWorld blimp, and Mission Bay thunderboat races. Bobby promoted Rogers to weekend DJ after he proved himself as a fill-in for several announcers sidelined by a flu outbreak.

During one of his air shifts, Rogers recalled, "I went to get a Coke from the vending machine and a little girl in the lunchroom asked me if I had any money. She didn't have any quarters, so I bought her a soda." Not long after, Rogers said, station owner Chris Meyer came into his studio and inquired, "Are you the young man who gave my daughter money for a soda?"

The DJ confirmed he had coughed up coins for a cola. He recalled that Meyer told him, "Her mother and I don't let her have those. I'd appreciate it if you don't give her any more money."

Meyer's daughter Elisabeth later joined the family business, eventually succeeding her father as owner and president of Midwest Television. A graduate of Stanford University and Harvard Law School, Elisabeth Kimmel operated the company's three San Diego stations (KFMB-TV, KFMB-AM, and B-100 FM) until 2018 when she sold them for a reported $325 million in cash.

In 2019, Kimmel was arrested in connection with her involvement in the college admissions scandal known as Operation Varsity Blues. She pleaded guilty to conspiracy to commit mail and wire fraud, was fined $250,000 and sentenced to six weeks in prison.[10]

Radio bug and a foot in the door

John Fox (no relation to Jimi) started working at B-100 while in college. He contacted a half dozen program directors for a class project in 1975 and "Bobby was by far the most approachable and willing to chat and help out a kid in school," he remembered. Fox had multiple assignments before getting the overnight DJ shift in the early 1980s. After staying nineteen years at B-100, Fox called it "the best damn job ever."

Two other teens found their way into B-100 thanks to Bobby's sponsorship of an Explorer Scout program for students interested in broadcasting. Eleventh grader Roy Robertson, on a visit to the station, received a quick lesson in music programming from the FM jocks and their PD. "The exposure was unbelievable," Robertson said. "Bobby

---

[10]*Press release, U.S. Attorney's Office, District of Massachusetts, Dec. 9, 2021*
https://www.justice.gov/usao-ma/pr/parent-sentenced-college-admissions-case-1

showed us a book of playlists and told us to plot out a four-hour show as if you're on the air."

Robertson's involvement in the program led to his hiring and twenty-nine years of employment at the KFMB stations. He saved his original B-100 music log from 1978 and proudly showed it to Bobby at a reunion in 2024.

Bill Calhoun was another Explorer Scout with a microphone dream. "Every week in the program somebody would come in to explain different aspects of the radio and TV business to us," he said. "We got a presentation by Bobby and then went to see how things were done in each department." Calhoun started answering request lines at B-100 in 1978 and has been spinning records ever since.

Mark Gleason and Dave Sniff also started in entry-level positions and went on to become lifetime DJs, programmers, and broadcast production professionals.

Gleason, whose rookie responsibilities included wearing a gorilla suit to hand out Boogie Ball window stickers for B-100, worked for at least six local stations and as a TV camera operator for more than two decades with the CBS Sports and Fox Sports networks.

Fresh out of high school, Sniff began as a board operator and worked his way up to director of programming/operations of KFMB-AM. After twenty-six years in upper management, he appreciated Bobby's simple instructions to new employees on their first day on the job: "Have fun. Just go frickin' have fun on the radio," Sniff said. "And we did."

Ratings soar

To boost the station's reach when most cars were not equipped with FM radios, Bobby coordinated a B-100 converter box giveaway, distributing devices that enabled AM listeners to tune in the 100.7 FM frequency.

Before long, his high-energy DJs and blend of "bitchin' summer sounds" could be heard blaring from car stereos and echoing from boomboxes at the beach.

By late 1977, Bobby achieved the pinnacle of programming success as B-100 became the top-rated station in San Diego. He had taken the station from startup to market leader in two and a half years.

"We were number one in the October/November Arbitron survey. All ages and all day parts. B-100 was the first major market FM contemporary station in the country to do it, winning the 12-plus ratings battle. That was my proudest moment," Bobby boasted. The station placed a full-page ad in *Radio & Records*, promoting its ratings triumph.[11]

Reflecting on the achievement, he observed, "It was that magical combination of the right place, right time, right people, doing the right thing and having it all work."

Acknowledging the GM for believing in his vision, Bobby said, "Paul Palmer was responsible for allowing B-100 to be what it was. Paul saw that I loved being on the radio but also had developed the ability to put the pieces together and build a format. Other station managers would tell you how they'd do it, what they had in their mind already. Paul let me do my thing."

The ratings triumph earned nationwide attention for Bobby and B-100. It also led to the hardest decision of his career, when he received an offer in 1978 to leave San Diego for the largest radio market in America.

---

[11] *Radio & Records, Dec 23, 1975, pg 13 https://www.worldradiohistory.com/Archive-All-Music/Archive-RandR/1970s/1977/RR-1977-12-23.pdf*

B-100 staff, c. 1977. Clockwise: Shotgun Tom Kelly (in hat), Gene Knight, Just Kevin, Cherie, Danny Wilde, Doctor Boogie, Glen McCartney, JR Rogers. (Photo from Bobby Rich Radio collection)

Chapter 29

Philosophy of a Winning Station

"A Conversation with Bobby Rich—The Philosophy of a Winning Station" in the February 3, 1978, issue of *Radio & Records* described B-100 (KFMB-FM) as one of Top 40 radio's proudest recent success stories and the dominant station in San Diego. In Bobby's third year as program director, B-100 rose to number one in the market according to Arbitron data from the prior October/November ratings period.

John Leader, R&R Top 40 Editor, conducted the interview and noted, "Listening to B-100, it sounds like the people who work at the station are having a lot of fun doing it. I hear the pure enjoyment of being on the radio."

"That's my whole philosophy," Bobby responded.

He went on to describe his approach to building a creative work environment, coaching DJs, inspiring teamwork, programming music, and dealing with management.

"I believe that a jock can do a great show by following almost all of the basic rules that have been set up," Bobby said, "and still be allowed the opportunity to be himself, and that means sometimes bending, breaking, or twisting the so-called format around to make it work for him."

He focused on selecting and developing talent who shared his approach to entertaining listeners, "which is somebody who can be himself, relax, be friendly, be happy, be a positive-type person, be easy to get along with, and just generally a nice person—who also happens to be a damn good disc jockey."

Shortly after his conversation with Leader was published, Bobby was on the move again.

For another forty-five years as a jock and PD, he continued to apply his programming concepts at stations in New York City, Los Angeles, Philadelphia, San Diego, Seattle, and Tucson.

Bobby's winning radio philosophy, expressed in the three-page *R&R* interview in 1978, was a constant until his retirement in 2023.

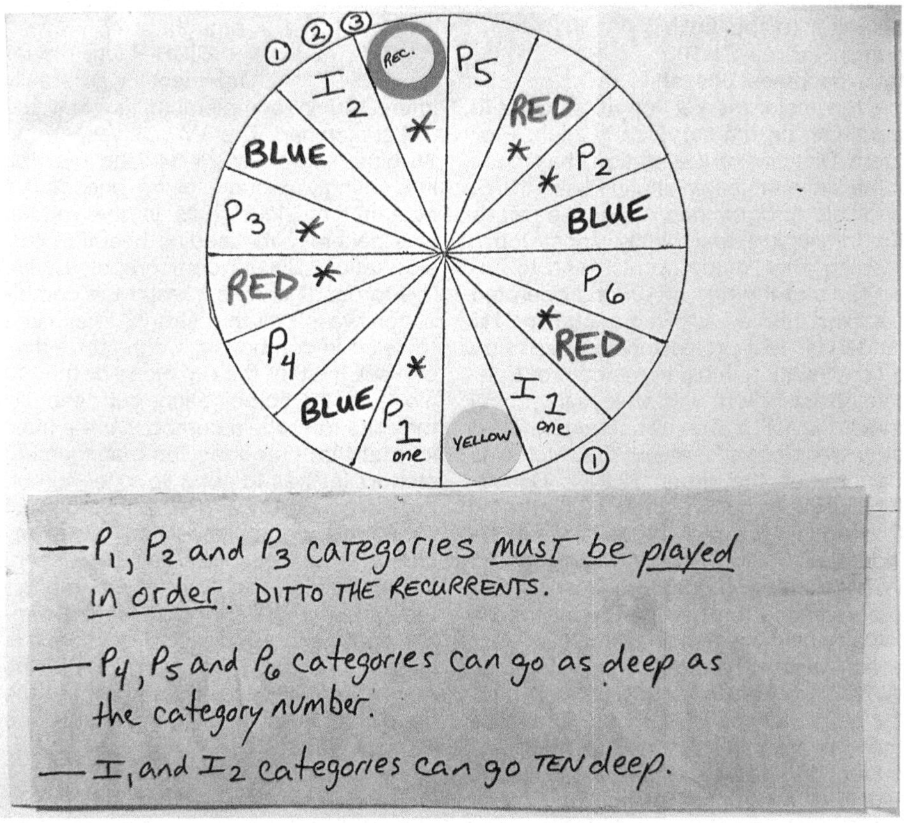

Hourly format clock designed by Bobby for music selection by DJs at B-100 and other stations.

THE INDUSTRY'S *NEWS*PAPER
February 3, 1978

A Conversation With Bobby Rich

The Philosophy of a Winning Station

B100/San Diego (KFMB-FM) is one of Top 40 radio's proudest recent success stories. The station gained three full points in the Oct/Nov Arbitron book, propelling it to top position in the city. B100 thus becomes one of the few major market Top 40 stations to dominate its market. Bobby Rich, Program Director of the station, has been there since the beginning in March 1975, and his programming theories make for interesting and highly constructive reading. Rich made up his mind to enter radio at the age of 10, and operated his own homemade radio station. He landed his first professional job at 14 on a small station in his hometown of Ephrata, Washington, and after high school moved to KFLY/Corvallis, Oregon. Next stop was Spokane, at KSPO (which was Country at the time), KDNC (Beautiful Music) and KXLY (then Top 40, now Pop/Adult). Leaving the Northwest, he worked at WJIM/Lansing. Michigan and WOHO/Toledo. In 1968 he won his first programming job at KSTT/Davenport, Iowa, where he remained for over four years. Then he worked at WMYQ/Miami, WAVZ/New Haven. and KHJ/Los Angeles before joining KFMB in 1973 as Operations Manager of the Pop/Adult AM outlet. The FM was originally a Beautiful Music station, until the decision to rock with it. Rich and R&R Top 40 Editor John Leader pick up the story...

R&R: Let's talk about B100 from the day the decision was made to chuck the automation and the beautiful music and rock with it. How was the subject first brought up?

RICH: Our management was really interested in complementing what the AM station had. The AM was very strong 25 plus, especially 25–34, and the FM, interestingly enough, being one of five beautiful music signals in the market was generally the leading beautiful music station. But its demographics were "49 to dead" and as a result the combination wasn't all that strong. They liked to sell it in combo, still do in fact – they can sell it either the AM alone or the FM alone, or the combination, but generally they like to sell it in combo. So the main idea at that time from the management standpoint was to get a younger combo buy. Knowing my Top 40 background – although I worked most formats in my career, most of my time had been spent in rock radio – so they asked me if I thought it would be good for the market and if so how I would go about it. I convinced them that I felt I knew the market well enough to know where the need was, which was a high energy Top 40 type FMer.

R&R: Bobby, when was this?

RICH: This was around October of '74.

R&R: When did the station actually hit the air?

RICH: It actually hit the air on March 3rd in '75. We had to get approval from our home office. We are a group of stations that is a family operation, run out of Champaign, Illinois – Midwest Television Corporation. They had to make the final approval, so I was asked to write a presentation listing the reasons why we should change, what kind of station it would be. I already knew in my mind what it would sound like and I tried my best to put that down on paper, talking about things like the energy of the station, the type of music we'd play, the type of jocks we'd have, the type of promotions we would do, the visibility in the community and the pace of the station, all those things.

R&R: Well, this was really a major step for them in terms of the fact the station was already a success.

RICH: Also, considering the fact that the AM was a Contemporary Pop/Adult station, they thought they already had a rock and roll station. I cringed when I heard them say, 'Why do you guys need another rock and roll station; you've already got one." Again, knowing what they'd think when they heard it. Because compared to KFMB-AM they were going to hear something they had never heard before.

R&R: So, the decision was made in March of 1975 and on it came.

RICH: Yes, we came on the air as if we'd always been there, we pulled the plug on midnight Sunday night and at 6 o'clock Monday morning we were B100-FM. We did a little pre-promotion on television over that weekend, showing our visual logo and playing some rock music behind it and I don't remember the exact line we used, it was something about "Beginning Monday, something like you've never heard before, Real Rock On FM," something like that. And then we hit with it. But preceding that, of course, we had already done some run-through shows. We had all the jocks sit in at the board and go through a few shows and then we went on the air. There was no "this is our first day on the air" type of thing, the attitude was "we've been here all the time, what took you so long to find us?"...

R&R: Interesting approach. So the whole thing was pre-practiced and ready to roll before it hit?

RICH: Yes, there was no first day jitters as such, because all the jocks had run through shows and the promos were already produced, the station was already up to par, right out of the gate.

R&R: What was the initial reaction to the station?

RICH: We had a bigger reaction than a lot of people expected. We of course had high hopes and they came through. Most of the people in that market, listeners and competitors alike, didn't really think that we would do that much. We are generally a pretty conservative company. I don't think that they knew all that much about me or my background. I was already here for a year programming the AM station in a Pop/Adult format. I don't really think anybody expected us to come on and be quite that strong, so we took some people by surprise. We came on the air with a really good sounding radio station, extremely high energy, we really came on screaming. We stayed with that high energy for about a year or so, and then slowly but surely we started to bring ourselves down to a more human level. I think we were always real, but we were also real up. We're certainly not real mellow now by any means, we're still definitely high energy, but we really have eliminated the yelling and screaming; we found other ways to project our energy. Several changes have occurred as we've grown up and that's really the way I feel it's happened, we've just kind of grown into it.

R&R: You came on the radio in the beginning with a high energy to get the visibility going, get people to notice you were there? The station was very exciting to listen to from a pacing stand point, the guys were cooking, the music was up. When did you make that decision to back away from that slightly? How did you know at what point in time to do that?

RICH: It wasn't so much a conscious

decision that we sat down and said, "OK, from now on we're going to eliminate some of this and get into more of this." Really, just like an individual human being grows up, we grew up by ourselves. It wasn't an overnight change, it was a very smooth transition and even today we are making the transition into what is a totally different radio station in a lot of aspects than it was one year ago. Really, this last year has been when we've really totally grown up and become adult. We still have a very useful energetic approach on the radio. There really was no point in time when it happened, it just happened automatically. As we started to see it happening, everybody kind of fell in line with it. It's like everybody shined off somebody else as far as the jock approach – one guy starts to bring himself down a little bit, and pretty soon it starts sounding good and feeling good and the others start doing it too, and then they are encouraged to do so; those who haven't caught on yet are encouraged to do so, also.

R&R: Let's get into philosophy. Listening to B100, it sounds like the people who work at the station are having a lot of fun doing it. I hear the pure enjoyment of being on the radio.

RICH: That's my whole philosophy.

R&R: How do you sit down with the guys you hire or the guys you have and say, "OK, I want you to sound like you're having fun on me radio"? It's like running into your morning man and saying "Be funny!" How do you get that feeling across?

RICH: I think you have to create an atmosphere, call it a "no hassle" atmosphere, you have to let the jocks know what you want from them. Some of the more encouraging moments of the growth of the jocks that have worked at B100 have come, for example, when an aircheck presentation was being put together, where I would take several hours of tape of each jock end then select certain sets that I wanted to put out for the advertising reps to hear on a national basis. Then when my jocks heard the presentation back, they suddenly heard what I liked best about them. We did the same thing when we put together a film a year ago. It was a home movie of the station that we shot with our morning man, Shotgun Tom Kelly's movie camera hooked into the audio. It's literally a visual aircheck. We have a new one now that we are just finishing up that we hope to be able to show this year. It was the same situation there, where we shot literally hours of sets and then I sat down and chose which ones I wanted to represent what the station was to those from the outside. The jocks, seeing the finished form and hearing the finished cut down aircheck suddenly realized what it was that I liked about them and then tried to do more of the same for me and for the station. I think that has a lot to do with the growth of the individual jocks on the station and therefore the overall sound.

R&R: Do you sit down with the jocks and go over tapes?

RICH: Not really that often. As a jock I never loved the critique sessions at all. Anytime I sat with a Programmer, listening to a tape of myself ... of course we as jocks are always overly critical of ourselves end most of us cringe everytime we listen to an aircheck of ourselves. To sit there cringing over your own aircheck and having someone pointing out everything that is wrong with it is not necessarily positive. I know a lot of programmers work that way and a lot of jocks like to be worked with like that, but I didn't like it as a jock and I really don't like it that much as a programmer. If I hear something really wrong, I am not likely to jump on it right away. I feel the guy has got to have a chance; we all make mistakes, I've made a lot of them. Jocks have a tendency to not stop and think. When we are on the air and doing an air shift there are a thousand things on your mind and I think it's unfair to a disc jockey to expect perfection. A lot of our rules are silly rules. but they're there for important reasons. I believe that a jock can do a great show by following almost all of the basic rules that have been set up for him and still be allowed the opportunity to be himself, and that means sometimes bending, breaking or twisting the so-called format around to make it work for him. To answer your question, I don't do the weekly critique sessions, I will do it occasionally, and generally I'll have jocks come to me asking me if I would please do it with them and I eventually get around to doing one. It's not part of my modus operandi.

R&R: In terms of your philosophy of people having fun on the radio, it sounds like the most important thing at B100 is the morale. You have to keep up the morale, but it's an intangible thing. It's very hard to say "Come on, guys, let's get our morale up," it doesn't work that way. Obviously you are protecting your staff so they can be more creative and not have to worry about the politics of radio.

RICH: Yes, I'm placed in a very difficult situation in this regard, almost on a daily basis, there are so many parts of me that want to make different decisions. There's the disc jockey part of me and there's the programmer part and the management part of me. I want to make money for the company on one hand, and on the other hand I want the jocks to go in and have a good time without any hassles whatsoever. On the other hand, I can't let a jock get totally out of control, because he's hurting not only himself but certainly the radio station and me. I have all these different thoughts and feelings and the barrage on a daily basis sometimes even hourly, sometimes becomes very difficult. But basically what I try to do is keep as much of the hassle away from the jock as possible. I also try to go out of my way not to baby the jocks, although sometimes that's what is necessary. But I treat them with respect and in return they treat me with respect. I make demands from management and I don't give in on a lot of things in arguments that I get into with management. Other times I do give in, because I know deep down it's probably the best thing to do; but I usually won't give in without a fight. I'll try to go out of my way to point out to people, either jocks or management, why I want to do something or why I think it is important, and whether or not they think I'm right, most of the time they'll go along with what I say and then I can prove myself out in the long run.

R&R: Let's talk about teamwork. Do you believe in it?

RICH: Absolutely, we couldn't do without it.

R&R: How do you handle it at B100?

RICH: By not telling them what to do but letting it happen. I had a Program Director at the biggest market I worked in who took over the job. I was one of the

B-100 fm

SAN DIEGO'S FAVORITE NEW MUSIC!

CLOSE ENCOUNTERS THEME — JOHN WILLIAMS
SERPENTINE FIRE — EARTH, WIND & FIRE
BEFORE MY HEART FINDS OUT — GENE COTTON
YOU REALLY GOT ME — VAN HALEN
LONG, LONG WAY FROM HOME — FOREIGNER
LET IT GO, LET IT FLOW — DAVE MASON
CURIOUS MIND (UM, UM, UM, UM, UM, UM) — JOHNNY RIVERS

SONGS LISTED UNDER 'FAVORITE NEW MUSIC' ARE NOW RECEIVING, OR BEING CONSIDERED FOR, AIRPLAY ON B-100

THE LISTING OF RECORDS HEREIN IS THE OPINION OF B-100 BASED ON ITS SURVEY OF RECORD SALES AND LISTENER RESPONSE

SAN DIEGO'S STEREO FAVORITES

VOLUME FOUR/NUMBER FOUR — JANUARY 27, 1978

LAST WEEK	THIS WEEK	SONG TITLE	ARTIST	WEEKS ON
1	1	WE WILL ROCK YOU/ WE ARE THE CHAMPIONS	QUEEN	6
3	2	Just The Way You Are	Billy Joel	10
10	3	Stayin' Alive	Bee Gees	6
4	4	(Love Is) Thicker Than Water	Andy Gibb	12
2	5	You're In My Heart	Rod Stewart	10
7	6	Turn To Stone	E.L.O.	10
9	7	Point Of Know Return	Kansas	11
13	8	Sometimes When We Touch	Dan Hill	7
5	9	Baby Come Back	Player	11
17	10	Come Sail Away	Styx	7
8	11	Sentimental Lady	Bob Welch	12
12	12	What's Your Name	Lynyrd Skynyrd	9
6	13	How Deep Is Your Love	Bee Gees	15
16	14	Isn't It Time	Babys	8
20	15	Don't Let Me Be Misunderstood	Santa Esmeralda	6
19	16	Peg	Steely Dan	8
22	17	Here You Come Again	Dolly Parton	5
15	18	Hard Times (I'm Falling)	Boz Scaggs	9
24	19	Emotion	Samantha Sang	5
11	20	Short People	Randy Newman	9
28	21	Back In Love Again	LTD	4
25	22	Slip Slidin' Away	Paul Simon	5
--	23	Desiree'	Neil Diamond	3
21	24	Swingtown	Steve Miller Band	13
30	25	Happy Anniversary	Little River Band	4
18	26	Blue Bayou	Linda Ronstadt	14
26	27	She's Not There	Santana	14
31	28	I Go Crazy	Paul Davis	4

Queen reigns on B-100 music survey, Jan. 27, 1978

jocks already there when this Program Director came in, and at his opening staff meeting he told us that we would be a family and that we would be brothers and help each other and all that. We all kind of looked at each other and thought that's a real neat idea, but we really don't like each other that much. We don't like this place, we're not really that happy here, there's a lot of things that we're disillusioned about and now this guy's coming in and telling us that we're going to be a family. It didn't work for us, and I don't think it would work in most any situation, but it certainly is the ideal situation. His idea was right, but you can't come in and tell somebody that you're going to like each other. You have to let it happen for itself. Thank God, here at B100 it did happen, from the very beginning. Now, we haven't had that much of a changeover, we've only changed over one entire staff in the three years we've been on the air. Considering our business, I think that's really fantastic. All the people that we've had from the beginning until the present time have been excellent people. But they've all known why they were here, they're all expert professional broadcasters. Even though many of them are very young and basically new in the business, working in this atmosphere of fun and professionalism has made them feel like they are a part of the success that we've always enjoyed. We were a success when we started, we're a much bigger success now that we're number one in the market. It's happened automatically, they've made it happen, it wasn't necessarily anything I've done or the atmosphere of the station, or anything else. It's having the right people, and I've just been really damn lucky to have the right people.

R&R: You say you've had one changeover since the beginning of B100 as a Top 40 station. When you look for a guy are you consciously saying to yourself, "I have to be careful that the person that I bring in will fit in with what already exists and will join the family and participate as part of the team?"

RICH: Yes, because of the relatively small changeover I really haven't had to worry about that too much. It's been like one new body at a time, separated by several months from any other new body, end there's plenty of time to get familiar and fall together. If I were to lose half or most of my staff all at once, it would probably be real difficult in that respect. But again, I'm only hiring people based on a good instinct that I have about people, that puts them in the same category of person that I am and the kind of person that all of my jocks are, which is somebody who can be himself, relax, be friendly, be happy, be a positive-type person, be easy to get along with and just generally a nice person – who also happens to be a damn good disc jockey. And there are a lot of them out there.

R&R: Yes, but very few of them have the situation you describe.

RICH: I know that. In the cases of some of my staff I have pulled them out of situations that were not like it and been able to put them where they deserve to be. But a lot of people who have come here have come from good situations too. When I listen to a tape, I listen for somebody who's doing what I want them to be doing here. I will not listen to a tape from a jock who says I'm doing this now, but really I'd much rather be doing that and I can really handle it. Jocks are really famous for doing that, no matter what format they're doing now, they can always do your format. But I don't hire people that can do my format; I hire people who are already doing my format. My feeling on that is if you're doing something now that is not right for you, then you are a fool, because if you're really that unhappy doing what you're doing now, you shouldn't be doing it. You should be out finding a way of doing it the way you want to do it.

R&R: You've become a success and in the latest Arbitron ratings you're Number One in San Diego. Where do you go from here?

RICH: We've been doing some research on it, and as near as we've been able to find we are the first Top 40 FM station to be number one 12 plus. Certainly in a major market we are; we've checked around and found a couple of FM rock stations that have achieved number one 12 plus in the markets, but they're all in the below top 50 markets, and San Diego is 19th, but we are finally beginning to realize that we really have done something here, which leads up to your question "What do we do next?" The answer is a lot more of the same. You don't change a winner, but a lot of our success has come because we are not being tied into staying exactly the same. We try to be flexible, not to the point of wild and radical changes that the casual listener will notice on a day-to-day or week-to-week basis, but on a constant reevaluation of what we're doing and why we're doing it. It's generally true in Top 40 radio that a lot of programmers are doing a lot of the things they are doing merely because they have always done them that way, or because Drake did it that way, or Buzz did it that way or because everybody does it that way. I have found myself with a situation in programming where somebody will say to me, "By the way, why do you play 10 powers?" and I said, "I don't know, I guess because we've always played 10 powers." Now wait a minute – there must be a reason for it. Maybe we should look to this so we can start looking at audience turnover and the number of records that are really hot today and this and that, end finally we realize that maybe we would be better off if we had 9 powers. So we'd have 9 powers for a while and that worked pretty well, but that started to burn and we were burning out some records a little too fast, so we went to 11 powers. Now it's a minor change, to say the least, but at least we're admitting the flexibility of it. My big words are, in programming and in life, is it realistic? Am I being objective and am I being fair? If it has those factors going for it, then it's probably right. But a lot of us don't stop to think about those things.

R&R: How do you deal with management?

RICH: All of the factors have to be right to have this seemingly almost ideal situation at a radio station, and the General Manager is a very important part of that. I am learning and growing on a day-to-day basis. I've never stopped learning and I feel as though I probably never will. I love radio and I've been doing it now for 18 years, so I really don't want to get out of it and I also don't want to stop learning. At no point in my career has the learning process ceased; it has slowed down a couple of times. Some of the people I have learned most from have been General Managers, specifically the ones who were over me when I was a Program Director. My current General Manager, Paul Palmer, has made it possible for me to do a lot of the things I felt the need to do. Without that kind of support from a GM it matters not how idealistic or great or realistic or positive your ideas are as a person or a programmer. Management has to be there to support you. One of the main reasons I was able to demand the clout that I had in putting B100 on the air is that I had already been here a year and they had a chance to get to know me. This is a situation unlike almost any in programming, when you think about it. When you get a programming job, you walk in the door, day one, after an interview and usually from out of state. They don't know you as an individual, they don't know what you are capable of or the type of person you are, all they know is your résumé, your letters, your interview and your phone calls. I don't think I could have ever achieved in as rapid time, what we have done with B100 if they hadn't known the way I was already. To answer your question further as to what do we do next – we have to try a lot harder, except we won't be making any major changes. We will continue to have a no change/change policy, meaning not to change B100 is really to be in a constant state of change, but to the listeners the station will sound basically the same. We realize we will have to work a lot harder now. Fighting your way up is always easier when you've got someone else there to shoot at. In the beginning when KCBQ was so huge it was inspirational to us all to say, "'We're going to kill those guys." But once they lost it and we took over, then there really wasn't anyone else to shoot for. Now we just have to shoot to keep ourselves up there, and that means a lot more work. And we are going to try to have fun and work at the same time.

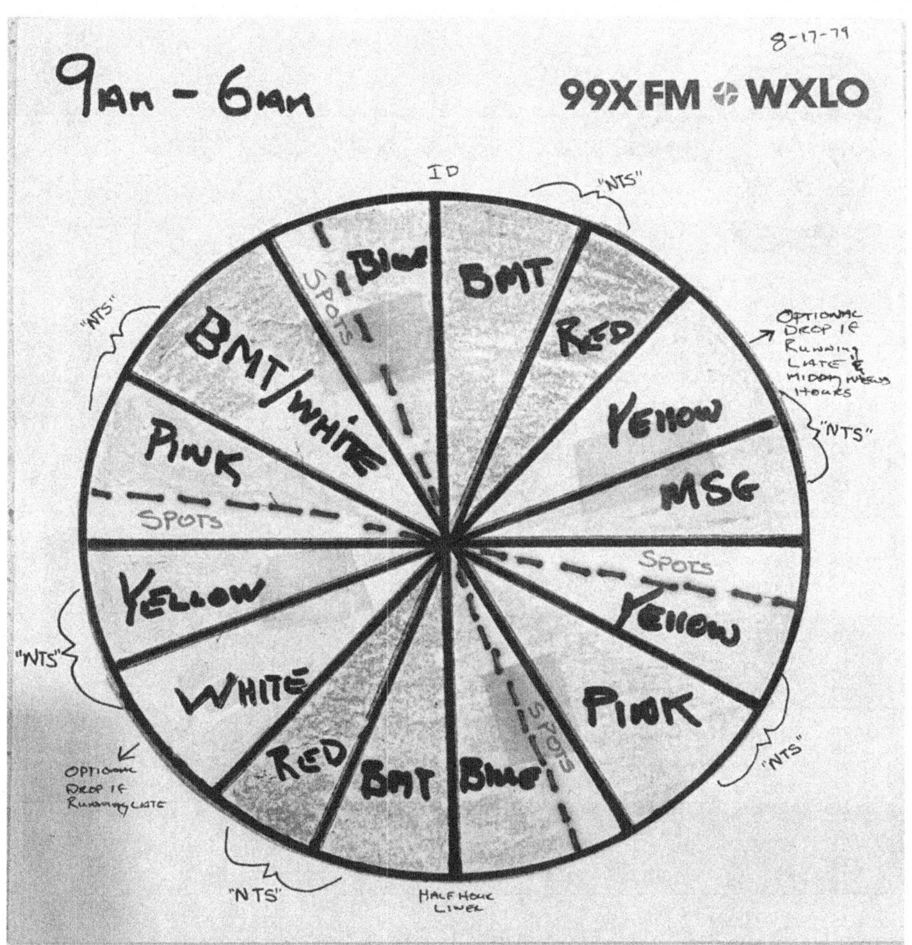

Music format clock customized for 99X New York. August 1979. (*NTS = No Talk Segue)

99X-FM/WHERE THE MUSIC COUNTS!
WEEK OF MARCH 1, 1978

LW	TW		
1	1	STAYIN' ALIVE	BEE GEES
2	2	JUST THE WAY YOU ARE	BILLY JOEL
3	3	LOVE IS THICKER THAN WATER	ANDY GIBB
7	4	NIGHT FEVER	BEE GEES
4	5	BABY COME BACK	PLAYER
5	6	SOMETIMES WHEN WE TOUCH	DAN HILL
6	7	COME SAIL AWAY	STYX
11	8	CLOSE ENCOUNTERS OF THE THIRD KIND	MECO
8	9	YOU'RE IN MY HEART	ROD STEWART
9	10	POOR POOR PITIFUL ME	LINDA RONSTADT
10	11	DON'T LET ME BE MISUNDERSTOOD	SANTA ESMERALDA
20	12	JACK & JILL	RAYDIO
13	13	FFUN	CON FUNK SHUN
26	14	CAN'T SMILE WITHOUT YOU	BARRY MANILOW
15	15	THE NAME OF THE GAME	ABBA
21	16	LAY DOWN SALLY	ERIC CLAPTON
14	17	PEG	STEELY DAN
22	18	LOVELY DAY	BILL WITHERS
16	19	TOO HOT TO TROT	COMMODORES
17	20	WHAT'S YOUR NAME	LYNYRD SKYNYRD
18	21	STREET CORNER SERENADE	WET WILLIE
19	22	RUNNING ON EMPTY	JACKSON BROWNE
12	23	I LOVE YOU	DONNA SUMMER
25	24	HOT LEGS	ROD STEWART
23	25	THUNDER ISLAND	JAY FERGUSON
27	26	DUST IN THE WIND	KANSAS
30	27	SWEET TALKING WOMAN	ELO
29	28	YOU REALLY GOT ME	VAN HALEN
32	29	WE'LL NEVER HAVE TO SAY GOODBYE AGAIN	ENGLAND DAN & JOHN FORD COLEY
31	30	HAPPY ANNIVERSARY	LITTLE RIVER BAND
33	31	ROCKET RIDE	KISS
34	32	ALISON	ELVIS COSTELLO
--	33	FANTASY	EARTH, WIND, & FIRE
--	34	I GO CRAZY	PAUL DAVIS
--	35	OUR LOVE	NATALIE COLE

ALBUMS

1	SATURDAY NIGHT FEVER	VARIOUS ARTISTS
2	THE STRANGER	BILLY JOEL
3	NEWS OF THE WORLD	QUEEN
4	RUMOURS	FLEETWOOD MAC
5	AJA	STEELY DAN
6	FOOT LOOSE & FANCY FREE	ROD STEWART
7	RUNNING ON EMPTY	JACKSON BROWNE
8	EVEN NOW	BARRY MANILOW
9	ALL IN ALL	EARTH, WIND, & FIRE
10	ONCE UPON A TIME	DONNA SUMMER

1440 BROADWAY · NEW YORK, N.Y. 10018 · (212) 764-7000 WXLO-FM · AN RKO RADIO STATION

Bee Gees stayin' atop 99X playlist, March 1, 1978.

Chapter 30

Big Apple and Meat Loaf

Putting B-100 on the air in San Diego and making it the city's top-rated station within three years earned Bobby a ticket to the top radio market in the nation.

Erica Farber, vice president and general manager of New York's WXLO, contacted Bobby in 1978 when the RKO radio group needed a program director to turn its flagship 99X FM into the dominant Top 40 in the New York, New Jersey, and Connecticut region.

"He had really made quite a name for himself," Farber said in a 2024 interview, "and the head of programming for our company was Paul Drew, who made it his business to know which stations across the country were doing something different. That's how I got connected to Bobby."

"I wasn't looking to leave a great situation in San Diego," Bobby said, "but Erica was persistent. And my closest friends told me I'd be crazy not to go to New York." It took more than a month of phone calls and in-person lunch meetings before he said yes to 99X.

"We finally agreed," Bobby recalled, "when Erica said: 'What if I throw in a car?'"

Farber clinched the deal by throwing in her 1973 Lincoln Continental. After another cross-country move with his family, Bobby was soon driving the land yacht to Broadway and 40th Street in Midtown Manhattan. The high-rise studios of WXLO were two blocks from

Times Square and two floors downstairs from its legendary sister station, WOR.

Bringing hipness to Gotham

He arrived in February of '78 and immediately began carving a new identity for 99X, which was considered a teenybopper station. "They'd been doing Top 40 for quite a few years and were successful at it but usually placing second or third in the market behind WABC and WNBC, both of which were AM stations," Bobby said.

"As an FM, I wanted to keep it mass appeal but make us hipper and more mature, playing songs right off the albums and longer versions of the hits, not the shorter versions edited for AM airplay."

To capture a bigger share of the target 15 to 34-year-olds, Bobby planned to create an image of "street hipness" with a playlist that balanced rock, ballads, and soul. In a memo to the staff, he described the future of 99X as a "middle of the rock road" station, playing "album-oriented hits."

Another part of his image refresh was a new articulation of the call letters in the station's legal ID that aired at the top of every hour. "I voiced it as 'W-X . . . L-O New York' to sound like 'Hello New York' (with a silent H)."

Field trip for disc jockeys

Bobby brought Rob Sisco from San Diego to be his assistant program director, and they introduced the jocks to their new format on a weekend getaway to all five boroughs of New York. Departing from 99X on a Friday afternoon, they traveled by subway, train, bus, and limousine, exploring well-known and lesser-known places in Manhattan, the Bronx, Brooklyn, Queens, and Staten Island.

"I wanted the DJs to feel like they owned the city. Many of the jocks had already lived there for a while but never had the chance to discover the diversity of New York neighborhoods," Bobby said. "We also went to Long Island and New Jersey, stayed in a couple of hotels, visited nightclubs, and everyone came home with local experiences to share with our audience."

Farber thought the field trip was a smart way to energize the air personalities about the station's new direction. "At each stop Bobby would present the format and explain the programming clock," she said. "We had a blast. There was a picture of us at a White Castle getting burgers at one in the morning."

The team-building exercise reinforced a Metropolis mindset in the music format that Bobby and Sisco unveiled. Songs in their Gold category were designated "BMT" or "IRT," named for the original Brooklyn-Manhattan Transit and Interborough Rapid Transit subway lines. "Big Apples" was their song category for red hot currents and "MSG" was a classification for records by top-tier artists that could be booked for concerts in Madison Square Garden.

"None of those names were used on the air, but they were just my way of keeping it fun and local, helping the jocks stay focused on the New York market," Bobby said. He also introduced no-talk segues, adding a spot in his hourly programming clock for back-to-back songs without DJ chatter.

Air personality with multiple personalities

Jay Thomas was the morning man on 99X, and Bobby hired Charley Steiner from WERE in Cleveland to do news and sports on Thomas's show. Steiner had previously worked with Bobby at KSTT in Davenport and WAVZ in New Haven. He went on to become a national sportscaster at the RKO Radio Network and ESPN and a play-by-play announcer for the Los Angeles Dodgers.

Thomas left 99X in 1979 to pursue his TV acting career as a cast member on the *Mork & Mindy* show starring Robin Williams and Pam Dawber. Before departing for Hollywood, Thomas surprised his radio boss when Bobby attempted to give him a performance evaluation.

"With any wildly popular personality like Jay, you pretty much let them go and do their own thing on the air," Bobby said. "But all PDs need their jocks to do the basics, like saying call letters at the designated times. So, I suggested to Jay that it might be a good idea to tell millions of people where you work so we can get credit in the ratings.

"That's when Jay replied with a straight face: 'Bobby, I'm gonna stop you right there because you're not talking to Jay Thomas right now. You're talking to Jon Terrell. As Jon Terrell, I totally understand what you're talking about. I will communicate this to Jay.'"

"He really threw me," Bobby remembered. I thought either Jay's crazy or so clever that he's found a way to take criticism using an alter ego." Thomas's real name was in fact Jon Terrell.

After Thomas quit, Dick Sloane moved into the morning show. The 99X lineup also featured Glenn "Bumper" Morgan, Bobby Messina, and "The Italian Stallion" Al Bandiero. Jay Stone, who had worked at KCBQ in San Diego, was another staff member.

"I was proud to hire Sue O'Neal from WGCL in Cleveland as one of the first female Top 40 DJs in New York," Bobby said, "and I told her she was selected not for her gender but because she was a really good jock. I also brought in John Larrabee, who I knew from WAVZ in New Haven before he went to WPRO in Providence."

Rick Bisceglia was Bobby's choice for music director at 99X when Roxy Myzal resigned to work for a record company. Bisceglia, Sisco, and Bobby met regularly to review the latest albums and pick the hit singles to play. Before adding new songs, they had to get approval from Dave Sholin, RKO national music director.

"(Push Push) In the Bush" by the disco band Musique required corporate signoff because of its sexually suggestive title and lyrics. "On our weekly call, I told Sholin about this dance record that was gaining popularity in the clubs and selling well in New York," Bobby said.

Sholin gave the green light, and the song quickly became a hit on 99X, cracking the station's top ten list just two weeks after being added to the rotation. "In the Bush" performed better in New York than it did nationwide, never peaking higher than number fifty-eight on the *Billboard* Hot 100 chart.

For much of 1978, the Bee Gees were riding high with "How Deep Is Your Love," "Stayin' Alive," and "Night Fever." Each of the three songs climbed to the top of the station's music survey, and the band held the number one spot for sixteen consecutive weeks. During their peak popularity, Bobby decided to break the *Saturday Night Fever* fever and give the brothers Gibb a rest. He put the Bee Gees on hiatus for one weekend, knowing their 48-hour absence from the airwaves would be an attention grabber for 99X.

Music celebrities were frequent in-studio guests, with the DJs interviewing Elton John, Dolly Parton, The Commodores, and other artists who performed in New York. "The Blues Brothers presented us a gold record for 'Soul Man,'" Bobby said, "and our jocks joined the Village People singing 'YMCA' on a float in the Macy's Thanksgiving Day Parade."

Just call me Meat

The atypical rock album *Bat Out of Hell* by Meat Loaf captured Bobby's attention. Music director Bisceglia and assistant PD Sisco invited their boss to a Meat Loaf listening session. "The minute Rick played *Bat Out of Hell* in the office, Bobby knew it was something special but not necessarily obvious for a Top 40 station," Sisco said.

"He added it in the number one market in the country. Then the floodgates opened." The album sold more than fourteen million copies in the U.S., making it one of the all-time best-sellers in the record business.

"*Bat Out of Hell* was a radio smash because of Bobby Rich," Sisco insisted.

Meat Loaf's single "Two Out of Three Ain't Bad" debuted on the *Billboard* Hot 100 in early 1978 and quickly climbed the 99X hit list. "Paradise by the Dashboard Lights" reached number one on the station's music survey in September. A third single, "You Took the Words Right Out of My Mouth," also peaked higher on 99X than on the *Billboard* national chart.[12]

After becoming friends with Meat Loaf, Bobby welcomed the wild and theatrical rock star to 99X as a guest DJ several times. On a fun and freewheeling Sunday night show in November, Bobby introduced the singer as "Mr. Loaf", and his guest replied, "Just call me Meat."

In between giving New York weather forecasts and reading commercials for K-tel Records, Bobby and Meat cracked jokes, took listener phone calls and played songs by Patti Smith ("Because the Night"), Bruce Springsteen ("Born to Run"), Bob Seger ("Night Moves"), Queen ("We Will Rock You"), 10CC ("I'm Not in Love"), Billy Joel ("Moving Out"), Foreigner ("Cold As Ice"), Exile ("Kiss You All Over"), and Cheap Trick ("Surrender"). Meat Loaf's "Heaven Can Wait" also got a spin.

Meat Loaf rejoined Bobby for a 99X countdown of the top ninety-nine songs of 1978. "I took the New Year's Eve shift so my jocks could go party," Bobby remembered. "Meat Loaf was out on the town and called to ask if he could stop by with a couple of friends. I said sure, so

[12] *Billboard* *https://www.billboard.com/artist/meat-loaf/*

he showed up at the station with his songwriting partner Jim Steinman and KISS drummer Peter Criss.

"I had the show timed out to play all ninety-nine songs by midnight, and I told Meat he could pick the final record of the countdown. He scoured our studio looking at all the music, but instead of choosing a current hit, found an oldie and said to me, off-mic: 'Oh man, Bobby, you're about to play the last song of the year and welcome in a new era! It's got to be historic, something really important, why not the first rock'n'roll record ever to hit number one—"Rock Around the Clock," by Bill Haley and the Comets!'"

Bobby pondered.

"That wasn't one I was considering. But the more I thought about it, the more it made sense to play a song that represented a historic shift in America and the beginning of a new generation in music. So, we finished the countdown with a pre-produced shoutout from all the jocks screaming 'Happy New Year!' as 'Auld Lang Syne' faded right into 'Rock Around the Clock' on 99X New York."

Heads roll as disco dominates

Little did Bobby know heading home early that New Year's Day that another seismic shift in music was about to cost him his job.

The disco craze of the late 1970s presented a challenge for radio programmers: how much dance music to play on contemporary stations without driving away loyal listeners who hadn't bought into the disco phenomenon. Bobby took a careful approach.

"The Village People were on the pop side, and we were safe with 'YMCA' and 'In the Navy', but I was cautious about not adding too much disco," Bobby explained, "because it hadn't gone mainstream yet."

Mellow rocker WKTU had less than 1 percent of the metropolitan area's total audience in the summer of '78 when it flipped formats and turned into New York's first twenty-four-hour disco station. Within a few months, it soared to an eleven share in the ratings and dethroned long-time Top 40 powerhouse WABC. The industry was taken by surprise as WKTU became the first FM station to reach number one in the Big Apple.

"Overnight they turned the market upside down and forced everybody playing contemporary music to decide whether to get on board with disco," Bobby said.

"We couldn't compete by sticking with the hip album Top 40 hits that I was programming, and that led to my demise at 99X." Six months after ringing in the new year of 1979, he was fired.

With disco winning the war for radio ratings, WNBC General Manager Charlie Warner also got the axe. He and Bobby were featured in a July 7 *Billboard* magazine article with the headline: Heads Roll as Disco Sound Dominates New York Market.[13]

Farber, the GM of 99X, commented in a *Radio & Records* article at the time: "The direction we need to be going and the area of Bobby's expertise were somewhat in conflict, but I still feel that Bobby is one of the finest program directors in the country. I learned a lot from him, and as I told him, I sincerely hope we can work together again someday."[14]

Looking back on the situation forty-five years later, Farber said the disco disruption was not the only reason for Bobby's firing. "There was a lot of discussion going on behind the scenes at the corporate level that really didn't involve the local station.

"As much as we tried to defend what we were doing, they had other ideas about the programming," she explained. "One of the greatest disappointments of my career was having to let him go."

---

[13]*Billboard, July 7, 1979, pg 4 https://www.worldradiohistory.com/Archive-All-Music/Billboard/70s/1979/Billboard%201979-07-07.pdf*

[14]*Radio & Records, June 29, 1979. Pg 1 https://www.worldradiohistory.com/Archive-All-Music/Archive-RandR/1970s/1979/RR-1979-06-29.pdf*

Going back to Cali

As Meat Loaf had pointed out, a new era of music was indeed looming at 99X.

Management added more soul and R&B music and adopted a black-oriented urban contemporary format in 1980. Failing to gain FCC approval to reclaim the original call letters WOR-FM, the company gave up on WXLO, switched to WRKS the following year and rebranded as 98.7 KISS.

Jilted by 99X, Bobby kissed New York goodbye and planned his return to the West Coast.

"Which one of you is Kiki Dee?" Charley Steiner and Bobby welcome Elton John to 99X, 1978. (Photo from Bobby Rich Radio collection)

1978 aircheck of Meat Loaf and Bobby on 99X at bobbyrichradio.com.

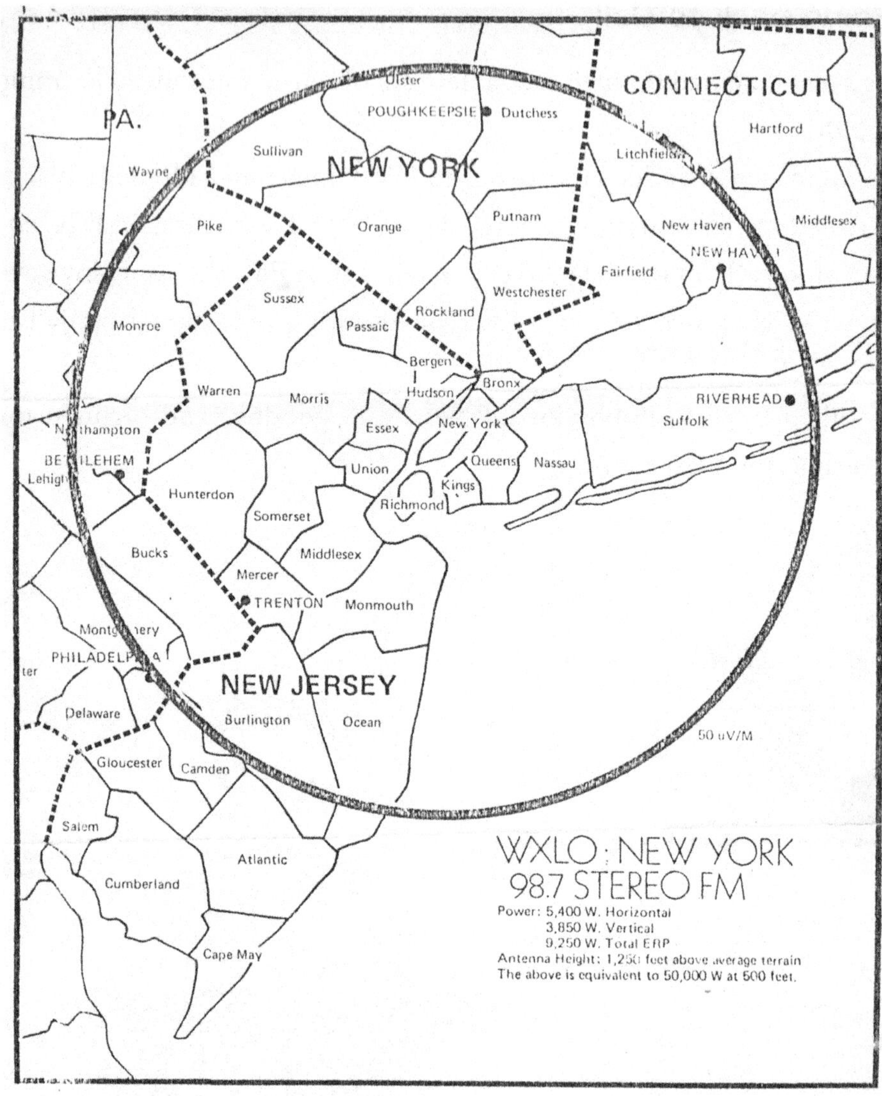

Coverage map showing WXLO 99X broadcast power, antenna height, and signal range, c. 1978.

Rob Sisco and Bobby, breaking another record at 99X.

Visibly disappointed Bobby after failing his audition to join The Village People, WXLO 99X, New York, 1978. (Photos from Bobby Rich Radio collection)

Chapter 31

Bobby's Ten Secrets for a Winning Radio Personality (and one free bonus*)

Being "on the air" is not the only important content creation position at a radio station. Somebody must also be in charge of setting up the format, determining the music library, and clocking turnover times so the same songs don't get played too often or not enough.

Someone (the boss, a.k.a. the program director) has to make big decisions, provide directives to the staff, and make sure they're followed through properly. I'm talking about philosophical direction, station image, and brand representation (both on air and in the community). The PD has additional responsibility for coaching the DJs for better performance, growth, and improvement.

As in any business, an effective boss needs to understand and be able to handle sensitive employees and members of the public. (By the way, ALL radio employees and listeners are sensitive!) The PD is accountable for getting the right talent for each air shift, encouraging camaraderie among the staff, often being their cheerleader, and delivering both good and bad news as necessary. Yes, it's true, ultimately everything starts at the top.

All the stations where I was the person making those decisions or had a boss who believed in me and trusted me had certain common characteristics.

Many of the things that I tell programmers today NOT to do are the very same things that I did when I had my biggest successes. Yes, embracing change is a thing.

Here is my never-before-revealed list of DO & DON'T suggestions for DJs, circa 2024:

1. Don't talk over the intro of every song you play all the way to the vocal. Every jock of a certain age has done this in the past and some are still talking up to the vocal in the 2020s. It's really hard to stop doing because it's so damn much fun! But frankly, only other radio people think it's cool.

2. Do talk over some of the intros some of the time, when appropriate. You can still "hit the post" but not the primary lead vocal. It sounds twice as good to the listener because they're hearing parts of the song that they rarely hear without the DJ "talking up" every intro.

3. Do talk to your listeners as if it were a one-to-one conversation. Avoid the expressions "ladies and gentlemen" or "hey everybody." Steer clear of phrases such as "hi guys" that are overused by YouTube video creators and social media influencers. If you feel the need to identify who you're talking to, just use "you", but for the most part that's not even necessary. Just say what you would if you were talking to someone face-to-face.

4. Do know who your target audience is. If you don't know or aren't sure, double-check with your manager, program director, operations manager, or station consultant. And if they don't know either, get out of there fast!

5. Don't go to work for someone who is unaware of radio's history. While there's always room for fresh new ideas, every operation needs someone who knows tried and true elements of programming.

6. DO love the music you are playing. If you must fake it, at least be believable. Listeners love the music you're playing, that's why they're listening! No one wants to hear you copping an attitude. For a jock to say, "I hate this song, but we have to play it because it's in the power rotation," is self-serving and has no place on a music radio station.

7. Do be nice to your listeners. They are your listeners! Without them, you are totally irrelevant. Treat them, all of them, even the difficult and annoying ones, like they are the most important aspect of what you do, because they are! Whether you're responding to a text, email, or a conversation, they are your customers, and you wouldn't be here without them. If you treat them poorly, they're going to tell everyone you're a jerk. Said another way, people won't necessarily remember exactly what you did or said, but they will always remember how you made them feel. It's your job to make them feel great! This is especially true when you meet them at an event or a live broadcast.

8. Do know what the songs are about, who the artists are, and in the case of oldies even if you're not old, when they were popular. It helps to know what the lyrics were intended to mean, and how to present the song on the air.

9. Do listen to each of the jocks and shows on your station. Get to know them as the listener does so you can effectively cross-promote their shows and convey your positive relationship with

them. Listeners love camaraderie between DJs. It makes them feel like you are all friends. Many years ago, a very talented PD taught me the concentric circle theory of cross-promotion: If your listeners really like and relate to you and you let them know that you really like and relate to your on-air colleagues, then they will like the other DJs too—because you do!

10. Don't spend a lot of time listening to the stations or jocks that are your direct competition. It can do one of two things: make you feel superior to them because you're so good or make you insecure because they ARE so good and better than you. Either way, it's not helpful or authentic. Instead, make it your goal to sound great and fresh and better than yesterday, every day that you're on the radio.

*And oh, by the way, DON'T eat all the food that listeners give you. It's not that it will all make you sick—but most of it will make you fat!

—Bobby Rich, November 2023

Chapter 32

Peter Tork Punchout and Leif Garrett Grabathon

As a disc jockey for over half a century, Bobby interviewed legions of pop stars and rock legends on the air and introduced hundreds of performing artists and bands at clubs and arenas in more than two dozen cities.

His home studio is adorned with album covers of favorite singers and a framed platinum version of his friend Meat Loaf's first record, *Bat Out of Hell*, which sold more than forty-three million copies worldwide.

Hanging nearby is a black satin jacket from the Grammy-winning rocker's 1978 concert tour. Meat Loaf was a regular guest on Bobby's radio show in New York and a party guest at Bobby's house in Connecticut.

Gold and platinum records from The Blues Brothers, Styx, and Rick Springfield are also in a memorabilia collection that includes photos of Bobby with Dolly Parton and the Village People, and backstage passes from concerts by Crosby, Stills & Nash, Aerosmith, The Eagles, Fleetwood Mac, Eric Clapton, KISS, and Queen.

New York concert connections

His first encounter with fame was seeing TV actor and pop singer Ricky Nelson. "I was maybe eleven when he came to Seattle and Tacoma and my sister Jan took me to Sea-Tac Airport to watch him get off the plane," Bobby said. "Ricky didn't sing or anything, and we just stood on the tarmac. But it was a thrill for me because I was a really goofy fan of his and thought he was so cool in the *Ozzie and Harriet* show."

As Nelson's music and film career took off, he changed his name from Ricky to Rick. In 1979, he hosted *Saturday Night Live*, performing with his Stone Canyon Band. Bobby was working at 99X and scored tickets from the record label plus an invitation to meet Nelson in the green room at NBC's Studio 8H. "I can't remember a single thing we talked about," Bobby said, "but he was totally as cool as I thought he'd be."

Another perk of being on the air in New York City was getting invited to The Music for UNICEF Concert at the United Nations General Assembly. Rod Stewart, Olivia Newton-John, Abba, the Bee Gees, Andy Gibb, Donna Summer, Rita Coolidge, Kris Kristofferson, and Earth, Wind & Fire performed at the 1979 benefit, recording an album to raise money for the UN's global anti-hunger programs.

Blood, sweat, tears, and cold feet

Entering the world of big-time celebrity as an eighteen-year-old DJ in Corvallis, Oregon, Bobby introduced Paul Revere and the Raiders at a concert in a roller rink in nearby Philomath. "Because Paul Revere was from Boise and Marc Lindsay was born in Eugene," he said, "it was a big deal for a Northwest band to get airtime on KFLY and a gig in the Corvallis area."

At his next stop in Spokane, broadcasting from a studio in the Davenport Hotel, Bobby encountered comedian George Burns. "It was pretty cool seeing George get a round of applause just for walking through the lobby puffing on his cigar," he said. Burns has three stars on the Hollywood Walk of Fame and a place in the Television Academy Hall of Fame.

Later in his career, Bobby introduced shows by Rock & Roll Hall of Famers the Beach Boys and Dick Clark. "Over the years, I welcomed onstage Johnny Mathis, the Association, Bobby Sherman, and Herb Alpert and the Tijuana Brass," he said.

"Fans always think it's glamorous and envy us DJs for having access to stars they pay to see in concert and whose records they buy and listen to on the radio," Bobby said after his retirement in 2023. "But people would be surprised and even shocked to see what goes on behind the scenes sometimes.

"One night in Iowa, I was getting ready to introduce the first of two shows by Blood, Sweat & Tears while they were taking a backstage vote on whether to bail out on the gig. They didn't think the crowd at the Davenport Masonic Temple was big enough. Canceling the concert would have been a big embarrassment for my station, KSTT, because we were sponsoring. In the end, the band decided to go on with the show."

Monkee gets cold-cocked before stadium gig

The Monkees, on a twentieth-anniversary reunion tour in 1986, played a concert in San Diego Jack Murphy Stadium following a Saturday afternoon baseball game between the Padres and the Phillies. The show was presented by B-100, which arranged for Bobby and the Rich Brothers to transport the Monkees in electric golf carts to a midfield stage constructed immediately after the game ended.

"The golf carts had no roofs, so the Monkees stood on back, waving to the crowd as we drove them around the stadium," Bobby said. "I was assigned to Micky Dolenz, and Scott was chauffeur for Davy Jones. Frank and Pat shared a cart with Peter Tork. Mike Nesmith didn't join the band for that show."

"I remember Micky was not happy when he found out we had enjoyed a few beers during the ballgame. But we safely delivered the

Monkees to their stage, and the concert for 25,000 fans went off without a hitch. Well, almost … ”

The Rich Brothers didn't know that during the game—which lasted twelve innings—Tork got into an altercation with Whitey Wietelmann, longtime Padres player, coach, and clubhouse staffer.

As reported by Kirk Kenney of *The San Diego Union-Tribune*, in a remembrance published in 2019, Tork was being escorted to the Monkees' dressing room when he and Wietelmann in separate golf carts approached from opposite directions in a narrow tunnel under the stadium. Unable to squeeze past each other, the sixty-seven-year-old baseball veteran ordered the forty-four-year-old guitar player to "Back up." Tork replied, "No, you back up, old man."[15]

According to a Padres official, Wietelmann got out of his cart and cold-cocked Tork, hitting him in the face with a right hook. Andy Strasberg, the team's promotions and marketing director, was summoned to the dressing room to check on the pop star. He said Tork apologized for his inappropriate language.

After applying an ice pack to his face, Tork performed alongside Dolenz and Jones in the late afternoon concert with no mention of the offstage skirmish.

By playing extra innings that day, the Padres and the Phillies allowed the Monkees more time to recover from the brawl before belting out their own hits in the post-game concert.

All hell broke loose when Leif Garrett showed up

Bobby had an earlier wild experience with a pop star when he organized a San Diego appearance for 1970s teen heartthrob Leif Garrett. After

---

[15]*San Diego Union, February 23, 2019*
https://www.sandiegouniontribune.com/2019/02/23/the-day-padres-whitey-wietelmann-made-the-monkees-peter-tork-a-believer-with-his-fist/

signing his first record contract at age fifteen, Garrett rode a wave of popularity in *Tiger Beat* magazine, cracked the *Billboard* Top 40 chart, and received airplay on B-100 with cover versions of "Runaround Sue" by Dion and "Surfin' USA" by the Beach Boys.

"His record company brought him to our station, and I was responsible for getting him to the pizza place where we'd invited listeners to meet him," Bobby recalled. "It started out as a friendly event, but right after the limousine arrived and Leif Garrett started signing autographs for a throng of overexcited girls, all hell broke loose."

B-100 programming assistant JR Rogers remembered that the crowd of teenyboppers was much bigger than anyone expected at a brand-new Shakey's Pizza Parlor on Mission Bay Drive. "The girls went absolutely batshit crazy when Garrett walked in," Rogers said. "They were swarming on him, pulling his hair. He was totally freaking out." Rogers assumed the role of bodyguard, leveraging his self-described "stature that resembled Mongo in *Blazing Saddles*."

"The record promotions guys wanted to get him out of the mayhem ASAP," Rogers said, "so they rushed out to bring the limo around, and I picked up Leif Garrett and threw him on my back. Surrounded by screaming girls, grabbing and tripping me, we managed to escape out an emergency exit on the side of the building. I carried Garrett on my back to his limo, threw him in the back seat, and they rolled out of there."

"It was like the Secret Service trying to hustle the president out of harm's way," Bobby said. "Girls in the autograph line getting their bikini tops signed might have contributed to the hysteria."

After his popstar piggyback rescue, Rogers returned to the pizzeria to assess the broken tables and other debris left behind by zealous fans of a teen idol. He and Bobby agreed that higher-level security planning would be a good idea for any future celebrity appearances.

Chapter 33

Difficult Undertaking: Station Resuscitation

Performing for the biggest audience on the biggest stage is the ultimate career objective of many broadcasters, but it was never Bobby's dream to work in New York or Los Angeles. Nonetheless, scarcely a month after getting sacked at WXLO, he said goodbye to the Big Apple and moved back to LA in the summer of 1979.

There was nothing glamorous about his return to the City of Angels.

He was recruited to program KHTZ 97.1 FM (formerly KGBS), which Greater Media Inc. had recently bought for $4 million from Storer Broadcasting Company. That price did not include the KHTZ building, its on-air studio, or its music library, but Storer allowed the temporary use of its antiquated facility and equipment.

Morticians worked here

Until new studios could be constructed, the station operated out of a run-down ex-mortuary in Koreatown.

The shadowy two-story building once used by undertakers was repurposed for live broadcasters in the late 1930s.

A creaky wooden staircase led to an improvised announce booth and several closed-off rooms that most employees dared not enter. Believing the place to be haunted by ghosts, several DJs got creeped out while working the graveyard shift in the former funeral home at 338 South Western Avenue.

Bobby knew KHTZ General Manager Tim Sullivan from their time at KHJ in 1973, but he was not expecting to get the cold shoulder from his new GM.

"When Tim told me, 'You were not my first choice for PD,' I realized the decision to hire me had come from higher up in the chain of management," he recalled.

First, get rid of all the DJs

Before selecting his air staff, Bobby's first responsibility was to make some cuts. Greater Media ordered him to fire the Top 40 announcers who joined KHTZ from Storer's KTNQ "Ten-Q" (formerly KGBS-AM) when it was switched to a Spanish language format.

"It wasn't my decision to get rid of the jocks, but I was told by corporate that I had to do it."

He remembered the mood was truly morgue-like on the day that six jocks were terminated. Jack Armstrong, Dave Sebastian, Nancy Plum, Lou Richards, Phil Conrad, and weekender Mike Carson (Dave Skyler) got the axe.

"Having to fire Big Jack Armstrong was really hard because he was a great afternoon jock and I'd been a longtime fan of his," Bobby said. Upper management allowed him to keep only two full-time DJs: morning man Charlie Tuna and midday jock Jim Conlee. Their shows were pre-recorded for several weeks until the station's relaunch.

Shaky transition to K-HITS

Bobby's vision was to combine the best songs from the Top 40 and Adult Contemporary (AC) music charts in the rebranding of KHTZ as K-HITS. "I was trying to invent a Hot AC format for a target audience of 18 to 49-year-olds," he said, "but Greater Media had already decided what they wanted me to do with the station and how to do it."

Without access to a music library, proper studios, and an advertising budget, Bobby could not plan a typical Tinseltown red carpet, star-studded premiere for K-HITS. An article in *Billboard* with the headline "Woes at KHTZ" revealed difficult conditions including the makeshift on-air workspace, mismatched equipment, and a lack of promotional resources.[16]

Radio & Records reported that the staff was "operating at a technical handicap" during the 1979 fall ratings period. The report continued, "The station is running no contests of any kind for this book."

To create some buzz for the revamped FM, Bobby hired eminent announcer Charlie Van Dyke to voice a set of dramatic promos with a ticking clock countdown to the K-HITS kickoff. Airing ninety-seven consecutive hours of Beatles songs before going live, the new PD kept people guessing while he finalized his music playlist.

The new K-HITS format was finally unveiled in October of 1979. Bursting with adrenaline, Bobby was behind the mic for the inaugural broadcast.

Busted for cussing on day one

"Of course, I had to be the first live jock," he said, "and I selected 'Beginnings' by Chicago for my sign-on song. Well, I cranked up the volume so loud on the studio monitor that things were falling off the walls. In that moment, unable to contain my extreme enthusiasm, I inadvertently screamed into the microphone, 'God damn, I've waited a long time for this!'"

The outburst brought a reprimand from the front office and a stern

[16]*Billboard*, Nov. 24, 1979, pg 28 https://www.worldradiohistory.com/Archive-All-Music/Billboard/70s/1979/Billboard%201979-11-24.pdf

warning against any more hard-core cussing. "It was the last time I ever used that phrase on the air, anywhere," Bobby confessed.

He put himself in afternoon drive for the first few months of K-HITS, then handed over the shift to Daniel West. In the original lineup, West was the 7-to-midnight personality. Dave Skyler returned to handle the overnight show, using his new air name—Dave Montoya.

Bobby then hired a series of jocks including Pat Evans from KHJ, Jeff McNeal from KUTE, and Gene Knight from 91X. He brought in Stephen Mitchell from KIQQ, whom he knew from WMYQ in Miami. Danny Moffett, Steve Scott, and Christine Becker were also on the staff.

Knight, also known as "The Greener," had worked for Bobby at B-100 in San Diego. He did late-nights at K-HITS before moving to the 4-8 p.m. shift. Another San Diegan, Cathy Derouville, music director at KMJC Magic 91, moved to LA to be program department coordinator.

Bobby soon found out his bosses were not on board with his plans for Hot AC.

"They sent me off on a cool trip around the country to listen to the company's well-established stations in Detroit, Boston, and Dallas. I stayed in hotels, listened to the radio, and took notes," Bobby said. "Greater Media had already decided what they wanted me to do as PD in Los Angeles—make K-HITS sound like KVIL in Dallas, a basic bright AC with big personality."

Bobby's biographer worked here, too

Thirty-four years before I started writing this book about Bobby's career, I was a college student with a part-time job at K-HITS writing traffic reports for Greener to read on his afternoon show.

Bobby hired Rollye Bornstein as the station's first news director and she hired me as a news assistant. Rollye and I had previously worked together at KPOL on Sunset Boulevard. Our newsroom at K-HITS, next door to Bobby's office, was equipped with phone, typewriter, tape recorders, wire service teletype machines, and police scanner radios. The scanners provided me with real-time traffic information from the dispatch centers of the California Highway Patrol, Los Angeles Police Department, and LA County Sheriff's Department.

I also wrote and recorded two news stories every afternoon for playback in Rollye's morning newscasts. The pay of four dollars per hour helped cover my tuition for two years of journalism classes at Cal State Northridge. I took on additional responsibilities as captain and center fielder of our station softball team, the K-Hitters, in games against Loni Anderson and her co-stars from *WKRP in Cincinatti* and a squad of LA Lakers and Kings players led by Magic Johnson.

Within six months, Bornstein left K-HITS and went on to be radio editor of *Billboard* magazine. She later returned to the airwaves as Rollye James at KFI Los Angeles, KOA Denver, KLBJ Austin, and WGN Chicago.

Her departure opened the door for Boyd R. Britton, formerly of Ten-Q, to reunite with Tuna as morning newscaster and sidekick. After K-HITS, Britton spent more than two decades at KROQ as "Doc on the Roq." He eventually retired from radio and became an ordained minister in the Anglican Church.

Music for you and your unicorn

In 2024, Bornstein recalled a curious conversation from her brief term at K-HITS. "One day I'm in Bobby's office and he wants the station logo to be a unicorn," she said. "So, he turns to Kathy Derouville and says, 'Can you go to the Los Angeles Zoo to see what a unicorn looks like?!'"

When reminded of the episode, Bobby responded, "That's hysterical. I'm pretty sure I did not send my assistant to the LA Zoo to get a picture of a unicorn. But it wouldn't be the craziest thing to happen at K-HITS."

To publicize their refreshed LA station, the company sprung for a TV commercial produced by Chuck Blore, the former Top 40 personality and programmer turned advertising wizard.

He created a quirky spot featuring an eclectic bunch of Angelenos sitting in front of a graffiti-covered wall, grooving to the music of 97 FM on their personal radios. Actors portraying a housewife, a weightlifter, a man in a tuxedo, and a high-fashion female model were joined at their sidewalk get-together by a unicorn wearing earphones. The commercial ended with the tagline "K-HITS Los Angeles—Music for people like you and your unicorn."

Blore's eye-catching ad, Bobby recalled, "certainly made people in LA aware of us, and that's the most important thing, especially when you have a new product. It was ingenious, just like Chuck."

Orders from above

Greater Media was not so great for personal autonomy, he discovered. "The company had all these levels of upper management above me, about seven executives in cities around the country who had their fingers in everything we did musically. I had a manager who didn't believe in me, plus a national PD, several consultants, and a guy in charge of music testing who ran the research operation from somewhere in Minnesota."

Bobby believed that overbearing management led to certain songs getting overplayed on K-HITS and staying too long in the power rotation. He cited "Rise" by Herb Alpert and "Still" by the Commodores as songs that performed well but got stale from repetition.

To get around company-imposed limits on his ability to add new records and keep K-HITS sounding fresh, Bobby decided to secretly tinker with the playlist.

With help from Derouville and Skyler, he modified the rotation—removing worn-out songs and inserting new releases without permission from headquarters. He reverted to the company-approved music only when the corporate bosses flew into town to check up on their station.

"This sneaky behavior wasn't exactly what they wanted," Bobby explained, "but I thought why waste time on an LA station doing things that didn't make sense to me. They kept insisting on a softer format, and I kept playing more Top 40 hits with a harder edge."

The mischief led to his firing in the summer of 1980 while he was on vacation.

Bobby found out he'd be getting the boot in an awkward phone conversation with Assistant PD Conlee and received an official termination notice after returning from vacation. Sullivan, the GM, cited "philosophical differences" as the reason for his exit.

Conlee then took Bobby's job as PD as the K-HITS staff settled into their brand-new studios at 3580 Wilshire Boulevard.

Getting blown out in LA did not stifle Bobby's radio dreams but strengthened his belief that a successful programmer needs a fully supportive general manager.

It would take another four years to reunite with such a leader who embraced his vision and let him make it a reality.

KHTZ's Pat Gaffey and Los Angeles Lakers rookie Magic Johnson at July 24, 1980 celebrity softball game, K-Hitters vs. Forum All Stars, El Segundo, California. (Photo from Pat Gaffey archives)

Chapter 34

Bobby's Boss Radio Bosses

Bill Drake and Gene Chenault introduced their "more hit music" Boss Radio format in 1965 at KHJ in Los Angeles, with Robert W. Morgan and the Real Don Steele as the ultimate boss jocks and the legendary Ron Jacobs as program director. They quickly turned the station into a ratings winner in the highly competitive LA market.

Boss Radio's success at KHJ was replicated by Drake and Chenault at top stations including KFRC in San Francisco, KGB in San Diego, WRKO in Boston, WHBQ in Memphis, and CKLW in Windsor-Detroit. By 1970 the Drake-Chenault partnership had expanded their consulting business to more than forty stations. They hired Bobby to join their company in 1980.

"I first met Bill Drake at the Billboard Radio Convention in New York in '68," Bobby said. It was a career-defining moment for the rookie program director at the helm of a Top 40 station in Davenport, Iowa.

"After he revealed some of his innovative programming and music rotation methods during that conference, I went back to KSTT and immediately revamped the format and improved our on-air product with techniques I'd learned from Drake."

Return to live and local programming

By the time Bobby went to work at Drake-Chenault Enterprises in

Canoga Park, California, the firm was providing automated equipment systems and music on reel-to-reel tapes to hundreds of client stations throughout North America. They also produced a ten-part syndicated radio documentary, *The History of Rock and Roll.*

"They valued my on-air and PD experience," Bobby said, "since I had jocked in ten cities and programmed stations in Davenport, San Diego, New York, and LA.

"When they hired me as director of specialized programming and consultation, they didn't have any live stations, only taped formats. My job was to build a new part of the syndicated business, consulting with clients who wanted to improve their ratings by returning to live and local programming."

Talent scout crowns Stern, Brandmeier, O'Dell, Greaseman, Adele

Bobby's bosses at Drake-Chenault approved his idea to conduct a national talent search, and he collected hundreds of aircheck tapes from up-and-coming DJs hoping to be discovered or recognized as major market air personalities.

"I judged all the jocks who entered the contest, listening to stacks and stacks of cassettes they sent in. Our goal was to find the leading and most promising talent in five formats. I picked winners in each category—Top 40, adult contemporary, album-oriented rock, and so on. Several of them became really big names in the business."[17]

Howard Stern at WWWW in Detroit, Jonathon Brandmeier at WOKY in Milwaukee, Willy B of WBSB in Baltimore, and The

[17]*Billboard, Mar 7, 1981, pg 26* https://www.worldradiohistory.com/hd2/IDX-Business/Music/Billboard-Index/IDX/1981/1981-03-07-Billboard-Page-0026.pdf

Greaseman of WAPE in Jacksonville were among Bobby's selections as best in the business.

Other contest winners were DJs Linda McInnes at KLOS Los Angeles, Adele (Arakawa) at WRJZ Knoxville, Randy Miller of WXKX Pittsburgh, Vinnie Brown of WOL Washington, DC, and Spike O'Dell on KSTT Davenport.

Three talent search winners would follow Bobby at key stations and cities in his career.

"I was amazed to learn that Spike O'Dell had grown up listening to me on KSTT while he worked overnights as a security guard at the International Harvester plant in Rock Island, Illinois," Bobby recalled. "After I left Davenport, Spike did mornings at KSTT. And he kept his overnight security job at the tractor factory!"

O'Dell's radio career later blossomed in Chicago, where he hosted the morning show on WGN.

Brown, recognized as the top talent among contestants from black-oriented stations, became program director at KISS 98.7 FM (WKRS) in New York, which was previously 99X (WXLO) when Bobby programmed the RKO outlet.

Miller landed in San Diego in the 1980s when Bobby was well-established as PD and morning man on B-100 FM. "As a jock on a competing station, Miller said some rude things on the air about me and my *B Morning Zoo* co-hosts," Bobby remembered, "but we chose to ignore him, and he never could match our ratings."

'Stealing albums again?'

Selecting audio samples from the best airchecks, Bobby produced a vinyl album featuring the winning DJs and sent the collector's item as a sales pitch to Drake-Chenault clients and prospective customers.

While carrying an armload of talent search albums to the company mailroom one day, he passed one of his bosses in an office hallway and was caught off guard by a well-timed zinger. "Stealing albums again?" Drake joked to his newly hired director of specialized programming.

"I freaked out, muttered something like, 'Hommina hommina hommina . . . ' and Drake just got a huge smile on his face," Bobby recalled.

Introduced to his other boss for the first time, Bobby greeted him with, "It's a pleasure to meet you, Mr. Chenault." To which the senior partner of the business responded, "Call me Pappy."

Oops, slight miscalculation

A later encounter with Pappy was less cordial.

As a consultant to client station KYNO in Fresno, the famous Top 40 powerhouse that Chenault owned and Drake programmed during their early days developing Boss Radio, Bobby came up with what he called a "brilliant suggestion."

His plan was to one-up a competitor station whose contest promised one lucky listener the chance to keep as much money as they could grab from a bank vault in a limited amount of time.

"I said we should double KFRE's prize total. Pappy asked me what it would cost, and I assured him that they had a promotion budget of $12,000 max. He said okay, and we launched our contest guaranteeing KYNO would award twice as much cash as any other station in the Central Valley."

The stakes turned out to be much higher, Bobby told *R&R* columnist Bob Shannon. "KFRE loaded the bank vault with too many large-denomination bills, and the winner scarfed up $54,000. We were stuck giving away $108,000 to one winner," he admitted.[18]

---

[18]*Radio & Records, Jul 12, 2002, pg 17* https://www.worldradiohistory.com/Archive-All-Music/Archive-RandR/2000s/2002/RR-2002-07-12.pdf

Bobby's miscalculation didn't cost him his job at Drake-Chenault. At least not right away.

Off the radio but not out of it

He devised another plan to expand the company's business model by creating a customizable live broadcast for a national audience. "I envisioned a personality radio show simulcast to all time zones, originating from Universal Amphitheatre in Los Angeles, hosted by a prominent DJ with guest appearances by musicians, movie stars, TV actors, and other entertainers," he said.

"I proposed that every station carrying the syndicated program have a local jock to insert brief weather, news, and sports updates for their listening area. With an automated equipment system using inaudible tones to cue the local drop-ins and commercials, the show would sound and feel like a blend of Hollywood and hometown."

Summoned to a meeting on his first anniversary at Drake-Chenault, Bobby assumed he was about to get the green light to proceed with the project. "Oh man, they're going to put me in charge of the whole thing," he said to himself. Instead, he was informed that his one-year contract would not be renewed.

"My bosses thought it was a cool idea, but their syndication model was designed to save money for local operators, so they didn't support my idea for retaining local announcers."

Nor did they support retaining Bobby.

The year at Drake-Chenault was longer than he'd ever gone without being on the radio. His self-esteem was low after being fired from his last three jobs.

"Getting blown out by stations in New York and LA, then losing the consultant gig was difficult. And there were marital problems," Bobby acknowledged.

His closest friend at the time was Mike Kinosian, also a national programming consultant at Drake-Chenault.

"When I was struggling, Mike listened to my whining, calmed me down, and refused to let me stay in the cellar of darkness. He pulled me out of some deep, dark times. To this day he's a lifetime, genuine friend.

"Looking back at my time there, I did a bunch of cool stuff and learned a lot. It was an interesting experience to be at Drake-Chenault, but I really missed being on the radio," Bobby said.

Two months after getting canned in Canoga Park, he would return to the airwaves on one of the most powerful stations in the country.

Chapter 35

Skydiving into Cake and Turning on Dr. Ruth

A friendship born in West Texas led to Bobby's return to Southern California. Jhani Kaye, assistant program director at KFI (AM 640) in Los Angeles, recommended Bobby when the station needed a night jock in late 1981.

"Jhani and I became friends in 1976 in El Paso, where he was program director of KINT and I went there to poach his 7-to-midnight guy Danny Wilde for B-100 in San Diego," Bobby said.

"I felt bad for Jhani because I was taking away his biggest star, but when we met, he told me it would be a great move for Danny and perfect for B-100. We both cried a bit, but it was very professional, and Jhani and I have shared a mutual respect ever since."

Kaye suggested Bobby to KFI program director Tom Bigby for the 6-10 p.m. shift that Big Ron O'Brien, a.k.a. "The Ayatollah of Rock & Rolla," had exited earlier in 1981.

KFI was Bobby's third LA station in eight years, following stints at KHJ and KHTZ.

Before going on the air each day, he and Kaye spent hours in the KFI lunchroom, writing clues for contests and promotional copy for the jocks to read. Collaborating with Bobby was enjoyable, Kaye said, "because he understood that a radio station should be fun."

Beyond brainstorming promotions, they shared ideas on programming elements that would play best with Southern California audiences. "We worked together very well because we both had West Coast ears," Kaye added, noting that very few programmers achieved success in LA if they weren't attuned to the listening habits and lifestyle of Angelenos.

On the day they awarded a $10,000 prize to a contest winner who parachuted into a KFI birthday cake, "Bobby really shined, ad-libbing for a couple hours straight, wonderfully describing the excitement for everyone listening on the ground," Kaye said.

50,000 watts of amazingness

With a clear channel 50,000-watt signal, KFI was the most powerful station that Bobby had ever worked at. His nightly show could be heard in more than thirty states, and listeners from the Pacific coast to the Midwest called the request line asking him to play their favorite song.

"People in rural areas of Minnesota, Michigan, and Montana told me that we were their 'local station' because KFI was the only clear radio signal they could pick up late at night. One night a guy called in from a small town in South Dakota to ask if I could emcee their high school prom! It was a thrill knowing my voice reached all the way to Mount Rushmore, but I had to politely decline the invitation," Bobby said.

"Another time, a listener called from Iowa wondering if I was the same Bobby Rich he used to listen to on KSTT in Davenport. He was blown away to hear me again more than ten years later and all the way from Los Angeles. That's the power of KFI's signal at night."

His boss changed Bobby's air shift a couple of times. "I did early evenings, late evenings, and overnights at KFI," Bobby said, "and when Bigby left, I went back to early evenings."

KFI branded itself as "The Amazing AM", and industry newspapers chronicled a tight ratings battle with five competitors: KIIS, KIQQ, KRTH, KRLA, and KWST.

While working the all-night shift, Bobby got to know the station's biggest stars, Al Lohman and Roger Barkley, who signed on at six every morning. LA radio personalities since 1968 at KFI, Lohman and Barkley amazingly held the morning drive time slot until 1986.

"When I got to the 50,000-watt blowtorch," Bobby said, "KFI was playing a more contemporary blend of music than most other LA stations that were going for adult listeners. Kind of like a grown-up Top 40 with energy and fun DJs and wacky stunts."

Seemingly naked woman skydives into giant cake

To celebrate its sixty-one years in the City of Angels, KFI sponsored a contest in 1982 asking listeners, "What's the Most Amazing Thing You Would You Do for $10,000?" Entry letters poured into the promotions department and were read on the air.

One prize seeker offered to bathe in a tub full of liver outside the Hollywood Boulevard landmark previously known as Grauman's Chinese Theater. Contestant Sandra Doyle of Escondido said, "A runner-up offered to mow the Rose Bowl grass with his teeth. Another guy offered to kiss 10,000 cows on the lips."

Doyle won the contest with her letter promising, "For $10,000 I will personally bake KFI a 300-pound birthday cake and place it delicately in the station parking lot or someone else's parking lot. I'll then catch a ride up into the blue with Bruce Wayne and parachute into the cake wearing only a banner that says Happy Birthday Amazing AM!"

A professional skydiver, Doyle had more than a thousand jumps under her belt and made some of them wearing only her birthday suit. But the station's lawyers insisted there could be no public nudity, so she wore a flesh-colored body stocking for the daredevil stunt.

Amazingly, the attorneys did not object to a listener jumping out of the airplane piloted by Wayne, KFI's traffic reporter. Weeks before the 1983 event, Doyle secured a million dollar liability insurance policy from Lloyd's of London and obtained necessary approvals from the FAA.

TV news crews and thousands of cheering spectators turned up at the designated landing area, a Puente Hills Mall parking lot in the City of Industry. As Doyle made her leap from about three thousand feet, Wayne described the action from "KFI in the Sky" and Bobby did live play-by-play at ground level.

They were joined by KFI's Steve LaBeau, Kim Kelly, Mark Taylor, Karen Sommers, Marv Collins, and Byron of Byron & Tanaka, adding color commentary on the skydiver's descent and perfectly executed touchdown in the 8-by-10-foot birthday cake.

Doyle not only nailed the landing but pulled LeBeau into the cake with her, smearing him with frosting as he presented an oversized check for $10,000 to the parachutist.

Air tragedy

In a 2022 interview, Doyle praised Wayne's professionalism and punctuality in delivering her to the designated exit altitude on the prize-winning adventure. "Bruce was a wonderful pilot," she said.

In a tragic accident three years after the parachute jump, Wayne lost contact with KFI during his morning traffic shift and died when his Cessna single-engine aircraft crashed shortly after takeoff from Fullerton Municipal Airport.

Bobby was on the air at San Diego's B-100 when he heard the shocking news of his former coworker's death. "It hit me hard," Bobby said of the 1986 plane crash. "Bruce was such a good guy, covering Southern California traffic for eighteen years and helping millions of people with his reports. He really was their eye in the sky."

Morning show fill-in finds his favorite shift

When Lohman's longtime partner Barkley called in sick early one day in 1982, Bobby was asked to stick around after his overnight shift and fill in for a couple of hours on the KFI morning show. "Al just needed me to play along as a straight man with his character voices, and I handled the basics like time checks and weather," Bobby remembered.

"That experience changed my life. Oh, my God, to be part of a show with talent like Lohman and Barkley's, I knew right then morning radio was for me!"

The Cox radio group, parent company of KFI and sister station KOST-FM, made some programming changes that November. "Jhani got promoted to PD of KOST when they switched formats to Adult Contemporary," Bobby said. "He later named me assistant PD of KFI."

Sexually Speaking, Dr. Ruth introduced to LA by Bobby

A sex talk show cut into Bobby's airtime in 1983 as Dr. Ruth Westheimer signed a deal with KFI to expand her popular "Sexually Speaking" program to the Los Angeles market. A smash hit in New York, Dr. Ruth's show on WYNY was presented as "a forum for the mature discussion of human sexuality."

As the late-night jock on Sundays, Bobby was offstage announcer for the LA debut of the sex therapist's hourlong weekly show at 9:30 p.m. "So, turning Dr. Ruth on for the West Coast was my assignment," he teased.

"We'd talk by phone, mostly about radio, and Ruth was very nice. She did it live via satellite from her apartment in New York, with me as board operator at KFI. We'd chat while I was finishing up my music show, I'd check her mic levels, make sure she was ready to go on the air, and introduce her.

"I was responsible for keeping the show on time, letting her know when to break for commercials, and announcing the Toyota dealership that sponsored "Sexually Speaking" with Dr. Ruth on KFI. Somebody else screened the incoming calls from listeners wanting to talk about their sex lives."

Bobby's next exciting career move was a corporate transfer to Philadelphia, where he was again given the reins of program director and took one last crack at the East Coast.

Audio of 1983 KFI parachute jump at bobbyrichradio.com.

Chapter 36

Michael Jackson Gets Put on Time Out

In the summer of 1983, Cox Broadcasting appointed Bobby as program director of WWSH in Philadelphia and revealed plans for a format change. Known as "Wish FM," the station had already evolved from Easy Listening to a soft Adult Contemporary (AC) format, and General Manager Bill Phippen announced, "We're going to be an AC Hit station."

"Under Bobby's programming expertise and consultant Mary Catherine Sneed's guidance, we'll be moving to a more contemporary sound in presentation and music," Phippen told the industry magazine *Radio & Records.*[19]

"Even after fifteen years as a programmer," Bobby told *R&R*, "I get very excited when the right opportunity comes along at the right time, especially when the chemistry is so perfect." Eager to try out a concept he'd been working on since 1979 at KHTZ in Los Angeles, Bobby wanted to distinguish WWSH with a playlist of up-tempo hit songs, big personality DJs, fun promotions, and heavy community involvement. It was a format that he would later refine as Hot AC.

Given several weeks to generate buzz and prepare for the debut of

---

[19]*Radio & Records, July 15, 1983, pg 1 https://www.worldradiohistory.com/hd2/IDX-Business/Music/Archive-RandR-IDX/IDX/80s/83/RR-1983-07-15-OCR-Page-0001.pdf#search=%22wwsh%20rich%20phippen%22*

the new WWSH, Bobby selected a solid lineup of jocks, wrote and recorded fresh promos, and invited TV coverage of the kickoff.

He informed *R&R* that a plan was in the works to replace the WWSH call letters. "Yes, I was promoting a call letter change in the media before I had permission to do so," Bobby openly admitted. He wanted a fresh image that was not associated with the station's prior beautiful music format.

When the Cox radio group rejected his proposal to retire their well-established WWSH call sign, he persuaded them to rebrand as "The Top FM 106," reflecting the station's uppermost position on the radio dial. "I made a change in identifying the product without using the formal call letters," Bobby noted.

It was a party atmosphere in the control room when the entire air staff celebrated the premiere on August 8 and a news crew from Philadelphia's NBC affiliate KYW-TV simulcast the first three minutes of Top FM. Once again, Bobby played "Beginnings" by Chicago as his ceremonial sign-on song for station reincarnation.

Freak accident sidelines new boss

His first month as PD was interrupted for several days by a rare bowling ball mishap. Despite boyhood experience as a pinsetter at his father's bowling center in Ephrata, Washington, Bobby lacked the body English to avoid serious injury on a visit home for his twentieth high school reunion.

"My dad stored bowling balls on a high shelf in the basement, and my mom was trying to clean out the cabinet. She couldn't reach the top shelf, so called me to help," Bobby said.

"When we moved one of the boxes, a sixteen-pounder rolled out and dropped about seven feet onto my foot, causing severe toe trauma. The reunion was that night, and I was the emcee. My dad gave me some pain pills, and as soon as I arrived at the party, I started drinking. Apparently, it made for a memorable evening, as my classmates later told me."

Top FM talent

For his first big hire at WWSH, Bobby recruited a two-man morning show from Hawaii, Kelly Randall and Dan Cooke. At KKUA and KQMQ, they competed against Honolulu radio legend J. Akuhead Pupule (Crazy Fish Head), affectionately known as Aku, who was born Herschel Laib Hohenstein and also used the name Hal Lewis.

Following Aku's death in 1983, Randall and Cooke were delivering solid ratings, Cooke remembered, but Bobby managed to lure them from the Big Island to Philly. Their show featured several characters voiced by Cooke, including astrology buff Dwayne, boorish Ted Wallace with Moron Sports, and Muppet-like weather amphibian Kermit the Fog Frog.

Harriet Coffey worked middays, and Bobby did the afternoon air shift. He added to the staff by hiring David Lankford, who had previously worked for him at KSTT in Davenport, and brought J.R. Russ from Buffalo for late-nights. Art Tiller was newscaster, assistant PD, and weekend DJ. He went on to work as an on-air host at C-SPAN.

Sam Milkman, another Bobby hire at Top FM, remembered taking a surprise phone call during a Saturday night air shift. His program director was on the studio hotline to inquire, "Sam, are you depressed?" A perplexed Milkman responded, "No! I'm on the air in Philadelphia, having a great time! Why, what's the matter?"

"You just played fourteen ballads in a row," Bobby informed him. The boss then instructed the young DJ, "Be in my office on Monday morning. I'm going to teach you about tempo."

During his coaching session with Milkman, Bobby wrote the reminder "Never on Saturday night, Sammy!" on at least one notecard in the DJ's playlist of sleepy song selections from the record library. "I learned there was much more dimension to it than just picking the next card in the stack," Milkman recalled.

"Other jocks would skip a dirge by Lionel Richie," Milkman explained, "but not me." A newcomer to the station, he had been reluctant to break format even if it meant playing two or more slow songs back-to-back.

Another of Bobby's protégés in Philadelphia was Matt Farber, who chose radio over Wall Street while studying at the Wharton School at the University of Pennsylvania. Farber started as producer for Randall and Cooke's program on WWSH and graduated to a career as a TV programming executive at MTV, VH1, and Viacom.

Finding the hot spot in the middle

Philadelphia Daily News columnist Dave Bittan was quick to criticize the station's morning show as outrageous, offbeat, and amateurish while insinuating that Bobby's Los Angeles approach to radio wouldn't fly in Philadelphia.

"My approach in Philly or any other city was always to get involved in the community right away, give listeners a reason to smile, and say or play something to brighten their day," Bobby responded. "That's the power of radio, and it's what I love most about what I do."

Answering to multiple bosses in upper management at Cox Broadcasting, he struggled to meet their expectations and achieve his own vision for differentiating the new Top FM from the old WWSH.

"Cox wanted a softer sounding Adult Contemporary format, but I took a more aggressive approach, programming music with a harder edge. It's what I've always done, trying to find the hot spot in the middle. Our sound had the feeling and imaging of a Top 40 station but wasn't aimed at teens at all."

As examples of "perfect Philly songs" in his rotation, Bobby pointed to "You Dropped a Bomb on Me" by the Gap Band and "Ain't No Stoppin' Us Now" by McFadden and Whitehead. But when it came to playing "Miss You" and "Shattered" by the Rolling Stones, he said the corporate honchos got uncomfortable.

Phippen, the GM who hired him, was Bobby's strongest advocate with top brass at headquarters who resisted his blend of pop, rock, urban, and softer fare. "I loved Phip for being such a supportive boss. Just a fantastic guy, lots of fun, a cheerleader always encouraging his staff.

"One other thing about Phip," Bobby recalled fondly, "he had loose teeth, and whenever he laughed really hard, his teeth would fall out."

Visit to the zoo of Scott Shannon

While struggling with the corporate hierarchy in Philadelphia, Bobby was fascinated with Scott Shannon's wildly popular *Z Morning Zoo* that had taken the New York market by storm. He called the Zoo format creator at Z100 and asked if they could discuss it.

Shannon arranged a meeting at WHTZ in Secaucus, New Jersey, and generously answered questions about his successful orchestration of an entertaining, fast-paced morning show with multiple co-hosts. In the *Z Morning Zoo* studio, Shannon let Bobby observe their blend of on-air banter, music, news, weather, traffic, commercials, zany antics, and interaction with listeners.

"Scott was very helpful, and I decided to design a morning show like his, but with a stronger team player concept." The meeting in Secaucus provided valuable insights for Bobby's later creation of the *B Morning Zoo* with the Rich Brothers in San Diego.

Message to Michael Jackson: Beat it!

At the peak of Michael Jackson's domination of the *Billboard* Hot 100 chart with a record-setting seven singles from his *Thriller* album reaching top ten status, Bobby imposed a WWSH moratorium on playing all songs by the King of Pop.

"You hear him on the radio, see him on TV, and read about him in magazines. Let's face it, he's tired. He needs some time off," Bobby said.

The "No Michael Jackson Weekend" was advertised with a tongue-in-cheek promo and round-the-clock repetition of WWSH jocks calling attention to the absence of Michael Jackson music.

"Of course we were talking about him all weekend," Milkman noted. The no-play order was lifted after seventy-two hours.

By making the station a Jackson-free zone, even refusing to air a Pepsi commercial featuring the Jacksons, Bobby attracted national media attention for WWSH. But the stunt turned out to be his swan song in Philadelphia. He had lifted the ratings but felt constrained by corporate bureaucracy and could sense he was about to be fired.

Thanks a lot, Mrs. Fox

That feeling was confirmed when Bobby arrived at work one day and the woman who sold coffee and newspapers in the lobby of the WWSH building told him, "We sure are going to miss you around here."

The newsstand operator, Mrs. Fox, had overheard station executives discussing plans to let him go that day. The bosses had not yet officially informed Bobby of their plans to replace him.

Choosing to resign, he agreed to stay on while Cox selected his successor. In April of 1984, after a year in Philly, he again set eyes on Southern California.

Confident he could win with a Hot AC format, Bobby was determined to find a GM willing to give him a shot. That dream job opportunity would come into view at the end of another coast-to-coast relocation.

Gloved up for No Michael Jackson Weekend. WWSH, Philadelphia, April 1984. (Photo by Owen Lampe Jr.)

Chapter 37

Back to B-100 for Hot AC and B Morning Zoo

"I'm a great believer in the 'You can go back to the place, but not to the time' philosophy. Times have changed, and so has programming . . . and so have I," Bobby announced in a front-page *Radio & Records* story about his return to San Diego in 1984.[20]

After proving himself in New York City and subsequent gigs in Los Angeles and Philadelphia, he chose to revisit the place where he enjoyed his greatest success as a programmer.

"About that time, I started thinking how silly it was to be moving around the country when the only place I really wanted to be was in San Diego," Bobby said.

"I'd been tossing around a lot of concepts for music formats, and one was really beginning to take shape. I also became convinced that if I was going to be on the air, only in mornings could I continue to grow. So, I decided to move back."

A career-assessing, soul-searching road trip from Pennsylvania to California was followed by a deep dive analyzing the radio market he had conquered in 1977.

---

[20]*Radio & Records,* Aug 24, 1984, pg 1; https://www.worldradiohistory.com/Archive-All-Music/Archive-RandR/1980s/1984/RR-1984-08-24.pdf

Perfect landing . . . but not right away

"I arrived in San Diego without a job but with a plan. I was hoping somehow to have another go at B-100." He began by analyzing the competition.

Bobby identified a handful of stations with mediocre ratings that might be open to a turnaround strategy. Three general managers agreed to meet and hear his proposal for a new format to expand their target audience.

"They all told me the same thing," he said. "Gee, Bobby, you're terrific, well-known in this market, got those huge ratings at B-100, everybody loves you, but we don't need you.

"The funniest part was talking to GMs whose stations were rated third or fourth in female listeners aged 18-34, and they were happy with that. Maybe there were other reasons not to take a chance, but I thought what a bunch of losers who don't have the guts to be better. They settled for good enough, fearful of losing what they already had."

Bobby's prior programming dominance in the market didn't seem to matter in his quest for a new gig. When four months of job searching yielded no offers, the disheartened Doctor Boogie wondered if he might end up at Pacific Stereo, selling home and car audio systems. But there was one more door to knock on.

Paul Palmer, general manager of KFMB's AM and FM outlets, had recruited Bobby in 1975 to launch B-100 as a Top 40 rocker. In just two and a half years under his direction, it rose to number one in San Diego, the first FM contemporary station to top the 12-plus Arbitron ratings (all age groups).

That triumph had punched Bobby's ticket to New York, where he programmed 99X and introduced his Album Oriented Hits format. He stayed in touch with Palmer as a friend and programming consultant for the next six years.

After unproductive conversations with other station managers in San Diego, Bobby got an appointment with B-100's GM and made his pitch to overhaul the station. Over the course of three or four meetings, Palmer agreed to rehire him as PD and replace the station's light rock Adult Contemporary music with a more up-tempo format that Bobby labeled Hot AC.

"Hot AC, combining harder-edged Top 40 songs with softer pop-oriented AC tunes, is what I tried at K-HITS in LA. But they told me it wouldn't fly. Then I tried it at WWSH in Philly, and again it got me fired. It wasn't until I returned to B-100 in 1984 that I was able to refine the format and make it work," he said.

San Diego's other zoo

Completing the transformation of B-100 was Bobby's concept for the *B Morning Zoo*. No other station had yet put a "zoo" show with multiple co-hosts on the air in San Diego.

"Scott Shannon set the bar in Tampa with his *Q Morning Zoo* at WRBQ and in New York with the *Z Morning Zoo* at WHTZ (Z100). Scott was kind enough to let me sit in on his show to see how he did it. I also loved elements of John Lander's *Q Morning Zoo* at 79Q in Houston. But I had in my mind more of a team show where everyone had an equal role," he said.

Influenced by the humor and on-air skits of Pat O'Day and Lan Roberts at his favorite station, KJR, Bobby had also studied the on-air chemistry of two-man teams Lohman and Barkley at KFI, Charlie and Harrigan at KFMB and KCBQ, and Hudson and Bauer at KFMB.

"Paul Palmer wanted to know how many people I had in mind to hire for our new B-100 morning show. When I replied more than one and less than seven, he didn't object. Paul was willing to try something groundbreaking that his competitors shied away from," he said.

Future biographer rejoins Bobby for B-100 reboot

B-100 is where I once again crossed paths with Bobby Rich.

He decided that the *B Morning Zoo* should have four co-hosts. Bobby selected Scott Kenyon (Benjamin Gall), Frank Anthony (Frank Catalfo), and me to be his on-air partners. Collectively, we would call ourselves the Rich Brothers. Individually, we were Bobby, Scott, Frank, and Pat. The four of us hunkered down for several weeks of show prep and rehearsals before the premier of our show on B-100.

Scott had programmed KYA in San Francisco and KIMN in Denver after breaking into radio with Bobby at WOHO in Toledo and at KSTT in Davenport.

"Back in those days," Bobby said, "people always thought we looked alike and would ask if Scott and I were related. We'd say we're brothers with different mothers . . . and fathers. At KSTT I asked him to consider changing his air name so that we could be the Rich Brothers, Bobby and Benjie. The timing wasn't right, but twelve years later Scott was off-the-chart giddy when I invited him to come to San Diego and join me on the show."

Frank, who had previously jocked at KCBQ and was doing the night shift at B-100, feared he would be fired in his first meeting with our new PD. Instead, he was offered a spot on the morning show as the third Rich Brother.

"I was completely surprised, because Bobby didn't know me from Adam," Frank said. "I had a sense of humor, a knowledge of music, and could write parody songs. He needed someone with a background in production and editing who could run a tight board and complement Scott with the technical value of the show. I jumped at the chance."

Over the next five years, Frank composed dozens of parody songs that we recorded and played on the *B Morning Zoo*. Handling all our musical arrangements, he earned the nickname Quincy Catalfo, a nod to renowned composer and producer Quincy Jones. As the only one on the show with any singing ability, Frank took lead vocals and applied his mastery of multitrack mixing to hide the ear-splitting voices of his melodically challenged brethren.

Our biggest hit was "The Rich Brothers San Diego Song," borrowing the tune of "Kokomo" by the Beach Boys and highlighting the ample sunshine and kickback lifestyle of California's second-biggest city. Another popular parody song was "Day-Oh San Diego." Inspired by the 1988 movie Beetlejuice, the silly ditty was a remake of Harry Belafonte's classic calypso number.

I was Bobby's final choice to complete his quartet for the Zoo debut. Already on the B-100 staff, I had joined the station in 1982 as newscaster for prior morning host Larry Himmel. Bobby knew me from KHTZ in Los Angeles before I spent a year in Fresno at "Kickass Rock & Roll" KKDJ.

Another KKDJ alum who landed in San Diego was bombastic sports personality Cookie Randolph. After acquiring the nickname "Chainsaw," Randolph joined Jeff Prescott and Mike Berger on 101 KGB and later starred on the long-running Dave, Shelly, and Chainsaw (DSC) show at KGB and Jack 100.7 FM.

As a former competitor of B-100 in the 1980s, Randolph complimented Bobby and the Rich Brothers for "killing it" with camaraderie and compelling content. In a 2025 interview, he recalled a parody song presented with good-humored repartee and crisp timing. "I remember listening one day and the guys went from banter into the bit, followed by a jingle into spots. Damn, it was perfect," Randolph said.

Traffic reporter Steve Springer in "the Stevebird" added his personality to our *B Morning Zoo*, relaying an aerial view of rush-hour snarls. Recurring bits included wisecracks about congestion on the Casa de Oro connector and backups at La Bajada Dip. Springer's signature "All

Clear" announcement wrapping up his last Airwatch traffic update each day marked the official end of San Diego's morning commute.

Recipe for Hot AC

A memo to all KFMB employees (FM, AM, and TV) in August of 1984 announced Bobby's return. Most of the management and air staff on B-100 were the same as when he left in 1978, so it felt like a homecoming. In a familiar place with familiar faces, he was back at the helm with the trust of a general manager who knew him, believed in him, and let him do his thing.

Palmer's memo also announced Glen McCartney's resignation as PD and credited him for building B-100 into the leading AC station in San Diego. According to *Billboard* magazine, five challengers competing for the AC audience were KFMB-AM, KBZT, KIFM, KYXY, and KLZZ.[21]

Palmer told *Radio & Records,* "It's very difficult to make a programming change when things are going well," but added, "I felt Bobby was the one guy in the country that could take what we have and move us to a new level."

Because of his Top 40 track record, many competitors and industry observers expected the new PD to adopt that format in his encore at B-100. But Bobby had something else in mind, telling *Billboard*, "My plan, simply, is to keep the station AC and make it better."

To come up with his Hot AC playlist, he researched a decade of music charts from *Billboard* and other industry publications including *Cashbox, Radio & Records,* and *The Gavin Report*. "This was before computers," he said, "so I made two columns on yellow legal pads and wrote down the titles of one hundred hits that charted in both the Top 40 and AC lists in each of the previous ten years."

[21]*Billboard,* Sept 1, 1984, pg 12; *https://www.worldradiohistory.com/Archive-All-Music/Billboard/80s/1984/BB-1984-09-01.pdf*

"I assigned a point system for songs. To make it into my library, they had to show up in both formats. If a song was number one on one chart and number 100 on another, it made it. But if a song was number one in one format and didn't appear in the other, it got eliminated. From that stack of yellow legal pads, we ended up with a playlist of probably four hundred to five hundred crossover hits that I believed would appeal to younger adult listeners or an older Top 40 audience."

Welcome to the jock lounge

After choosing his morning show co-hosts, Bobby solidified the lineup for other day parts, reuniting with two of San Diego's best-known DJs. He hired Gene Knight, "The Greener," for middays and Gary Kelley for afternoons when Danny Wilde resigned. The four of them were Boogie Brothers in the first incarnation of B-100 in the mid-1970s.

Wilde made a career change after eight years at the station, leaving to attend medical school. Trading his microphone for a stethoscope opened the door for Kelley's return.

For the 6-10 p.m. shift, Bobby took Danny Romero from KYNO in Fresno, and Romero brought his dog Roscoe with him to San Diego. The well-behaved pup sat in the studio and was given occasional speaking parts in the nightly show, barking on command.

Romero later segued from radio DJ to TV weatherman at KFMB and KGTV in San Diego. He then moved to Los Angeles to work at KCOP, KNBC, and KABC. In 2022, his seventeenth year on the air at ABC7 Eyewitness News in LA, Romero said in an interview, "Bobby absolutely put me on the path to where I am now."

Kathy Aunan worked the late-night shift and John Fox handled overnights for the 1984 reboot of B-100. Part-timers included Don Pia, Gary Hamilton, JR Rogers, Roy Robertson, Dave Sniff, and Tony Pepper. Pepper hosted the *Saturday Night Dance Party* show. Rob Actis was later added to the weekend schedule. Longtime DJ and programmer Mike Novak joined the air staff in 1986.

Bobby brought Ellen Thomas from Modesto to San Diego that same year, following Aunan's crosstown move to KYXY. Thomas did late-nights until 1989 when she left B-100 for middays at X-100 in San Francisco. Taking the name Ellen K, she relocated to Los Angeles and co-hosted mornings at KIIS-FM from 1990 to 2015, first with Rick Dees and then with Ryan Seacrest, before getting her own show at KOST-FM. In 2025, the iHeart station noted that Ellen K on KOST was the longest continuously airing morning personality in the LA market.

Gary Kelley, a radio host for nearly three decades in San Diego and LA, called Bobby "the best PD and the best boss that I've ever worked for. He's a motivator who doesn't order you to do things, he just makes you want to try harder, and that's how he gets the best out of everybody." Hired three times by Bobby, Kelley had a second career in TV as a San Diego weathercaster on two stations in his hometown.

Because it's a jungle out there

Bobby contracted voiceover artist Ernie Anderson, known for his dramatic ABC-TV network promos (*The Love Boat*), to record liners reinforcing B-100's promotional events and programming ("*The B Morning Zoo* . . . because it's a jungle out there!")

The station was defined by Anderson's vocal imaging that emphasized frequent on-air contests with heavy repetition of the catchphrase "Music, Money, and Fun!"

"Ernie really sold it," Bobby said. "He did more with those four words, emphasizing the three things we wanted to be known for."

Little buddy Dwayne

Long before "working remotely" was a thing, Dan Cooke joined us as a virtual fifth Rich Brother, making regular appearances from Philadelphia. After finishing his own morning show on WWSH at ten Eastern time, Cooke brought his stable of fictional characters to life for San Diegans.

Over a long-distance phone line, he portrayed quarrelsome sportscaster Ted Wallace, redneck Bucky from Santee, and amphibian weather puppet Kermit the Fog Frog.

Cooke's most popular character was Dwayne, a whimsical busboy at a famous beach-area watering hole whose playfulness and on-air friendship kept our audience laughing and guessing.

We affectionately referred to him as "Our little buddy Dwayne." Flamboyant, sensitive, and unpredictable, he served up romantic relationship advice, party planning ideas, holiday decorating tips, and humorous reviews of the TV series *Dynasty*. His daily escapades made the network soap opera seem tame by comparison.

Listeners who went looking for Dwayne at Bully's restaurant and bar near the Del Mar racetrack were disappointed to find that he was never working when they stopped by.

"The thing about Bobby," Cooke said, "is he came to play every day. Of course, there were always distractions in our lives, but he taught us to give it our best shot, put everything aside, and bring positive energy to each show."

Cooke went on to be a TV weather anchor and realtor in Hawaii. He credited Bobby for inspiring a spirit "I take with me in my life no matter what I'm doing. That consistency and professionalism he demonstrated daily has helped me to survive and thrive."

Deliveries B Us

Full-service radio took on a new meaning the day our morning show sent overnight jock John Fox to run an errand on his way home from the station. "It started with a listener who called us right after six because she needed a quart of milk or something," Bobby said. "John agreed to stop at a convenience store and take the item to her house. He put her on the air with us, and that was the start of Deliveries B Us, which became a recurring segment on the show."

When a major snowstorm hit the San Bernardino mountains, Fox was dispatched in the B-100 Boogie Van to check out snow conditions at Big Bear. For the sake of a good bit, he pretended not to realize the Rich Brothers wanted him to drive to the ski resort in the San Bernardino National Forest. In a series of live reports stretching over several hours, Fox finally arrived at "Big Bear," only to report there was no snow to be found.

"No snow?! Where exactly are you, John?!" we demanded. An exasperated Fox, calling from a San Diego supermarket in the Big Bear grocery chain, screamed into his phone, "I'm at 54th and El Cajon stinkin' Boulevard!"

"Oh, come on, we meant Big Bear MOUNTAIN!" we replied in mock frustration. The bit ended with Fox's icy retort, "You never said anything about a mountain, you just said go to Big Bear."

Another field trip took Fox to Northern California to find out why Yuba City was ranked dead last out of 329 U.S. cities in Rand McNally's 1985 Places Rated Almanac. His live reports back to San Diego featured interviews with Yuba City's mayor and a long-distance operator named Lolita, who connected Fox's collect call from a phone booth on Main Street.

Wedding bells

The start of Bobby's second run in San Diego coincided with the end of his first marriage. He and Judy had split up before he moved to Philadelphia in 1983. They divorced after his return to B-100.

In February of 1985 he remarried, exchanging vows with Debbie Sisco in a Balboa Park garden ceremony. Their wedding party included

Bobby's sons Bryan and Jeff, and Debbie's daughter Laine. The Rich family celebrated the birth of their daughter Lesley the following year.

Debbie was project coordinator for our *Rich Brothers Funny Song Album*, a collection of twenty-four novelty tunes and comedy bits from the show. The vinyl record was a high-profile charity project, generating more than $12,000 in sales. All proceeds were directed to the YMCA's Cara-Net and Juvenile Crisis Center, which promoted child safety and funded a hotline to assist parents of missing children. We dedicated the album to the memory of Cara Knott, a San Diego State University student murdered by an on-duty California Highway Patrol officer.

Bobby, Scott, Frank, and I lent our voices and support to many other humanitarian causes and nonprofit organizations. Hosting a golf tournament with the Del Mar Kiwanis to benefit Canine Companions for Independence, provider of service dogs for people with disabilities, we invited listeners to play in "the Rich Brothers Celebrity Pro-Am … heavy on the am," repeating the self-deprecating tagline in unison. Former Chargers quarterback Dan Fouts joined us in the golf outing at Lomas Santa Fe Country Club.

Over the years we accepted dozens of invitations to community events, turning up in our matching Converse red sneakers to participate in holiday parades, serve as celebrity waiters for charity galas or judge high school science fairs and air band contests.

When tragedy strikes

"It's not always fun and games being on the radio," Bobby noted, reflecting on the space shuttle Challenger disaster of January 28, 1986. "We were talking about the mission for days, and the launch that morning was televised live, so the explosion that killed all seven astronauts including schoolteacher Christa McAuliffe was a shock to everyone, just heartbreaking.

"Because it happened during our show, we had to react immediately, turn on the mic, and be there for our radio family. You can't stay in entertainment mode at a time of national tragedy, but you owe it to the audience to keep people informed. Fortunately, we could turn things over to Pat, an experienced and trusted reporter," Bobby said.

For the remainder of our show, I provided updates on the shuttle explosion and casualties. I did not mention that three weeks earlier I had mailed an application to NASA's Journalist in Space Project. My focus that day was on reporting the tragic event, not on disclosing any personal interest in the civilian astronaut program. More than 1,700 reporters across the U.S. applied for the Journalist in Space Project in 1986. NASA ended the program that summer because of the Challenger tragedy.

Which Bobby sang that song?

One of the songs most representative of B-100 and the *B Morning Zoo* in the late 1980s was also one of the happiest records to top the music charts during that era. "Don't Worry, Be Happy" by singer-songwriter Bobby McFerrin became a San Diego favorite thanks to a tip from a DJ on a competing station.

"My friend Wild Bill Calhoun, who was a guest turkey on the *Bobby Rich Turkey Hour* show at KFMB in 1976 and stayed in touch over the years, was working late-nights at smooth jazz KIFM when they got an early copy of McFerrin's breakthrough album," Bobby recalled.

"The first time Bill played "Don't Worry, Be Happy" over at KIFM, he immediately thought the song had the real good, feel-good sound and vibe of the Rich Brothers. So, he brought me a reel-to-reel tape the next day and we started playing it on B-100, ahead of all the mainstream AC and Top 40 stations."

McFerrin's a cappella single made it to number one on the *Billboard* Hot 100 in September of 1988. "Bobby Rich helped it become a national hit that summer," Calhoun said, "because people paid attention to Bobby and his station.

"B-100 then used 'Don't Worry, Be Happy' in a marketing campaign with the Rich Brothers lip-synching the catchy lyrics in a TV commercial," he added. "It was so successful that many San Diegans actually thought they wrote and sang the song!"

Picnic time for teddy bears

Under Bobby's direction, the mandate of the *B Morning Zoo* was to wake up the people of San Diego with a smile. "We're here to entertain," he told an interviewer, "by being spontaneous, locally relatable, often silly but equally pseudo-intellectual. We can be a little edgy at times, but overall family oriented."

He chose "The Teddy Bears' Picnic" as the Rich Brothers' official theme song and played the Bing Crosby version on a regular but rotating basis, with a few well-placed giggles, train whistles, and other sound effects added for good measure. The song's child-friendly lyrics evoking images of playful teddy bears lent an element of nostalgia and wholesomeness to the program while providing a counterbalance for our edgier content.

Dale "the Voiceman" Reeves, who DJ'd with Bobby in Davenport, provided a touch of adult humor with interactive comedy bits he customized for the San Diego audience. His characters included Rhonda La Fonda, a sassy secretary with an annoying New York dialect, and Leon Freon, a hipster who sounded like Eddie Murphy. Reeves also did celebrity impressions of Elvis Presley, President Reagan, Mr. T, and Mister Rogers.

Letting the listeners glisten

"We don't see ourselves as the star of the show," Bobby told students at

Point Loma Nazarene College who invited us to a broadcasting seminar. "We see ourselves as coordinators of mayhem." Referring to the menagerie that appeared on the air each day, he said the Zoo crew presented original comedy material and welcomed listeners to play along.

At least a dozen contributors created characters for the show, participating by phone in interactive live skits and routines recorded on tape.

Jim Hershey, a street magician and juggler who entertained tourists in Balboa Park, called in to perform tricks while providing his own play-by-play as we pretended to be dazzled by his acts of illusion. A daring escape from a straitjacket and an elaborate ruse to "levitate" all the residents of Ocean Beach were two of Hershey's illusory stunts.

Twice each week, a gruff-voiced Sergeant Charlie Delta made contact via an "unsecure phone line" at Marine Corps Base Camp Pendleton, berating the Rich Brothers and barking orders at the grunts in his platoon.

Another character, South of the Border Traffic Reporter Chico Ramon, told borderline jokes accompanied by helicopter sound effects.

Surfing golfer Radout provided beach reports and random wisdom with a stoner voice and bro-cabulary resembling Jeff Spicoli's in the movie *Fast Times at Ridgemont High*.

Lotto Bob, an overnight clerk at the 7-Eleven convenience store on Reynard Way, recited winning numbers on the air from the weekly California lottery.

Pseudo-Caribbean crooner Doctor Knife brought an island vibe to the show, shimmying to the beat of his own steel drum.

From Imperial Beach, vocal duo Linda and Debbie (a.k.a. the Friday Singers) kicked off each weekend with their stirring rendition of "The Friday Song," which became an anthem on the Zoo.

Psychic Samara, resident clairvoyant, made frequent in-studio visits, interacting with audience members who called to ask questions about their future or fortune.

A loyal listener using the pen name Sue Fari submitted numerous creative ideas via handwritten letters mailed through the U.S. Postal Service. Her frequent correspondence contained suggestions for funny bits, songs, and lyrics, many of which we used on the air.

Tuning in every day on her commute from Carlsbad to downtown San Diego, Joyce Middlested contributed to our show by delivering one-liners and carne asada breakfast burritos. She joined a Rich Brothers guided bus tour of the greater Grantville neighborhood and described the outing as "inane and so ridiculously stupid that it was just a kick in the butt. Just so much fun."

Ratings rise rapidly

Hot AC was an instant hit for B-100. Just seven months after its 1984 debut, Arbitron reported a cumulative ("cume") audience of 337,100 listeners per week, the station's best ratings since Bobby left for New York six years earlier.

"It was a huge shot in the arm when he came back to B-100," remembered Sales Manager Chuck Cotton, "because he was always thinking ahead to build ratings and find one more thing to make the station better."

While on the air, Bobby refused to let the sales staff enter our studio to talk about upcoming promotions or sponsor opportunities. He did it to prevent any distractions in the four-hour show. Across the hall at KFMB-AM, morning hosts Hudson and Bauer allowed salespeople to drop in unannounced and schmooze during commercials or newscasts.

"Bobby didn't like talking to us," said account executive George Essig, "and was very protective of the sound of the station. To his credit, he was strict with the sales team in terms of what went on the air. If there were any commercials running that didn't measure up, he'd let you know."

Cotton agreed that Bobby's primary focus was on programming. "He didn't go on client calls and wasn't a sales-oriented PD, but he was collaborative and creative, and we all evolved and learned how to support each other."

By the spring of 1987, B-100 had the number one morning drive show in San Diego. The Rich Brothers captured the highest market share among all listeners in age groups 12-plus. During the most desirable advertising hours of 6-10 a.m., we placed first in adults 25-54 and women 18-49.

In that same Arbitron survey period, B-100 had become the market's most listened-to FM station with a weekly cume of 391,000 listeners.

Awards, elephants, and underwater pumpkins

Billboard magazine was next to recognize the staff's success. In the 1987 *Billboard* Radio Awards, Bobby won Program Director of the Year and B-100 earned Station of the Year in the Medium Market Adult Contemporary category. The Rich Brothers were named Air Personality of the Year, Gene Knight was awarded Music Director of the Year, and Joan Hiser was honored as Promotion Director of the Year. The awards were the result of voting by industry peers, readers of the magazine.[22]

Hiser and Promotions Manager Sandi Banister coordinated an annual "Win an Elephant for a Day" contest when the traveling Circus Vargas came to town. Listeners sent in their best reasons for needing a three-ton elephant. One contestant proposed a public art project, offering to dip her naked butt cheeks in paint and decorate with colorful "double-zeros" marking the tail end of B-100's call letters. She lost out to a PTA president who proposed a pachyderm playground ride for her principal's retirement party.

---

[22] *Billboard,* Sept 19, 1987, pgs 19–23; *https://www.worldradiohistory.com/Archive-All-Music/Billboard/80s/1987/Billboard-1987-09-19.pdf*

The next year's contest winner climbed onto the circus elephant and made a successful marriage proposal to his girlfriend.

An underwater pumpkin carving contest and live broadcast from La Jolla Shores was the station's most memorable Halloween promotion. Ocean Enterprises owner Werner Kurn sponsored the event, providing scuba training for the DJs, plus wetsuits and dive gear.

Station engineers devised waterproof microphones, but JR Rogers remembered that the breathing equipment interfered with audio quality from the sea floor, "making it sound like the world's largest obscene phone call."

"The most amazing thing I ever saw was when Scott Kenyon threw up during a scuba certification dive and a big white cloud just enveloped him in the deep water," Rogers recalled.

Blue Angels jet jockey

Ever the thrill seeker, Scott owned a white Corvette and boasted that he'd once driven naked in an open convertible across the entire state of Ohio. Of the four Rich Brothers, he was the only one of us brave enough to fly in a supersonic fighter jet.

His next big chance to "blow chunks" came with an invitation from the Navy's Blue Angels Flight Demonstration Squadron to go up in an A-4 Skyhawk from Miramar Naval Air Station in July of 1986.

Scott eagerly climbed into the backseat for his ultimate thrill ride with a Blue Angels pilot, and they soared over San Diego in the combat aircraft capable of speeds faster than 670 miles an hour. Upon landing he went straight to the studio and created a dramatic recap of his heart-pounding flight, set to the song "Danger Zone" from the *Top Gun* movie soundtrack. Filmed in San Diego, the Tom Cruise action drama had been released in theaters just a few weeks earlier.

Raquel Welch and the Rich Brothers

San Diego Magazine profiled the Rich Brothers in a list of eighty-five San Diegans to Watch in 1985. The article described our show as "a wacky mix of music, conversation and comedy that brings back memories of the zany Top 40 men of the golden days of hit radio back in the '60s."

Raquel Welch was on the cover of that issue, posing in blue jeans and a long-sleeved blouse. A 1958 graduate of La Jolla High School, she was a weather presenter on B-100's sister station KFMB-TV six years before donning a fur bikini in the movie *One Million Years B.C.*

The Rich Brothers appeared again in *San Diego Magazine* with an April 1986 cover photo and feature article on the city's most popular morning shows. Demonstrating a keen sense of fashion, we sported safari outfits later popularized by TV star Steve Irwin, the Crocodile Hunter.

"Who's Zoomin' Who?"

One of Bobby's favorite bits occurred when a listener called us one morning to question the origins of the *B Morning Zoo*. "I was on vacation in New York and heard a Z Morning Zoo," she said. "Now which came first? Come on!"

Bobby spun a twisted tale of radio piracy. "I gotta tell you something," he began. "There's this guy in New York, his name is Scott Shannon. He came on vacation to San Diego about a year and a half ago and spent some time in Hotel Circle. And he listened to us on the radio and liked the idea so much that he took it back to New York!"

Alleging that Shannon's Z Morning Zoo on Z100 was a copycat of the original *B Morning Zoo* on B-100 in San Diego, Bobby indignantly claimed, "He ripped us off!"

The outrageous accusation of zoo poaching was captured on tape by Art Vuolo, professional videographer and "Radio's Best Friend," who happened to be an in-studio guest that day. Vuolo promptly shared the recording with Shannon in New York, as Bobby knew he would.

Shannon then played the audio on his show on Z100 and offered proof that his Z Morning Zoo preceded and inspired the San Diego version.

The audience did not know that Bobby's allegation was made entirely tongue-in-cheek to amuse his friend Shannon. The bit started with Ro Catalfo, B-100 traffic department manager and wife of Rich Brother Frank, placing the phone call that set up the inside joke.

Ron Cey wake-up call

Timing could not have been better to launch our show in the summer of 1984 when the upstart San Diego Padres were making a surprising run to the World Series. The hometown baseball team captivated the city by posting its winningest record since becoming a major league club in 1969.

The *B Morning Zoo* debuted three days before the Padres clinched the National League West, with ten games remaining in the regular season. San Diego had never experienced baseball fever in September. After finishing last in their division eight times in fifteen years, the Padres were finally best in the West, with Tony Gwynn, Goose Gossage, and Steve Garvey coming through in the clutch.

Because our sister station KFMB aired the Padres' radio broadcasts, B-100 had access to star players for interviews and hundreds of baseball game tickets to give away, which helped boost the FM ratings. "We certainly rode the team's momentum," Bobby acknowledged, "adding to that buzz and attracting lots of new listeners eager to jump on the bandwagon."

The Rich Brothers scored a hit with our first parody song, "(The Padres Are) Ballbusters." Frank wrote the baseball-themed lyrics and adapted them to the *Ghostbusters* movie theme, which hit number one on the *Billboard* Top 100 that summer.

San Diegans were thrilled with their winning ballclub and our on-air antics extended to the parking lot of Jack Murphy Stadium, where we entertained thousands of tailgating Padres fans before postseason games at "The Murph."

With a prank phone call to Chicago Cubs third baseman Ron Cey, the Rich Brothers may have unwittingly contributed to baseball history during the 1984 playoffs.

Chicago had a commanding lead over San Diego in the National League Championship series after trouncing the Padres 13-0 in the opener and winning the second game 4-2 at Wrigley Field. Cey, whose nickname was The Penguin, socked a home run, hit an RBI double, and scored three times in Chicago's early victories. The Cubs needed only one more win to clinch the pennant.

When the series shifted to San Diego, so did the momentum. With both teams arriving the night before their third game in three days, Cey's sleep was interrupted by an unwelcome wake-up call.

Thinking it would be a funny bit at 7:05 a.m., Bobby took the lead in dialing the Cubs' hotel and asking to speak with Mr. Cey. We never expected to reach the VIP guest, but the hotel's unsuspecting operator fell for the gag and put our call through to the ballplayer's room.

When the phone was answered, Bobby blurted out, "It's a wake-up call," and promptly hung up. Surprised by what had just happened, Scott, Frank, and I nervously reacted with shrieks of "Whoops!" and "Uh-oh!" fearing we might be in big trouble for our live broadcast of the on-air prank.

Later that day the Cubs lost to the Padres 7–1, with Cey getting only one hit in four at-bats. He went hitless in the next two games as San Diego came roaring back to claim the National League pennant.

The Penguin left town without filing a complaint. The Padres advanced to their first World Series but got clobbered by the Detroit Tigers four games to one.

B-100 scored a big win in 1985 with a different kind of game, California's inaugural state lottery. The station bought $10,000 worth of the first scratch-off cards and gave away 100 lottery tickets every 100 minutes. The introduction of weekly lotto games a year later had the audience once again listening for a chance to win free tickets and potential jackpots.

Sewer station serenade

Seeking to supplement our salaries, the Rich Brothers signed a well-known publicity agent as personal manager in 1987. Sonny Sturn quickly generated a burst of publicity about his hiring. A *Los Angeles Times* article included an announcement of our availability for appearances at local business events and social occasions. "We'd like to do grand openings, like for new dry-cleaning establishments. It's an industry that's under-represented, and we think we can bring dry cleaning out of the closet."

The article went on to quote our pitch to companies looking to boost sales with celebrity endorsements. "We can do testimonials to say we like your product. If you think it would be better for you if we say we don't like it, we can say that too."

With savvy PR agent representation, the Rich Brothers secured a major gig to perform at a local sewage treatment plant. The appearance resulted from our protest song ragging on San Diego's broken-down sewer system that repeatedly spilled millions of gallons of waste into a lagoon near Torrey Pines State Beach.

To the tune of "Love Potion No. 9," we harmonized on lyrics about the beleaguered Pump Station 64.

We dump our sewage on the ocean floor
Then wonder why our water tastes so poor
When it comes to sewage, we really know the score
We gotta pull the plug on Pump Station 64
Who said our coastline was a bottomless pit?
With all that waste it really smells like *it*
Now Sorrento Valley will smell forevermore
Unless we pull the plug on Pump Station 64
The fish hold their nose in Peñasquitos Lagoon
They know that a toilet flush will end up there soon
The water is polluted yet nobody blinks
It burns your eyes, it stings your nose
It really stinks ...

When the city completed a $23 million overhaul of the plant that caused the environmental fiasco, the Rich Brothers were the featured entertainment at a grand re-opening ceremony.

We invited San Diego Mayor Maureen O'Connor, City Councilwoman Abbe Wolfsheimer, and other attendees to "go with the flow" as a new set of five hundred horsepower pumps was activated, increasing the facility's capacity to treat fifty-three million gallons of raw sewage per day.

Dressing up for the sewer plant ribbon-cutting, we chose bedazzled fluorescent orange construction worker vests and matching hard hats adorned with fuzzy dingle balls made of red yarn.

Station manager Palmer often said of the Rich Brothers' fashion sense, "Success certainly hasn't gone to their wardrobe."

Taking the high road

Rival radio hosts took verbal swipes at B-100 on the air, but Bobby directed us to ignore them. So, when KKLQ (Q106) morning men Jack Murphy and Terrence McKeever, who had worked on Zoo shows in New York and Tampa before arriving in San Diego, made disparaging comments about the *B Morning Zoo*, their cheap shots failed to elicit any response.

Randy Miller of KSDO FM (KS103) attempted to belittle us on a call to TV host Stanley Siegel when we were in-studio guests on Siegel's nighttime talk show on Channel 51 (KUSI). Bobby, Scott, Frank, and I responded by pretending not to know the scornful DJ or his station.

Taking the high road was an attribute later summarized by renowned programmer Bob Henabery, who told *Radio & Records*, "Bobby's stations are fun to listen to and never talk trash."[23]

New shoes for a big job

Having reestablished a strong public identity for B-100, Bobby realized he was ready for the next big step in his career. "I didn't go looking elsewhere," he said, "but once again, they found me."

In the summer of 1989, a national broadcast executive called to recruit him as general manager of an AM/FM combo in Seattle. "I felt as though I'd been waiting my whole life for an opportunity to work there," Bobby said. "I grew up listening to Seattle radio."

It wasn't easy to break the news to Palmer, the GM who had trusted and empowered Bobby to make a winner of B-100, first in 1975 and again in '84.

"I'd say Paul was devastated when I told him that I had to take the

---

[23] *Radio & Records, July 12, 2002, pg 17;* https://www.worldradiohistory.com/Archive-All-Music/Archive-RandR/2000s/2002/RR-2002-07-12.pdf

job in Seattle. I wasn't hoping for a counteroffer, and he knew there was no changing my mind."

Palmer threw a going away party at his home in La Jolla so station staff and clients could say goodbye.

"That's where Paul presented me with an expensive pair of Florsheim shoes as a farewell gift," Bobby said. "He told me if I was going to be a GM, I'd have to wear proper shoes to executive meetings, not my size thirteen red sneakers."

Palmer's leadership and the entire team at B-100 were a source of great pride for Bobby.

"Those five years, from 1984 to '89, were the most fun I had ever had. The success we achieved and the people working there on and off the air, just the whole atmosphere, the vibe in the building, was extremely positive and a high point in my career."

Paul Palmer, KFMB Radio VP/GM, and the Rich Brothers celebrate Paul Palmer Day, American Diabetes Association Man of the Year tribute/roast, San Diego, Apr. 18, 1985. (Photo from Bobby Rich Radio collection)

B Morning Zoo and a Lockheed C-5 Galaxy. Naval Air Station Miramar Airshow, San Diego, July 26, 1986. (Photo from Bobby Rich Radio collection)

February 4, 1985

PAT

TO: B-100 Talent
FR: Bobby
RE: Stuff

1. There are three things people are afraid of: death, speaking in front of other people, and being publicly humiliated. In the past few days I have heard examples of people being humiliated on two different radio stations: one of them ours. Having a conversation with a winner and/or listener should be a great positive... it shows all listeners that we have a one-on-one rapport. Just remember to be NICE... even if the caller does sound stupid- let the listener figgure it out for themselves!

2. It is absolutely essential that you log all weathers, PSA's, traffic reports, and any legitimate news content. We really need to get credit for everything that runs. Keep this in mind when you ad lib stuff that could qualify as any of the above!

3. Please be thinking about your vacation plans for 1985. I would like a tentative schedule from you by February 28.

4. A great quote I heard and have been saving:

   There are only two categories of people...
   Those motivated to achieve success, and
   Those motivated to avoid failure.

   Which are you?

5. We choose to show the social conscience of B-100 by avoiding liquor oriented promotions. That is why I took off the Weekend Warmups. Now it is time for you to carry this responsibility a step farther by avoiding comments about social drinking, unless it is accompanied by a not too subtle disclaimer about moderation.

   I would very much like to have B-100 take a leading step in this very important area. Your suggestions are welcome.

6. ...what else...

   HAVE FUN--- AND SOUND LIKE IT!!!!

Bobby

Program Director's memo to DJs, encouraging positivity and responsibility. B-100, Feb. 4, 1985.

Library patron thumbs through the Rich Brothers cover story in April 1986 issue *San Diego Magazine*.

FOR IMMEDIATE RELEASE

B-100 Radio Sweeps BILLBOARD Magazine Awards in 5 Categories
"BEST A/C STATION OF THE YEAR"

San Diego, Sept. 14 - B-100FM is pleased to announce the winners of Billboard Magazines 1987 National Radio Awards. The winners were determined by their peers within the entertainment industry - and will be published in the Sept. 19th issue.

B-100 led the polls by sweeping all five possible catagories in the Adult Contemporary Radio classification. In addition to the prestigious "RADIO STATION OF THE YEAR AWARD", B-100 swept the top honors in each of the following catagories:
Bobby Rich/ "PROGRAM DIRECTOR OF THE YEAR"
The Rich Brothers/ "AIR PERSONALITIES OF THE YEAR"
Joan Hiser/ "PROMOTION MANAGER OF THE YEAR"
Gene Knight/ "MUSIC DIRECTOR OF THE YEAR"
The Billboard awards recognize the best talent in each of five formats for three different market sizes.

# # # #

Contact: S. Banister
292-8452

B100 FM

B-100 press release on sweep of five categories of *Billboard* magazine national radio awards, September 1987.

The Rich Brothers perform at Pump Station 64. From left, Scott, Frank, Pat, Bobby, and San Diego Mayor Maureen O'Connor. Nov. 4, 1987.

Chapter 38

Why Is It So Hard to Be Good?

I don't want to sound like a thin-skinned wimp, but words hurt, and when a listener complained about something that they heard, or thought they heard, or just assumed, I had to decide whether to respond or let it go.

Let's start with politics. When things started getting really nasty, and people even nastier, I stepped up my efforts to be a "nonpolitical" host on the radio.

I received comments from listeners who complained, "You're always talking about the right, being so right," and others who said, "You are such a liberal dolt." People accused me of being "a diehard Democrat" and at the same time griped, "I would expect nothing less than your obvious, Republican beliefs." Et cetera, et cetera. You get the idea. All of them were responding to things that weren't said on the radio by me or anyone on my show.

I've always been proud of being a middle of the road thinker. Proud of my independent standing and choosing the best candidate, not the ones that belong to a particular party.

Even for not expressing my political views, I was criticized for being wishy-washy!

Now, let's talk about the music that I chose to play on my radio stations. This is wildly diverse because of the different formats and different target listener groups that I set out to attract. I generally lean close to the center. Meaning not too hard, not too soft.

I'm not someone who pays too much attention to a song's lyrics. I'm more interested in how it sounds. And how it makes me or others feel. Sometimes that pays off and other times I find out that if I had paid more attention to the lyrics, I would've known that it was a mistake to play a particular record.

"I Want Your Sex" by George Michael was a song with a title and lyrics that were immediately and obviously controversial when it was released in 1987 during the AIDS epidemic.

Based on a programming philosophy of you don't get hurt by NOT playing a song, I chose to not play this one at all on our station. I was trying to protect our good, clean, fun image.

Unfortunately for us (and happily for George Michael and his record company) the hit was huge. Went to number one eventually. I was quoted in the local media that we would never play that song. So, I had to stick with that decision. And I did.

This created a real interesting situation when the song started climbing the charts and appeared on the *Countdown USA* national radio show that we aired on weekends. I was asked by the show's production company (coincidentally run by my brother-in-law Rob Sisco,) "Well, what are you gonna do about this, pal?" Taking the high road, I responded, "We're going to cut it out of the countdown, and anybody who cares can complain to me."

"I Want Your Sex" worked its way up to number one! And I still didn't play it.

"Into the Night" by Benny Mardones was another hit song that was extremely popular despite making many people uncomfortable because of lyrics they perceived as sexualizing a teenage girl.

I wasn't a PD when it peaked on the *Billboard* Hot 100 in September of 1980, but by then it had generated a controversy requiring his record company to issue a statement explaining the song's heartbreaking origin story.

Many years later I became friends with Benny. He used to tell me that he needed another single on the radio so he wouldn't be considered a "one-hit wonder." Sadly, he never had a successful follow-up.

In 2019 when putting together the playlist for KDRI Tucson, I needed to consider our audience and what they would think hearing that ballad nearly forty years after its release.

"Into the Night" went into my "Do Not Play" category.

Four years later I left the station, and one of the first things they did was add the song into the rotation.

—Bobby Rich, August 2023

Chapter 39

One of the Biggest Mistakes They Ever Made

"It doesn't make sense to hire smart people and tell them what to do; we hire smart people so they can tell us what to do." —Steve Jobs

As a teenager in rural Washington state and a disc jockey in a dozen cities across the U.S., Bobby always dreamed of being on the air in Seattle.

"My all-time favorite music radio station was KJR, which I first heard in my dad's Chrysler Imperial on family road trips to Seattle," he said.

"After hearing the Top 40 genius of Pat O'Day on afternoon drive and Lan Roberts their morning guy, KJR became the one and only station where I wanted to work.

"Pat was absolutely brilliant as a jock, program director, and general manager. The architect of KJR's longtime success in every way, shape, and form."

In the late 1960s, Bobby sent a tape to O'Day for an opening as a fill-in jock. He didn't get that job, but his dream to work in the Emerald City came true in 1989.

Needed: GM for AM/FM turnaround

"Rich and Noble" was the headline on an article in *The Gavin Report* on Bobby's "unexpected move" to join Noble Broadcasting as general manager of KMGI-FM and KIXI-AM.[24]

John Lynch, CEO and president of Noble, had known Bobby since the '70s when they both worked for Paul Palmer at KFMB and B-100. Lynch credited Bobby for taking B-100 to number one in San Diego and hoped he could do the same with his FM/AM combo in Seattle.

KMGI and KIXI had been acquired for $16 million, but ratings were in a slump. "Nothing was working," Lynch said. "I needed a turnaround."

Lynch's company also owned the San Diego combo of 91X FM and XTRA AM, so recruiting B-100's PD and morning show leader to Seattle was a potential double play.

"They wanted to get me out of San Diego," Bobby said. He nervously accepted Lynch's offer to be a first-time GM.

Objection overruled

Norm Feuer, Noble's chief operating officer, did not endorse Lynch's decision. "When it came time to hire Bobby, I suggested he not do that," Feuer said. Feuer acknowledged Bobby's winning track record as a programmer but said, "He had no sales experience and never had GM responsibility. Seattle was a pretty big market and to go up there was just beyond him.

"By the way, I like Bobby as a person. He's easy to get along with and he's good. The difference was that I had a business to run."

"It wasn't a good fit, and everybody knew it," Bobby admitted. "Probably one of the biggest mistakes they ever made. I didn't have the training needed, but I believed in myself, was confident in my

[24]*The Gavin Report*, July 28, 1989, pg 4; https://www.worldradiohistory.com/hd2/IDX-Business/Music/Archive-Gavin-IDX/IDX/80s/89/Gavin-Report-1989-07-28-OCR-Page-0004.pdf#search=%22gavin%20bobby%20rich%22

leadership qualities, and knew enough about the business having done radio my whole life. Plus, several people I trusted and respected in the industry who knew me quite well said that I could be a great GM."

In announcing the hire at KMGI/KIXI, Lynch said, "We will do whatever it takes to help Bobby ensure the maximum success of both stations. There is no one more qualified to lead our Seattle stations to a position of market dominance."[25]

In salary negotiations, Bobby had an advantage. "I wasn't looking to leave San Diego, and John really wanted me to reinvent B-100 in Seattle. So, I gave him a number that I thought was ridiculously high, and he agreed to pay it."

I-Radio before iPods and iPhones

Bobby's first move was to blow up the station's "Magic 108" identity and rebrand KMGI as I-107.7 to reflect its actual frequency on the FM broadcast band. The new name—"I-One-Oh-Seven Seven"—was not well-received by some in the industry.

"I got laughed at, put down, and criticized by several consultants and station owners who thought my i-idea was stupid," Bobby remembered. "Keep in mind, this was years before Apple introduced the first iMac, iPhone, iPod, or iPad."

"I imagine Steve Jobs probably listened to us on I-107.7 and said to himself, 'Hey, that's kind of a cool product name. I think I'll try that someday.'

"If he were alive, I'd sue his ass," Bobby joked.

With KIXI airing an automated beautiful music format and morning man Mike Webb the only DJ hosting a live and local show on the AM outlet, Bobby concentrated on his FM station.

---

[25]*Radio & Records*, July 28, 1989, pg 1 https://www.worldradiohistory.com/Archive-All-Music/Archive-RandR/1980s/1989/RR-1989-07-28.pdf

After rebranding KMGI, he hired Rob Sisco as program and operations director to succeed Magic 108 PD Steve "Smokin" Weed. Sisco was Bobby's trusted assistant in programming stations in San Diego and New York. The twin brother of Bobby's wife Debbie, he also ran a company that produced syndicated radio programs including the *Countdown America* show on RKO.

Launch of the I-Guys

Handing operational responsibilities for the AM/FM combo to Sisco freed Bobby to join KMGI's morning show.

"I couldn't not be involved on air because it's too important to me," Bobby told *Radio & Records* one month into his new gig. "Being on the radio is the first thing that attracted me to this business and remains one of my greatest passions."[26]

Co-hosting with Kelly Stevens and Alpha Trivette, he renamed the show *The I-Guys with Kelly and Alpha and Bobby.* Liz Summers was their newscaster, Storm Kennedy did weather updates, and Mark Carlson provided airborne traffic reports as "Commander Denny McFly, the I-Guys' Fly Guy."

"I didn't try to take it over but just add to Kelly and Alpha's very good morning show," Bobby said. His microphone was in a separate broadcast booth with a window adjoining their studio, built by chief engineer Dwight Small.

Rounding out the I-107.7 air staff were midday jocks Randy Lundquist and later Kevin Cassidy, afternoon DJs Stitch Mitchell and later Jeff King, followed by Ron Harris on evenings, Angie Good on late-nights, and Rich Ellis on the overnight shift. Greg MacArthur, production

[26] *Radio & Records,* Sep 22, 1989, pg 57 https://www.worldradiohistory.com/hd2/IDX-Business/Music/Archive-RandR-IDX/IDX/80s/89/RR-1989-09-22-OCR-Page-0051.pdf#search=%22bobby%20rich%20kmgi%22

director, was responsible for producing commercials, contest promos, and station IDs recorded by legendary voiceover artist Ernie Anderson.

Flying the I-Flag

Community involvement was a hallmark of Bobby's programming philosophy. In the summer of 1990, he sponsored a thunderboat in Seattle's popular Seafair hydroplane races, plastering an I-107.7 logo on the boat and broadcasting live from the shore of Lake Washington.

Another memorable promotion was a broadcast from atop the Kingdome where the Seattle Seahawks, Mariners, and Supersonics played. Overcoming his acrophobia for the sake of a good radio stunt, Bobby joined Kelly and Alpha in a treacherous climb up ladders and catwalks to the roof of the domed stadium 250 feet above the city. There the three DJs did their show and raised an I-107.7 banner visible to motorists on nearby Interstate 5 and other local highways.

To create an identity distinct from other FM stations in Seattle, Bobby commissioned a custom jingles package produced by Rainer Rey, a Seattle musician and ad agency owner. Rey composed and recorded a catchy song with a chorus of singers including Ned Neltner of the popular Northwest band Jr. Cadillac.

Bobby was delighted with the piece, which yielded at least five separate jingles, thirty seconds and sixty seconds in length. He selected one of the tracks to use in an unconventional TV spot for I-107.7 that garnered public attention but failed to boost ratings.

Hail Mary pass couldn't save game

"We were in a really difficult spot," Sisco said, "trying to fit in between several mainstream AC and Top 40 stations that were well-established in the market. Positioning I-107.7 as a grown-up Top 40, the only way to differentiate from KLSY, KPLZ, KUBE, KOMO, KSEA, and KLTX was by adding new songs earlier than the competition, playing hits no one else was on yet."

That approach led Noble corporate bosses and consultants to blame the unfamiliar music for I-107.7's lackluster ratings, Sisco recalled.

The timing wasn't right for a fresh blend of Hot AC and Top 40 in Seattle, Bobby soon realized. "A slight variation from the other stations was not enough to make a big splash," he said, "and upper management was impatient, demanding results that required more time and meddling with the format and strategy they hired me to implement."

Lynch, a former NFL linebacker, admitted it had been a Hail Mary pass to bring in Bobby and hope for a miracle. Reflecting on the situation thirty-four years later, he said, "I knew it was a risk, but you know what, we gave it a whirl. I thought he could recap that glory."

Lynch insisted he didn't hire Bobby in Seattle to hurt Palmer in the San Diego market. "No . . . I had my ass against the wall, I had to succeed. I borrowed a hell of a lot of money . . . It had nothing to do with Paul."

Bobby's time at I-107.7 came to an end when other executives at Noble Broadcasting finally convinced Lynch to let him go. "John was the only one holding on to the possibility that I could turn it around," he said, "but they insisted on firing me."

The big job in his dream destination lasted sixteen months. After fighting the front office for a generous payout, Bobby left Seattle in December 1990.

The ownership group switched the format to modern rock in 1991, changed the station's name to KNDD, and called it The End.

Chapter 40

Not a Doctor but Played One on Radio

Doctor Boogie was the on-air persona that Bobby adopted in 1975 when he diagnosed a Top 40 deficiency on the radio in San Diego and prescribed B-100 as the remedy.

The nickname outlasted his four years there. After taking the station to number one in the market, he took the honorary badge of boogie with him.

The next time he assumed a fictitious doctor identity for entertainment purposes was in 1991 for the relaunch of "the All New KZZU" in Spokane. Bobby conjured up the zany character Dr. Lenny A. Richman and hosted a marathon solo show from a hot air balloon, a bowling center, and a karaoke club. He even crossed the state line from Washington into Idaho to perform a wedding in a sock store.

"I was out of work and had nothing else to do," Bobby said. "My nephew, Mark Patrick, was part of the morning show at KZZU, and they needed a publicity stunt for the station's rebranding. So, they asked me to come up with a gimmick that would grab attention for the 'New Zoo.'"

That's how "The 25-Hour Day" featuring Dr. Lenny Richman was born.

"I had this crazy idea," Bobby recalled, "and management bought in on the whole concept, going so far as to buy advertising on competing stations to tease the mysterious doctor's arrival in Spokane and his highly unusual program.

"They flew me up there, got me a hotel, and gave me free rein to take over the station as Dr. Lenny, broadcasting nonstop from early one morning right through till the next day. I hardly spent any time at KZZU because the chief engineer set me up with a wireless microphone and drove me all around to explore the sights and sounds of Spokane."

The 25-Hour Day turned out to be a one-man variety show with Bobby constantly on the move. Hurrying from one location to another, he interviewed people downtown at Riverside Park, invited listeners to join him in bowling, and narrated an audio tour from a balloon flight over the city.

Meat loaf and a side of Do Wah Diddy Diddy

One of the station's DJs, Corey Cruise, volunteered to be his assistant and helped coordinate live phone calls from listeners. Only when Dr. Lenny needed a bathroom break were any songs played during the unconventional talkfest.

"We stopped at a family restaurant where I read the menu out loud, chatted with diners, and asked them, 'How's the meat loaf?'" Bobby said. "It was a little awkward to be eating my meal while carrying on a conversation with strangers before jumping back in the truck to head to our next destination.

"A local TV station invited me to come on their eleven o'clock news show and talk with the anchors and weather person about all the Dr. Lenny sightings around town." To their chagrin, the cantankerous doc became confused and quarrelsome while attempting to pinpoint his hometown of Ephrata on the weather map.

"I made a total ass of myself," Bobby admitted, "but my nephew and the station GM didn't seem to mind. They knew it was a wacky idea, and Dr. Lenny's unpredictable appearances got people talking and listening to the new KZZU, which was exactly what they intended."

The schedule also featured the eccentric guest DJ singing songs with a kindergarten class, emceeing a nightclub karaoke contest, and belting out his own rendition of Manfred Mann's "Do Wah Diddy Diddy."

With these socks I thee wed

Dr. Lenny's tour de force was a wedding ceremony on KZZU that he officiated for a pair of lucky listeners who volunteered to get married in a sock store.

"I solicited on the air for couples who had already obtained a marriage license and were ready to tie the knot," Bobby explained. "Two young lovers, maybe twenty-one or twenty-two years old, called in and agreed to take their vows on the air. For legal reasons, we had to drive to Idaho for the ceremony and held it in a strip mall just off Interstate 90 in Coeur d'Alene."

Surprisingly, the bride and groom did not receive any presents from KZZU. "Nope, no gifts. Only socks," Bobby said. "They just wanted their wedding day to be special. Of course, the sock store was packed with people who came to watch. And the store manager was happy for his business to get mentioned on the radio."

The 25-Hour Day marked a homecoming of sorts for Bobby, who as a young DJ worked at four stations in Spokane, including KZZU's predecessor, KREM-FM. His return appearance included a visit to a house where he lived in the mid-1960s.

When Bobby moved to Arizona in 1992 and landed his next job as a PD, he hired Cruise, the assistant to Dr. Lenny in Washington, to be the night shift DJ on KTZN in Tucson.

Chapter 41

Rufus the Weather Dog Fight

San Diego is the only city that Bobby Rich moved to three different times, to work at three different stations. His San Diego years were much like the summery temperatures there—in the 70s, 80s, and 90s.

He created B-100 and took it to number one before leaving for New York in 1978. Returning in 1984, he reinvented the station and delivered another five years of solid ratings for Paul Palmer, vice president and general manager of KFMB radio. In 1991, another GM in need of a turnaround expert brought Bobby back to the border city in California.

KKYY 94.9 FM, known as Y-95, was headed for a last-place finish among two dozen San Diego competitors for the 12-plus audience in the Arbitron winter ratings. Ownership group Sandusky Broadcasting decided to get rid of their call letters as well as their GM, PD, morning show, and other key employees.

Hired to revamp the format, Bobby said his new boss was secretive about plans for the station.

"I almost didn't sign because I didn't have a good feeling about the new GM, but I wanted the job and agreed to convert their station from Hot AC to oldies-based AC. Not until I signed my contract would he tell me the new call letters. That was strange."

The new call letters were KRMX, which new VP/GM Bob Visotcky unveiled as "MIX FM" in February. After welcoming Bobby back to

San Diego as PD and morning air personality, Visotcky told industry newspaper *Radio & Records*, "The chemistry with Bobby was instantly great. The entire staff is pumped . . . Bobby Rich brings instant recognition and credibility."[27]

Rich Brothers 2.0

KRMX purchased billboards to promote their new image and morning team, declaring "Bobby's Back!" and teasing that the Rich Brothers had returned to local radio.

Immediately after signing, Bobby hired Scott Kenyon from KKOS in Carlsbad, California, for a scaled-down version of the Rich Brothers show. Their other two partners from the *B Morning Zoo* on B-100 had since found new jobs in San Diego, and there was no effort to reunite the foursome.

"I didn't feel it was disloyal to use the name," Bobby said, "because it was something I had owned since the '80s. And my first concept of the Rich Brothers was with Scott back in 1968 in Davenport."

For his first wacky DJ stunt, Bobby broadcast from the top of a billboard on the main drag in Mission Beach over a three-day weekend, taking music requests and playing "the right mix of the '70s, '80s, and today."

KRMX never gained traction, while B-100 scored high ratings with new morning duo Jeff and Jer who had left Y-95 to succeed the original Rich Brothers show.

If dogs could talk

Bobby's downfall at KRMX was a make-believe radio character that he named Rufus the Weather Dog.

---

[27] *Radio & Records*, February 8, 1991, pg 3; *https://www.worldradiohistory.com/Archive-All-Music/Archive-RandR/1990s/1991/RR-1991-02-08.pdf*

In a recurring bit inspired by comedian Soupy Sales and his TV puppet White Fang, the "dog voice" of Rufus gave weather reports that were then "translated" by Bobby and Scott.

Visotcky pooh-poohed the pooch routine and demanded that they quit playing it.

"While the boss was on a sales trip, we ran another episode of Rufus the Weather Dog and announced on the air we did it because he was out of town," Bobby boasted. "Visotcky was mad enough to suspend me for a week, and then he tried to fire me for insubordination.

"By this time, he had acquired the nickname Smiling Firing Bob. I got a lawyer and sued for wrongful termination. We settled, and I resigned."

Three weeks after Bobby's departure from KRMX in June of 1991, Sandusky Broadcasting announced it was selling the station for $10 million.

Bobby's final act in San Diego lasted only five months, but he would soon find himself a new stage and a home in radio for the next thirty-two years.

Chapter 42

Danger Zone

Disc jockey is typically not ranked near the top on any list of the most hazardous occupations. But throughout his career, Bobby singlehandedly and singlefootedly defied the image of a DJ safely working three or four hours a day in a cushy studio.

He bravely survived a series of bizarre and bloody accidents, all of them self-inflicted. His run-ins with inanimate objects created severe pain, left permanent scars, and caused temporary workplace absences in three different cities.

1. A sixteen-pound bowling ball landed on his foot and spoiled Bobby's trip home to Ephrata, Washington, to emcee his high school reunion. While helping his mom move boxes in a basement closet, he dislodged the ball from a top shelf. Before he could jump out of the way, the Columbia 300 fell and smashed his big toe. The injury caused a brief absence from his new job as program director at Top106 in Philadelphia, but Bobby was back at work a few days later, wearing a cast and a sandal.
2. On another occasion, Bobby tore his hand open while rocking out to Van Halen's "Jump" at B-100 in San Diego. With his back against the record machine, he went ahead and jumped—to shred an air guitar solo. The song was blaring at maximum volume when Bobby caught his hand on a JBL speaker mounted in

the studio ceiling. His morning show co-hosts, the Rich Brothers, recoiled at the sight of bloodshed in their broadcast booth. After getting bandaged up, Bobby returned to work but was forced to retire his signature air guitar windmill move.

3. While a Roomba was cleaning his house in Tucson, Bobby tried to help the autonomous vacuum by rolling up a rug and moving it out of the way. Tripping over the Roomba, he fell on the cement floor, landed on a knee, and shattered his patella. Unable to drive to KDRI The Drive after emergency surgery, Bobby resumed work from his home studio. Morning show co-host Hill Bailey joked that the robot cleaner kneecapped Bobby to get on the TV show *Dancing with the Stars.*

Chapter 43

Love Letter to Tucson

I didn't know I'd love you until I met you.

It wasn't quite "at first sight." Rather, it took several months of being with you every day. Then I started to "get you."

And the more time I spent with you the better I liked you. Then it became love.

I love the looks of you, the scent of you, the unrelenting friendliness of you.

The east, west, north, and the south of you.

I love the mystery of you. Even after two decades of being with you I don't know nearly enough about you. Yet you know me, providing the familiarity I need when I'm feeling a little lost.

At the same time, I can become lost in your strange ways of twisted, turning arteries. And like the rest of us, you are a bit confused as to what you want to be when you grow up.

At any given time of the year, you can cry me a river or dry my eyes. Feed me, entertain me, and show your artistic understanding of colors at the beginning and end of the day.

I love reminding those who would criticize your hotness that they could be living in Chicago or Minneapolis.

And one thing I especially love is how you care for those who need help. Your empathy and concern for the helpless and underserved often proves your heartfelt desire to make yourself better.

I am at home with you. It feels right. Let's stay together.

—Bobby Rich, February 2014

Chapter 44

The Chosen City

Getting pink slips twice in six months from stations in Seattle and San Diego motivated Bobby to take a different path in making his next career move. "I decided to pick where I wanted to live instead of going where the next job offer took me," he said.

Radio had taken Bobby to thirteen cities across the Northwest, Midwest, Northeast, Southeast, and Southwest. He was ready to put down roots and make a permanent home somewhere geographically, professionally, and personally appealing.

With his wife, Debbie, he launched a ratings survey of desirable places. Family considerations would influence their rankings and ultimate decision.

"Debbie and I knew that we didn't really want to live in a city as big as LA or New York," Bobby said. "As much as we both loved San Diego and Seattle, we were looking for something smaller and suitable for raising our daughters, who were then five and ten years old. We preferred a university town, thinking that would be best for our kids to have quality schools and for the culture that comes with it."

They started by listing locations with impressive scenery, decent weather, affordable home prices, and reputations for friendly people. Places that seemed too fast-paced were ruled out. Bobby studied the broadcast landscape in each city—number of radio competitors, winning formats, share of ratings, total advertising dollars spent in the market, and ad revenue earned by each station.

Nine cities made the list, including Colorado Springs, Albuquerque, Eugene, Spokane, Sacramento, and Las Vegas. After months of online evaluation and in-person visits, the Rich family chose Tucson, Arizona, as their new home.

"Tucson was a place where the girls would be able to ride horses and I could make a decent living in a competitive market, doing what I love, having fun on the radio," Bobby said. "With a population of slightly more than four hundred thousand at the time, I felt the city was just the right size that I could wrap my arms around it."

Ponying up for a piece of the action

Opportunity came knocking in January of 1992 with an invitation from his friend Jim Wood to join the ownership group of Tucson's KTZN 92.1 FM. As part of the deal, Bobby would also program the station and host morning drive. He had jocked with Wood twenty years earlier at WMYQ in Miami and was friends with Reg Johns, another KTZN co-owner and respected radio marketer across multiple formats.

"They knew me and my reputation, and hearing that I was in town checking out stations, they jumped at the chance to bring me on board."

Investing severance pay from his last two firings, Bobby joined as vice president of operations, program director, and morning personality. The first thing on his to-do list was replacing KTZN's soft music format with a higher energy, up-tempo, personality station that came to be known as Tucson 92.

Bobby hired Royce Blake to partner with him on a new morning show, *Rich and Royce*. He chose Adrienne Walker to host middays. She would go on to work with him for more than two decades at other stations in Tucson. His air staff also included Corey Cruise from Spokane and Steven K. Brown who later switched to country radio as Hopalong Cassidy.

As a newcomer in a dozen cities throughout his career, Bobby made a habit of quickly learning the local whereabouts, driving in rush hour traffic, and taking note of landmarks and neighborhoods to talk about on the air. In Tucson, earning credibility with listeners required extensive research in Mexican restaurants to find chilaquiles and margaritas worthy of mention.

"I always loved talking with my audience about things going on in the community or a small business they might want to try out. Volunteering to emcee at charity fundraisers, introducing myself to event organizers and community leaders, I got in front of as many people as possible, giving out our call letters, talking up the new KTZN Tucson 92."

Just right rock

Musically, Bobby tried out a hybrid format he'd never done before, straddling Adult Contemporary (AC) and Rock. "The best name for what we're doing is Hard AC," Bobby explained to attendees at the National Association of Broadcasters convention in June of 1992. "Like most other good contemporary stations, we're mainstream and hit-oriented in every way, shape, and form. The spice comes from the rock side."

His playlist included "One Night Love Affair" by Bryan Adams, "All This Time" by Sting, "Time, Love and Tenderness" by Michael Bolton, "Working for the Weekend" by Loverboy, "Don't Get Me Wrong" by the Pretenders, "Old Time Rock and Roll" by Bob Seger, and "Wind of Change" by Scorpions.

KTZN's slogan was "Not Too Hard, Not Too Soft. It's Just Right Rock." But the new PD soon found out that everything was just not right at KTZN.

"The FM signal wasn't strong enough to penetrate the entire Tucson listening area, and we'd get knocked off the air for several days at a time," Bobby said. "I'd go in for the morning show, and tell them, 'Hey, I couldn't get the station driving here and my house is only four miles away.'

"The transmitter would be off, and we had to wait for an engineer to get to the mountain and beat on the equipment. People who heard it really liked it, but not enough of them. Without good reception, we couldn't generate sufficient ratings or revenue."

The owners poured money into engineering studies, equipment purchases, and speculative signal improvement work. They even relocated the broadcast tower, but all the costly transmitter adjustments failed to fix their technical problems.

Knew when to fold 'em

A wrongful termination lawsuit filed by a former sales rep caused further economic drain on KTZN. When the partnership ran low on funding, Bobby and Debbie borrowed $10,000 to meet payroll for the staff.

"We thought we could save the station long enough to turn things around. I was naive to let our group president convince me that the bank loan would keep us afloat and prevent bankruptcy," Bobby admitted.

With technical, legal, and financial difficulties mounting, he resigned in late 1992. "I didn't want to be the last one to turn out the lights," he said. The station was sold the following year.

Losing his life savings in KTZN did not diminish his love for radio or his commitment to Tucson.

"We went into it with our hearts rather than our heads. It's only money. But to us it was everything we had," Bobby later told *Radio & Records*. "My family and I are ecstatic about living in Tucson, and that's very important to me. It's a great feeling being in a place where you feel at home and comfortable."

Even though it didn't end well at KTZN, Bobby believed the experience was worthwhile and led to his next prospect. "I made a positive impression in the market, got involved in the community, and met people who respected what I could do on the radio," he said.

Two months after walking away from the "Just Right Rock" station, he landed another gig at a higher-rated station in Tucson and stayed there for the next twenty-five years.

Chapter 45

Ronstadt Rant

I love Tucson. But I hate haters. I was excited to pass along the list of the most caring cities in America. We did that last week on our show. Out of the 100 biggest cities in the USA, Tucson was number three.[28] Always a joy to hear positive appreciation expressed for the town where I've performed wake-up duties early every morning since 1992. Good news always makes me feel good. It always puts a little extra kick in my step.

So, after sharing the news on our radio show last Friday, I hit Facebook and one of my first shares was to the Ben's Bells page. Of course, that's the nonprofit that brings the kindness message to us every day. Among the many gleeful responses, I was stunned to find a heaping handful of negative, complaining ones. Now imagine this, on Ben's page, the "Kindness Central" in this community, some people wanted to bitch about this achievement!

Every day, thousands of our neighbors make us proud by volunteering, opening their arms and their hearts to those with less, lifting up each other and this beautiful community. They don't have time to bitch. Every day, thousands invest their energy, money, and heart in this town to build a great, prosperous American

[28]https://www.movoto.com/blog/most-caring-cities-in-america/

city. Downtown is booming because of the gutsy, risk-taking capitalists and the visionary public servants who ignore the whiners and naysayers and instead have placed their full faith in America's most underestimated city. And they are right.

I agree that there is plenty of room for improvement around here but still shocked to see so many haters and naysayers. How anyone could find fault, in an attempt to change good news to bad is beyond me.

So, I wasn't alone on Facebook. Guy B. posted, "Looking for the wrong in everything tears the fabric of the individual and the community." And Michael B. added: "How have we as a society become so unwilling and unable to see the good in anyone or anything anymore?" For some people, complaining is such a habit that we become blind to the good. As David Fitzsimmons *[Daily Star cartoonist]* told me, "Sometimes I think we have more Eeyores in this valley than scorpions. At least a scorpion doesn't complain unless you mess with him."

Add to this former Tucsonan Linda Ronstadt, who is regurgitating her displeasure with her hometown again. Tim Steller writes in the *Arizona Daily Star* yesterday that "She can't help but keep talking smack about Tucson. She keeps expounding on our home's faults."

You know, when Linda Ronstadt sang with the Stone Poneys and she had her first hit, I fell in love with her voice then. But now I'm remembering that song "You're No Good." Was that her clue that she would become a Negative Nellie?

Well, I say Tucson "I Can't Help It (If I'm Still in Love With You,") I'm not standing around wondering "When Will I Be Loved" by Linda Ronstadt or any other negative voices anymore!

Of course, she has the right to say anything she wants. But she's been offering these types of comments for years. And apparently every time someone else asks her why she left Tucson, she has new reasons. But as Steller said in the *Star*, one year it's the strip mall she dislikes; another year it's the dust. One year it's the jet noise; another year it's the chain stores. This time it's downtown buildings so generic they look like Stalinist Russia, and Tucson is a car culture like living in Los Angeles.

Enough already! If you or Linda want to complain about my town, go right ahead. But first, pitch in, get your hands dirty with the work of building your family, your neighborhood, and your hometown, like the rest of us.

Linda gave us inspiration and happiness to so many people with her performances. But now I cannot hear her beautiful voice without remembering all this negativity.

Linda, until you march to the beat of a "Different Drum," I can't listen to you anymore. So as of now, I pledge to never again play another Linda Ronstadt song on 94.9 MIXfm.

Linda, the day you say something positive about Tucson, I'll play your music. "That'll Be the Day."

Tucson has timeless beauty. Make the time to see it. Tucson is kind. Tucson is creative, scrappy, gritty, and it's growing into an awesome city. Downtown is booming. The U of A is great. Our Wildcats rock. UMC and TMC are world leaders in health care. And our men and women in uniform at Davis-Monthan Air Force Base make us so proud. We are truly blessed to have them as neighbors.

I say we should all celebrate the good. When you're not happy about something, tell someone who cares. Ease up on the fault finding.

Tucson you're no good?—that's a broken record. And I beg to differ. And I'm saying that Tucson isn't just good, it's great.

P.S. Don't like Tucson? What are you doing to make it better? Find another place that has beautiful mountains, a unique lush desert, a rich history, killer salsa, and move there.

You'll miss the mountains. And you'll miss the people. There's no place like Tucson on this earth.

I'm Bobby Rich, and I approved this message.

(MIXfm, Aug. 25, 2014)

Chapter 46

The Longest Time

Like a jockey thrown from his horse, Bobby got right back in the saddle after an early exit from his first go-round in Tucson radio. The ride at KTZN was brief, but he soon took the reins of another Tucson station ready for a reboot.

"My friend Doug Erickson, the media consultant, let me know of a pending ownership change at KKLD, Cloud 95 FM," Bobby said. "They had a very soft adult contemporary style that was successful in the market but with a format that I used to make fun of because it was so mellow. You could say that their music was sleepy enough to play in a dentist's office.

"When Doug told me the new owners were open to transforming Cloud 95 and looking for a new PD and morning show, I was all in. He set up a meeting and I pitched my ideas for a big-energy, personality-oriented station with more up-tempo music and aggressive production and promotion.

"They agreed with all that and let me program a brighter sound that would attract the broadest range of listeners aged 25-54. We changed the call letters to KMXZ and rebranded as MIXfm, replacing what I called 'a dull contemporary' with a mainstream Adult Contemporary format that became a long-term success."

Walking in the door in January of 1993, Bobby never imagined that he would remain at KMXZ until 2017 and become Tucson's longest-running morning radio personality, working for ten different owners, general managers, and operations directors.

Good clean fun on MIXfm

After soloing on the morning show for the first few weeks while evaluating potential on-air partners, Bobby hired local radio veteran Brad Behan to be his co-host. "I knew the kind of talent I wanted for a partner," he said. "A strong news person who could do other stuff like write sketches and punchlines, do character voices, chat between songs, take listener phone calls, just an all-around morning personality."

Launching the *Bobby and Brad Good Clean Fun* show, they set out to reach a wide demographic of adult listeners. Bobby described it as "A family reunion type show that you felt safe having on the radio while taking your kids to school."

"Brad and I hit it off right away," he said, "and both of us felt good about the pairing. Our complementary talents, humor, and community focus made for a strong presentation on the air."

Their partnership at MIXfm was interrupted less than two years later when Brad left the show, moved to Oregon, and took a job at a country music station in Portland. "We had a good thing going," Bobby said, "and I felt it was way too soon to break it up."

After Behan's departure, Bobby again soloed in the morning shift while auditioning other prospective co-hosts. When he brought on Jerry "Eggs" Agar as his sidekick in 1995, the show became *Bobby and Eggs in the Morning*. They appeared in a TV commercial featuring a woman taking a shower while listening to her radio. "I shower with Bobby and Eggs first thing every morning" was the ad's tagline.

Bobby and Eggs did one of their shows from Biosphere 2, the giant research facility under glass in Oracle, Arizona. They used wireless microphones to transmit their radio signal from the ocean, rain forest, desert and savanna habitats inside the mega-terrarium designed for research into self-sustaining space-colonization technology.

Their wackiest radio stunt, Bobby remembered, was a parachute jump by Agar, who packed his own broadcast equipment, made the daredevil leap from a plane, and landed safely. Once again Bobby remained on the ground, providing commentary on a station-sponsored skydive. *[See Chapter 35 for previous skydiving broadcast.]*

Two years after Agar replaced Behan as Bobby's partner, he was replaced by Behan. Agar went on to a successful career in talk radio, at stations including WLS in Chicago, WABC in New York, and CFRB in Toronto.

On the same page but not in the same place

Behan became available after moving back to his home state of Colorado, and Bobby rehired him for a relaunch of their MIXfm morning show in 1997. This time there was a new twist to the pairing as they cohosted from two different cities, Bobby in Tucson and Brad in his home studio in a suburb of Denver.

Most of their audience in Arizona was either unaware or unconcerned that Brad was working remotely. "We didn't hide the fact that he wasn't in the same place as me," Bobby explained, "but we didn't call attention to it either."

Learning to deal with digital network compression that caused a slight delay in audio transmission of their long-distance ISDN phone connection, Bobby and Brad used a video link to talk with each other off the air and to help avoid talking over each other on the air.

With internet access to the daily news of Tucson, Brad wrote and delivered locally relevant headlines and updates twice per hour from his basement studio in Colorado. His interactions with Bobby and their listeners reflected the local knowledge of someone who had gone to high school and college in Tucson and had worked at other radio stations in the city.

Many listeners were surprised and some felt duped when an *Arizona Daily Star* article with the headline "KMXZ Radio Has a Secret!" revealed in 1997 that Brad was based not in Tucson but nine hundred miles away.

By then the morning men had earned the respect of Tucsonans who appreciated their community ties and ability to be fun and entertaining most mornings but serious and supportive in times of crisis. The duo remained a popular act for ten more years in the 5:30-9:00 time slot. In 2003, they added an executive assistant, and Bobby gave her the radio name Mrs. Grant.

"My job was to keep the show moving," Mrs. Grant said, "checking that the music and commercials aired, connecting the ISDN line to Brad in Colorado, and making sure the video feed was dialed in so he could see us."

A Tucson native with no prior radio experience, she became an integral member of the team, advancing from assistant to show producer and on-air contributor.

What the world needed: love, sweet love

When terrorists attacked the U.S. on September 11, 2001, Bobby and Brad broke format to provide their audience with developing news coverage and an opportunity to talk about the unfolding national crisis.

"Brad was brilliant in reporting the tragedy, relaying updates from Associated Press, eyewitnesses, and emergency responders in New York," Bobby said. "We dropped all songs and commercials for the rest of our show to focus on the terror attacks."

Throughout the day, MIXfm jocks played "What the World Needs

Now is Love" by Jackie DeShannon, "Heal the World" by Michael Jackson, and other special songs like "God Bless America" and "The Star-Spangled Banner."

They continued airing these and other poignant titles for weeks after the 9/11 catastrophe while the station's no-play list included Billy Joel's "Only the Good Die Young," Cutting Crew's "I Just Died in Your Arms," Kool & the Gang's "Celebration," and Kansas's "Dust in the Wind."

Radio & Records reported that Bobby adjusted his current and recurrent song categories to give more airtime to songs like "I Need You" by LeAnn Rimes and "You'll Be in My Heart" by Phil Collins.[29]

On September 15, KMXZ hosted an all-day broadcast from the Tucson headquarters of the humanitarian agency World Cares. Listeners donated more than $14,000 in cash and enough relief supplies to fill a 26-foot U-Haul truck. DJ Adrienne Walker volunteered to drive it to New York City and called in reports to the station when she delivered the goods.

"That was a shining moment in my career," Bobby said of his team's response to the crisis. "I'm really proud of the way we handled it, rallying together, doing the right thing, and being helpful to people who were hurting."

"To this day," Bobby recalled more than two decades later, "people still come up and tell me, 'I'll never forget hearing the news from you guys on MIXfm, and having you on the radio helped me through that trauma.'"

Wildcat prank and more morning show shakeup

Showing their lighter side, Bobby and Brad pulled several on-air pranks

[29]Radio & Records, Oct. 12, 2001, pg 77 https://www.worldradiohistory.com/hd2/IDX-Business/Music/Archive-RandR-IDX/IDX/00s/01/RR-2001-10-12-OCR-Page-0078.pdf#search=%22mike%20kinosian%20bobby%20rich%22

over the years. Early in their partnership, having fun at the expense of a local celebrity earned them national attention but angered fans during the 1994 NCAA basketball tournament.

"We made up a list of ten far-fetched jokes to run on April Fool's Day," Bobby said. "At the top of our list was the silly claim that University of Arizona basketball coach Lute Olson announced his retirement last night.

"A listener called in right away and played along with the joke, saying she'd seen the beloved coach on TV at the NCAA tournament, and he looked very concerned. Soon, fans were flooding our phone lines, begging Olson not to quit. By nine o'clock all the TV stations were in our lobby waiting for comment, and ESPN picked up the story. The whole thing backfired, but we never thought anyone would believe it."

Olson, hugely popular in Tucson, had taken the U of A to the Final Four and the Wildcats coach didn't need the distraction on the eve of his team's biggest game in their quest for a national championship. Arizona lost in the semifinals. Fans and sportswriters were mad at the jokesters. Bobby took the blame and was reprimanded by his boss for the April foolery.

Another time, he and Brad set up a make-believe broadcast from a downtown intersection where construction had purportedly begun on Tucson's first underground shopping mall. They selected a vacant lot on Broadway Boulevard surrounded by chain link fencing as the site for the imaginary subterranean development.

"Finally, a Nordstrom is coming to town!" Bobby teased. Excitement grew as the audience heard a constant stream of heavy equipment, cement trucks, reverse motion beeping alarms, jackhammers, and other sounds echoing from the "underground mall construction site" while the DJs fielded "live reports from the scene."

"In fact, we were broadcasting from our usual studios and playing sound effects to create theater of the mind," Bobby later revealed. Listeners who fell for the prank and drove to the location to see for themselves found the MIXfm van parked next to a sign marked Happy April Fool's Day.

After thirteen years as partners, the broadcasting duo had a falling out, and Behan left the station in late 2007. "I was really broken up about the split," Bobby said. "I thought our show would go on for years, and it should have.

"Like a long-distance relationship, the geographic distance between us added to the difficulty of staying together as partners. Brad was the best, and what we did together all those years was probably my best show ever, next to the Rich Brothers *B Morning Zoo* at B-100 in San Diego."

New mix of kindness, community . . . and diapers

Mrs. Grant continued with Bobby and his new partner, Greg Curtis, as the show was renamed *The Bobby Rich Morning Mix*. Curtis, born and raised in Tucson, had jocked at sister station KZPT and in Boston at WBMX. The new team maintained the "Good, Clean Fun" morning radio on MIXfm.

Protective of that wholesome public image, Bobby refused an advertising proposal from a shop selling sexy lingerie and adult toys, Mrs. Grant remembered. "He put his foot down quite hard. It was all about being safe radio to listen to in the car with your kids."

"A huge part of what we did and what I learned from Bobby was his philosophy of being fun, funny, and local," Curtis said. "Before working for him, I assumed community service was something that most program directors believed in. I later found out they only did it because they were told to, while Bobby understood the value of radio serving the local community."

"Kindness and community work were in the DNA of all our shows," Bobby said. When a grieving mother initiated a public art project shortly after the death of her two-year-old child in 2002, KMXZ promoted her campaign to distribute colorful wind chimes and encourage intentional acts of kindness.

In memory of her son Ben, Jeannette Maré established Ben's Bells, a grassroots organization of family and friends who created ceramic bells and placed them in public places for people to find and take home. They attached notes to the bells encouraging the finders to spread kindness in their community.

Bobby adopted the group's kindness campaign as a key feature of MIXfm programming and gave airtime to the weekly recognition of Tucsonans selected to receive bells for their kindhearted deeds.

More than twenty thousand people per year volunteered with Ben's Bells, and the organization grew from a local nonprofit into a national movement. On the first anniversary of Ben's death, four hundred ornaments were placed around the city. The organization has since distributed bells throughout the world, and its free educational outreach program has reached more than 1.6 million students with a simple message: Be Kind.

A community need for diapers got Bobby and his DJs wrapped up in an earlier kindness initiative. Organizer Hildy Gottlieb sent a fax to all of Tucson's radio and TV stations in 1994, asking for coverage of her December Diaper Drive. Only one of them responded. "I believed in the concept as soon as she told me about the urgent lack of baby diapers in a local crisis nursery," Bobby said, "so we broadcast the event on MIXfm and asked our listeners to donate."

Gottlieb explained that many parents living at or near the poverty line had to miss work if they couldn't afford personal hygiene products required by most providers to place a young child in daycare. She and her business partner, Dimitri Petropolis, brainstormed the holiday collection and with media support from Bobby established the Diaper Bank of Southern Arizona, the first of its kind in the nation.

"It did sound kind of funny during the holiday season to be asking our audience not for toys, coats, food, or money, but for diapers," Bobby admitted. But the response was overwhelming, with twenty thousand nappies donated in the bank's first year of operation.

The following December, he set a goal of eighty-six thousand diapers, for children at the city's Casa de los Niños and Pio Decimo Center.

Radio advertisers also answered the appeal, said James Barton, the station's marketing and promotions director. "Bobby would go to client meetings and tell people this is important to the community, and you need to write a check. He encouraged business owners to donate diapers, and we'd go get them."

The generosity of MIXfm listeners enabled the agency to expand services to seniors and disabled people.

Sixteen years later, at an award ceremony honoring Bobby, the diaper bank's executive director said, "With his unfaltering dedication, we have covered babies' butts and adult bottoms with over six million diapers." His award, a handmade ceramic bell, was presented by the kindness advocates at Ben's Bells.

"The thing I love most about this business . . . "

MIXfm's production of "*A Christmas Carol with a Tucson Twist*" was another major charitable event that became an annual tradition. Adapted from the 1938 radio broadcast starring Orson Welles as Ebenezer Scrooge, the play was conceived by Bobby and his friend Dave Fitzsimmons, political cartoonist at the *Arizona Daily Star*.

Of course, they had to create a role in their Christmas classic for Tucson's Jimmy Stewart. The city's first TV weatherman and morning meteorologist on MIXfm, Stewart joined the station's DJs performing onstage with local celebrities, community theater actors, and radio comedian Dale "The Voiceman" Reeves.

Tucson Mayor Bob Walkup and his wife, Beth, joined the ensemble. Cast members also included Pima County Sheriff Clarence Dupnik, former U.S. Surgeon General Richard Carmona, TV news reporter Lupita Murillo, meteorologist Erin Christiansen, and musicians Richard Marx and John Tesh.

The two-hour theatrical production was laced with parody songs and topical humor. "Every year it was an opportunity to satirize what was happening in Arizona," Fitzsimmons said. "We would weave fantasy storylines into the script and change the workplace setting of Scrooge. One year, he was a small-town newspaper publisher in the foothills, another year a city bureaucrat.

"It was social commentary," noted Fitzsimmons. He saw their reimagined Dickensian classic as "an enduring fable that argues for the virtue of all of us adopting a more charitable role in advancing social and economic justice."

Performed with a live audience at prominent venues in Tucson, the homegrown holiday special was recorded and aired three times during Christmas week.

One of Bobby's other jobs at KMXZ was director of community partnerships for the station's parent company, E.W. Scripps. He and a management committee reviewed hundreds of applications, choosing which nonprofit organizations to spotlight each month with public service announcements and free airtime on six local radio and TV stations.

Tucson Medical Center for Children was a key partner, and MIXfm hosted the local Children's Miracle Network Radiothon, raising funds for a new pediatrics unit at the hospital.

Listeners pitched in to replenish the pantry shelves of the Community Food Bank of Southern Arizona during MIXfm's annual "Thanksgiving on the Mayflower" broadcast. "It was a wonderful feeling," Bobby said, "to see so many folks fill our Mayflower moving van with donations." In 2010, the station accepted more than seven thousand pounds of food and $130,000 to set a record for the largest one-day collection in the food bank's history.

Of his impact as a DJ, Bobby said, "The power of radio is something I always took very seriously. I don't have any high opinion of what I do or what I say, but the thing I love most about this business is that I can talk to people and help out where there's a need.

"Even a little thing can make a difference. My place in the world is to spread the word. Sometimes it's a fundraiser, or just saying good morning, sharing a positive attitude, song, interesting story, or fun event."

DJs free to let their personalities shine

A big believer in full-service radio, Bobby enlisted Big Al "Your Traffic Pal" Kath of KGUN-TV and Jimmy Stewart of KVOA-TV to provide morning rush hour updates and weather reports.

His philosophy of "have fun and sound like it" carried over to middays with Marty Bishop, a fixture on the station for more than thirty-seven years, and the afternoon show hosted by Adrienne Walker for nearly twenty years.

MIXfm's on-air lineup featured nationally syndicated personality Delilah at night, and John Tesh's syndicated show in the overnight shift. The staff also included Jim Gilly, Bruce Daniels, and twenty-year personality and programmer Leslie Lois.

Walker credited their PD's leadership for the station's unique appeal. "He put together a team that knew Tucson and let them rip. You had a feeling when you turned on the radio it was your city, your community.

That was all Bobby. He really put the focus on charity and getting the public involved, doing good things for the community through radio.

"As PD, he let us be us. We were totally free to let our personalities shine," Walker said.

More than thirty FM and AM stations composed the Tucson radio market and in 2007, MIXfm topped them all in three of the four Arbitron ratings periods. Arbitron surveys measured weekly listening of people in age groups 12-plus, Monday to Sunday, from 6 a.m. to midnight.

When ratings occasionally took a dip, Curtis said Bobby didn't freak out but urged management to stay the course and not alter programming based on one down book. "His MO was to just wait it out, confident we were doing the right thing."

Contract renewal at twenty years

MIXfm's prime-time ratings success was recognized in the 2008 *Radio & Records* Industry Achievement Awards. KMXZ won adult contemporary station of the year for markets 51–100 and Bobby was honored as AC personality/show of the year for all markets in the U.S.

That same year, he was described in the trade publication *Inside Radio* as "one of this industry's most exceptionally gifted communicators." Special features editor Mike Kinosian wrote, "A more quality individual won't be found than gregarious superstar programmer/morning talent Bobby Rich."

For his twentieth anniversary, the station threw a pool party at Casino del Sol Resort, followed by an amphitheater concert by rockers Ann and Nancy Wilson of Heart.

Bobby signed a multiyear contract extension in 2013. "They seem to like how it is going," he said at the time.

Shaun Holly, operations manager for the station's owner, Journal Broadcast Group, praised him as "the leading force behind MIXfm's ratings success since 1993 and the most visible radio personality in the city."

MediaConfidential quoted Holly on the morning show's long-term popularity: "Bobby discovered the secret of radio success in Tucson by creating the ultimate bond with listeners, advertisers, and civic leaders. He's the best I've ever seen at that."

Tucson Mayor Jonathan Rothschild proclaimed November 8 to be Bobby Rich Day, citing his contributions to the city, the station, and the entire broadcast industry through "uplifting radio" and community service work.

Canceled after twenty-four years

At the time of his induction into the Arizona Broadcasters Association Hall of Fame in 2013, Bobby was the longest-running morning radio personality in Tucson. He went on to work another four years at MIXfm, outlasting at least six GMs and operations managers and surviving four changes in corporate ownership.

Of the high turnover rate in the front office during his tenure, he said, "There was a virtual parade of midlevel managers and consultants fighting about who got to give me a critique every day.

"Most of the owners took good care of me, giving me contract extensions for two to three years at a time and bonuses for delivering the right kind of ratings, exceeding performance in our target demographics. But as time went on, new managers inevitably tried to cut expenses on the morning show.

"They'd all ask why couldn't I do the show by myself, without partners. It wasn't about how good our show was and how well it was performing, they just wanted to save money by reducing head count. I'd always say why would you demolish a team that's been successful for years?"

Management prevailed in January of 2017 when *The Bobby Rich Morning Mix* with Greg and Mrs. Grant came to an end. "Mostly for cost-cutting purposes, I was moved into the afternoon shift, and the morning show continued without a replacement for me," he said.

Four weeks after the debut of his new afternoon program, *Bobby Rich Celebrates Tucson*, he exited MIXfm under mysterious circumstances.

The departure caught everyone by surprise and remained a secret for the next eight years.

Bobby's long-awaited explanation of why he had to leave is finally revealed in the upcoming pages.

Bobby and morning co-host Brad Behan, MIXfm Money Song contest mailer, Tucson, April 1999.

Joke book distributed by MIXfm co-hosts Bobby and co-host Jerry "Eggs" Agar, Tucson, c. 1996.

MIXfm co-hosts Bobby, Greg Curtis, and Mrs. Grant, in studio, Tucson, 2013. (Photo by Pat Gaffey)

Chapter 47

Firing Line

Getting fired in the radio business is pretty much a regular thing. There's very little job security in our line of work, for disc jockeys or station managers. Getting blown out just goes with the territory, and most of us have been shown the door more than once. In my fifty-plus years in broadcasting, I've been sacked nine times. I've also been the messenger of bad news an equal number of times. When it was my turn to get the axe, sometimes there was good cause. Other times I was let go for the flimsiest and funniest of reasons.

Corvallis, Oregon

After my freshman year at Eastern Washington State, I left college radio and moved to Oregon for a paying job as nighttime DJ on KFLY, a Top 40 station in Corvallis. Our crosstown rival, KLOO, hired another up-and-coming jock named Bwana Johnny for the same shift. Although we were competitors, Bwana and I became friends. We were both about nineteen years old and total radio nerds. After getting off the air at midnight, we'd meet several times a week at a nearby truck stop to drink coffee and talk radio.

I was so impressed with Bwana's on-air personality and

presentation that I recommended him for a gig at KFLY. Soon after, he got a call from my general manager, offering him my job! Before accepting the gig, Bwana insisted that KFLY keep me on the staff. Surprisingly, the GM agreed to his demand. The station created a midnight-to-6 a.m. air shift for me, and I was reassigned to overnights. Two months later, Bwana and I received another surprise when we both got the boot from KFLY.

Spokane

My next move was to Spokane, the second-biggest city in Washington. I returned to college, taking daytime classes while working nights at easy listening station KDNC and then overnights at country station KSPO. When they asked me to join the sales department in addition to spinning cowboy records on KSPO, I said no. Selling ads was not for me. That refusal led to my early departure. I got my walking papers when the boss called to say he'd found someone willing to play country music on the midnight shift and sell commercials during the day.

KXLY, the third station to hire me in Spokane, gave three reasons for letting me go. The first offense was telling a screaming teenybopper who called in and won tickets to a concert, "Boy, you're really excited, Maryann. You almost wet your panties there." The PD called me into his office and hollered, "You can't say wet your panties on the radio!"

The second offense was a radio column that I wrote for my college newspaper, reviewing Top 40 stations in Spokane. At the time, I was working nights at KXLY. My commentary praised a competing station, KJRB, for kicking our ass with highly professional jocks and a jingles package that put KXLY to shame. The boss saw a copy of the school paper and started preparing my exit papers.

My third and final strike was taking a late-night joyride in the brand-new Pontiac Tiger GTO loaned to the station by a local car dealer. Spokane police called him at 1:30 in the morning to report someone was drag racing his GTO. I returned the muscle car unscratched but was blown out by KXLY later that day.

New York

Fast forward to 1979 in New York, where I programmed an album-oriented hits format on 99X FM (WXLO) against Top 40 competitors playing shorter versions of songs edited for AM airplay. That's when the disco music trend peaked in popularity, and we lost the ratings war to WKTU. They went all disco and became the number one station in America's biggest city.

When 99X cut me loose after a year, *Billboard* magazine reported ours was one of several rock-oriented stations that suffered from the switch in audience allegiance. I said in the article, "It was a dumb time to come in with the disco thing happening."

Los Angeles

Less than a year after having to fire a half dozen jocks in Los Angeles due to a change in ownership at KHTZ, I received my termination notice from the new parent company. Actually, it was a conniving assistant PD who broke the news while I was on vacation. I called him long-distance, and he started hemming and hawing, being all weird on the phone. Then he put me on hold and left me hanging for about seven minutes. When he finally got back on the line still awkward and evasive, I asked, "Am I being fired?" and he said yeah. Wouldn't you know that weasel was in cahoots with the GM to take my job. And my bonus.

Philadelphia

When upper management at Top106 (WWSH) in Philly decided to get rid of me in 1984, I found out from the lady who sold coffee, cigarettes, and newspapers in the lobby of our building! Stopping by her kiosk on my way in to work to buy a copy of *The Philadelphia Inquirer,* I gave her the usual greeting, "Hi, Mrs. Fox, how are you today?" And she looked at me sadly and said, "We sure are going to miss you around here."

Obviously, the newspaper vendor had overheard my bosses talking about letting me go. I agreed to resign and stuck around for a couple of weeks to let them find a replacement.

Seattle

My departure from I-107.7 (KMGI) in Seattle was another case of getting fired by someone who wasn't my boss. The company president let two of his associates do the dirty work. The hatchet men called a meeting to get rid of me and dropped that Michael Corleone line from *The Godfather*, "It's not personal, it's strictly business."

They pressured me to quit after a year and a half as GM and PD. First, they took away my executive office and gave me a workspace in the jock lounge. Then they threatened to move me from the morning show to the overnight shift. I guess they figured that would be too humiliating to accept.

I refused to give in to their strong-arm tactics. The big boss overruled his associates and worked out a deal with me. The company eventually did the noble thing, and I left with a considerable severance package.

San Diego

Okay, here's the silliest thing I ever got fired for: Rufus the Weather Dog. Not a real dog, Rufus was a fictitious character on a short-lived morning show I did in 1991 at KRMX San Diego with my co-host Scott Kenyon. Rufus gave weather reports in a gruff, unintelligible "dog voice," which Scott and I "translated" for the audience. It was basically the same bit that Soupy Sales did with the puppet character White Fang on his 1960s TV comedy show.

Well, our GM thought the weather dog routine was stupid and told me to drop it. So, we waited until he went on a sales trip to do the bit again. And I said on the air that Rufus was making a return appearance because the boss was out of town. Of course, word got back to him, and he promptly canned me. But as they say, payback's a bitch. KRMX paid me a pretty good settlement because the GM's petty bullshit complaints didn't hold up and he couldn't prove that I had violated my contract.

Tucson

Well, that explains why I was fired by eight different stations, but there's one more where I've never explained what happened . . . until now.

—Bobby Rich, September 2023

Chapter 48

Finally Revealed: Why I Got Fired for the Last Time

I said earlier that getting fired was sometimes a badge of honor in the radio business. It meant you pushed the envelope or did or said something outrageous or controversial. Other times the boss was just looking for reasons to get rid of you so he could hire someone who'd be a puppet and not challenge his authority.

Then there's the manager well-known in our industry for lining up toy army men across his desktop whenever a DJ was going to be sacked. He would summon the next victim to his office and explain that one of those green plastic figures represented you. He then flicked his index finger and thumb as if he were shooting marbles and proceeded to fling YOUR toy soldier across the room as he blew you out.

Another management ploy was giving you a choice to resign rather than be fired. The assumption behind this form of ultimatum was that you would prefer to quit and be spared the shame of getting canned. Also, companies could save money by not having to pay unemployment or severance benefits because you resigned.

And then there were times when behavior was really deserving of termination.

My last firing was one of those I deserved, even though the whole thing was taken out of context.

It started with the hiring of a new general manager who was my sixth and final boss at the station.

To begin the story, I have to say he just did not like me. That and the fact he'd been given instructions to get my salary off the books. I could detail at least three times he outright lied to achieve the deed, but that would be petty and look like I was copping out.

In his first meeting with me and my programming staff, he told everyone that I had "a big personality and sucked the air out of the room." As if the staff didn't already know that! Somehow, he made my on-air job description ("a big personality") sound like it was a bad thing.

Weeks later he took me and the operations manager to lunch. That's when he announced to both of us, "By the first of the year MY station will have a TWO-person morning show."

There were three of us co-hosting the morning show at the time. When the GM revealed the two he planned to keep, my name was not one of them.

I'm not sure but I think the operations manager was more surprised than I was.

Adding insult to injury, the GM suggested, "Of course we'll want you, Bobby, to stick around. Maybe you could come in one or two days a week to do a short feature? Or we could set you up for a weekend shift, or to represent us as a pro bono emcee for community public service."

This exchange occurred during one of the lowest points in my personal life and professional career. Debbie and I had recently separated. My GM phased me out of the lead role on the morning show after twenty-three years. And I had given up my responsibilities as PD.

Demoted but still doing mornings, I was driving to work one day and heard a promo on the station teasing, "Our dysfunctional morning show coming up next." That was all I could handle. I felt as if I had been rudely stomped on, and a fuse had been lit.

I lost it. Walking in the door, I shouted something horrible to an intern, then popped into the studio to tell my team I was out of there, leaving them flabbergasted just seconds before our show was starting.

I went to my desk, left a voicemail for the operations manager, and composed a letter to my boss stating, "I can't perform today. I may be having a breakdown. I'll be back to work when I can, no later than Friday for the Children's Miracle Radiothon."

Four days later I returned for our radiothon broadcast, but that episode came back to haunt me when the GM fabricated an untrue report to corporate claiming that I simply disappeared without telling anyone. He stuck with that version even after I requested the opportunity to tell my side to the brass. He told me to send it to the HR regional office. I did and was told by HR they couldn't get involved.

All of this happened before my agreed-upon transfer from mornings to afternoon drive (3-6 p.m.) I was enthusiastic about building a new solo show called "*Bobby Rich Loves Tucson*"—a mix of music, talk, and information about local events, business, the nonprofit world, and fun things to do in town.

My final appearance on the morning show was the Friday before Christmas 2016. The plan was to take some mental health days and return in January to the afternoon slot. At that juncture, to say I was mentally unstable would be an understatement.

The realization this would be my LAST show after more than three decades in mornings became overwhelming. I got through it struggling to find the motivation to finish the show and be positive while telling our listeners of my move to afternoons. It came as a surprise how emotionally exhausted and mentally drained I was. Good judgment was nowhere to be found.

. . . and THAT brings us to WHY I WAS FIRED.

After that final morning show I wandered around chatting with coworkers at the other stations in the building. I ended up in a studio where a friend was starting their show. We had a long-running fun game trying to crack up the other by saying something inappropriate during a commercial break just before the microphones went live.

I leaned over her shoulder and whispered a variation of the punchline to a well-known dirty joke. It did not go out on the air, but someone nearby heard me say it.

What they overheard was immediately reported to HR and the GM.

No, I won't reveal the exact words. I will not say it to anyone, I never have said it since.

It was disgusting, completely improper, and embarrassing. I left the area immediately. I apologized profusely and admitted it was said in a moment of extremely poor judgment.

The joke is famously known as "the three biggest lies."

—Bobby Rich, December 2023

Chapter 49

The Bitchin' Better Boogie is Back

Bobby's first radio shows could be heard only inside his family's house in Ephrata. With an inexpensive home broadcasting kit from Radio Shack and records borrowed from his teenage sisters, the boy DJ did a nightly show from his bedroom. The signal reached as far as the dining room, where his parents and sisters comprised an audience of four.

Fifty years later, Bobby converted a bedroom of his house in Tucson into a home studio, launched an internet station, and beamed his own music to listeners worldwide.

Bobby's B-100, anytime and anywhere

Except for a brief spell as a DJ on his college station, Bobby's entire career was in commercial radio.

By 2010 he had purchased the necessary computer software and automation equipment to run a noncommercial station.

"Without any fees, subscriptions, or paid advertising," Bobby said, "my internet-only channel offered round-the-clock streaming music from a playlist of songs at least double the size of what most traditional broadcasters were using.

"My intent with the online station was the same as my philosophy for programming traditional radio. Have fun, play great music, and give people something to smile about whenever they tune in."

As a tribute to the illustrious San Diego station where he was known as Doctor Boogie, he named his web radio enterprise Bobby's B-100.

Commercial-free boogie

Claiming the URL of BobbysB100.com, he created the tagline "Bitchin' '70s and '80s Digital Radio" to conjure memories of cool vibes, retro music, and summer fun.

"Ears over forty-nine years of age" were invited to sample his curated selection of hit songs from the pop, rock, and soul charts. The playlist also included some favorite "midchart stiffs" that never quite made it into the Top 40.

Webcasting allowed Bobby to program his own personal music format with no corporate influence or interference and no FCC licensing or government regulation.

A labor of love

To help launch the home-based venture, Bobby brought his best friend, Scott Kenyon, on board. They had worked together at three stations in Ohio and California and remained close for forty-four years. Their reunion came at a time when Kenyon was experiencing major health problems.

"When Scott became ill, I knew he'd enjoy being on the air again and programming with me in a low-stress, easygoing situation, given his serious medical condition. Scott was the real inspiration for my online project, which continued for eight years after his death in 2011."

Because it could be heard only via the internet, the streaming audio outlet did not compete or pose a conflict of interest with MIXfm (KMXZ), where Bobby was PD and morning host since 1993.

"In my free time I did live and recorded shows. Jocks who had worked for me in San Diego volunteered to cut audio tracks. That gave the impression that we had a staff of air talent," Bobby said. "Nobody, including me, got paid for anything. It was just a labor of love.

"Adding the other DJ voices and a PAMS jingles package that I bought from Jam Creative Productions made Bobby's B-100 sound bigger and highly professional.

"I started it as a laboratory of experimental ideas for music programming. Like, would these songs play well together? Is there an audience that would like the spread of genres and musical eras that I had in mind?"

From webstream back to mainstream

Finding himself unemployed in 2017, Bobby had more time to collect audience research and refine a format that would eventually breathe new life into the terrestrial radio market.

"Those couple of years that I was in my home studio for hours on end programming the online station really paid off," he said, "because that was what we later put on the air at KDRI The Drive Tucson."

His experiment paved the way for a startup FM station in 2019. Unplugging his internet platform, Bobby returned to the local airwaves in his familiar role as programming boss and morning personality.

Gazing longingly into Dolly Parton's … eyes? (Photo from Bobby Rich Radio collection)

Captain Bobby looking for Tenille. (Photo from Bobby Rich Radio collection)

Chapter 50

Reinventing Radio, The Road Stops Here

Getting blown out as PD and morning show star after twenty-four years at MIXfm left Bobby in no hurry to jump back into the radio business.

"I knew from getting fired nine times in my career that I'd find another job," he said, "so I wasn't worried about that." And he wasn't looking to move to another city, having promised his family that Tucson would be their permanent home.

A two-year absence from the morning airwaves ended shortly after his friend Fletcher McCusker, a successful entrepreneur and Tucson civic booster, called one day to tell him, "We've got to get you back on the radio! You've done too many good things for this town, it's crazy that you're not on the air," Bobby said. "He believed I still had a lot to offer."

Music to his ears

"We started talking about buying a station, and Fletcher wanted me to have full creative control of it." They enlisted another local broadcast executive, Jim Arnold, to join them in forming a company called Radio Tucson and began shopping for available licenses.

"My concept for a new station," Bobby said, "was a presentation of music for people aged 45-64, baby boomers and pre-boomers, a demographic that was being ignored as corporate radio focused its attention on younger listeners.

"Being intimately familiar with the age group, I invented an uncommon format that would appeal to these folks with music from the mid-1960s through the mid-'80s. Fletcher and Jim agreed with the strategy."

At the age of seventy-three, Bobby was about to reinvent yet another radio station for yet another decade.

"I wanted to create a sound for the 2020s that would be familiar and at the same time fresh," he said.

"In the back of my mind I thought it might be my last station, which increased the importance of making something successful and long-lasting so I could go out a winner."

After months of searching, the trio found a Christian network willing to sell its AM-FM combination. They paid Family Life Broadcasting $650,000 for KFLT 830 AM and 101.7 FM.

The deal included FCC authorization for the FM to operate as a translator station and simultaneously broadcast (simulcast) the primary signal of the AM.

McCusker put up most of the money and took the lead as chairman of the board of Radio Tucson. Bobby made a financial investment in the partnership and assumed responsibilities as president, program director, and morning man. Arnold, known as "Sunny Jim" from his early days as a rock jock in Tucson, signed on as general manager.

Top secret startup

An air of secrecy surrounded the recruitment of experienced local DJs for the new station. Bobby withheld details about his unique format and proposed call letters.

"Until they were hired, I couldn't take the chance of word getting out. What we were doing was so different that it had to be hush-hush to prevent competitors from trying it before we could sign on," he said.

Bobby chose Hill Bailey to be his morning show co-host, Ken Carr for middays, Mikey Esparza for afternoons, and Tyler Russell for the night shift. All the announcers had deep Tucson ties, and most had jocked in larger markets. The original staff also included weekenders Maria Mendez and Brenda Catalina.

Bailey got her radio start at the University of Arizona, worked at another FM in Tucson, and had been on the air in Colorado Springs, Denver, Sacramento, and San Luis Obispo.

Carr brought eighteen years of experience at three Tucson stations and prior radio service in Kansas City, Salt Lake City, and Providence.

Esparza began his career in Tucson and returned after working at stations in San Diego, Dallas, and San Francisco.

Russell, son of McCusker, was born and raised in Tucson and mentored by Bobby before graduating to programmer jobs in Palm Springs and Laguna Beach.

How The Drive arrived

As their startup date neared, the PD revealed to his staff plans for a high hourly song count, frequent traffic and weather updates, and a heavy emphasis on in-car listening.

He credited Carr for suggesting an ideal brand name while they met for lunch and a beer.

"I was planning to call the new station Take It Easy Tucson, maybe with the call letters KTIE," Bobby said, "until I shared that name with Ken. His reaction was, 'Oh, I was thinking it could be called The Drive.' The second it crossed his lips, I literally froze, then blurted out, 'Oh my gosh, that's perfect!'

"That was the day I changed my mind, and we became The Drive Tucson."

For a station identity based on cars and drivers, the next task was finding appropriate call letters. A search of the FCC's database revealed that the call sign KDRI was available, and the ownership group immediately applied for it. With a green light from the FCC, the partners prepared to take the wheel of The Drive.

"Right away we started planning ways to connect things to driving," Bobby said. "For instance, instead of saying, 'Here's the traffic . . .' we'd have the jocks introduce road reports with something like, 'For your Drive, avoid the intersection of Speedway and Plumer.'

"I also coached the DJs to always include some kind of hook to Tucson whenever they opened the mic. That way anybody listening at any time would theoretically get a bit of interesting local information from us.

"I used this technique in San Diego, which, like Tucson, is kind of sexy. So, just mentioning 'It's another great Tucson Tuesday' can make a favorable impression to connect with the audience."

As the worm turns

Throughout the summer, Arnold interviewed candidates to join a small but motivated sales staff at KDRI as Bobby devised a scheme to build suspense, get publicity, and smooth the transition from a contemporary Christian format.

Before its reincarnation as The Drive, the station temporarily became "The Worm," playing the "greatest novelty hits of all time."

For their term on The Worm, DJs chose the wriggly pseudonyms Wormy McWormface, Nightcrawler, Red Wiggler, and Glow Worm. Bobby claimed the alias Dr. Willie B. Wormish.

For several days, the staff dug up songs such as "Hello Muddah, Hello Faddah" by Alan Sherman, "They're Coming to Take Me Away, Ha-Haaa!" by Napoleon XIV, and "My Ding-a-Ling" by Chuck Berry.

"It gave us a chance to get comfortable with the studio and equipment, test how loud to set our headphones, all that behind-the-scenes stuff," Bobby said.

After a long weekend unearthing "Fish Heads," "King Tut," and other silly songs, The Worm DJs reclaimed their regular air names for The Drive's premiere.

Timeless music

KDRI The Drive Tucson debuted with a library of approximately three thousand songs. Bobby chose about a thousand titles for his active playlist and sorted them into groupings based on genre, era, feel, tempo, and other musical characteristics.

Assigning identities to each song, he created a rotation schedule for every hour of every show to ensure that a tune wouldn't be heard twice in the same air shift or at the same time on consecutive days.

"My programming was entirely by gut," he said. "We didn't have a budget for music testing, which is a popular but expensive way to get audience feedback about the songs you're playing or thinking about adding."

In the station's kickoff announcement, McCusker offered his characterization of the format: "It's not classic rock. It's not golden oldies."

Competing with five rival stations playing Hot AC, mainstream AC, R&B, and alternative rock in Tucson, Bobby described his playlist as "a variety of '60s, '70s, and '80s rock, pop, Top 40, acoustic, some country, and even a touch of smooth jazz . . . blending genres in a way that makes sense and is fun to listen to."

"Certain songs have a lasting ability to evoke the sad and the joyful part of nostalgia," he said, citing "What a Wonderful World" by Louis Armstrong and the medley "Somewhere Over the Rainbow/What a Wonderful World" by "IZ" Kamakawiwoʻole as examples of timeless music in his soon-to-be-revealed format.

Known and unknown adversaries

On August 5, 2019, KDRI The Drive Tucson was born, with the *Bobby and Bailey Show* going live at 6 a.m. To mark their first day on the air, he played his favorite sign-on song, "Beginnings" by Chicago.

Going up against established broadcasters and new media challengers Spotify, Pandora, Sirius XM, and other music streaming services, Bobby expressed confidence in his management partners and DJs.

"It's crazy to start a new radio station, but we are just crazy enough and have the passion to make it work."

In hindsight, Bobby offered a candid assessment of their market entry with an invisible virus looming. "We knew the competition, but not the pandemic."

Pandemic relief radio

Seven months after The Drive's debut, the outbreak of coronavirus disease 2019 gripped the globe. COVID-19 was declared a pandemic by the World Health Organization in March of 2020.

Arizona Governor Doug Ducey announced a statewide public health emergency on March 12. Social distancing was implemented to prevent the spread of the virus. A stay-at-home order went into effect, with exemptions for travel to essential services and work. School schedules were disrupted. The University of Arizona extended its spring break and then switched to online instruction.

Tucson Mayor Regina Romero proclaimed a citywide state of emergency on St. Patrick's Day, causing many businesses to close and limiting restaurants to takeout and home delivery service.

Early in the pandemic, Bobby and Bailey mobilized their listeners to help feed local health-care workers and first responders. Bailey cooked up a grassroots restaurant assistance plan, starting The Drive's "Drive Thru for Tucson's Frontline" campaign to express appreciation and community pride.

"There's a group of people that have stood up and decided to take care of us," Bailey wrote in a GoFundMe appeal to donors. "Health-care workers and first responders have put aside their worries for their own families and health to show up for us every day . . . It's that positive energy and human spirit we need to continue to push forward."

Tucsonans responded with more than $40,000 in donations. Partnering with restaurants struggling to survive, Bailey coordinated the distribution of four thousand breakfasts, lunches, and dinners to forty local emergency agencies and care providers.

"I contacted every fire station, police station, and hospital, plus nursing homes around the city," she said. "The community showed up so big for us in supporting our health-care heroes. People just wanted to give back."

Yes to kindness and critters, no to politics

Bobby credited Bailey for originating the show's signature good news segment, Kindness Corner. "Hill introduced it; the concept was like wouldn't it be cool if every neighborhood had a place where the neighbors all gathered to share something positive they had heard so it didn't feel like everyone was mean and nasty?"

"Kindness was our thing, it was our way of helping people get through the pandemic years," he said. "We found good news stories to tell, mostly local but some national stories too. We'd set up the segment by playing the opening from the *Sesame Street* song 'The People in Your Neighborhood.'"

Animal Tails with Bobby and Bailey became another of the show's warm and fuzzy features. "It was my favorite bit," Bailey said of her popular news roundup from the animal kingdom. Typical stories involved long-lost pets reunited with their humans, a baby koala rescued by a golden retriever, and a "klepto cat" accused of stealing sunglasses and toys.

Wildlife conservation also had a place on Animal Tails, with the Arizona Game and Fish Department providing information on protection and adoption of desert tortoises.

Editorial cartoonist and columnist Dave Fitzsimmons of the *Arizona Daily Star* complimented Bobby for walking "a curious and amazing tightrope" as a public persona without a political agenda.

"I thought that was quite a skill to avoid anything that hinted of partisan speech yet be able to fill the airwaves for hours with entertaining content," Fitzsimmons said. "It also helps to have a beautiful voice."

The DJs followed the lead of their PD in focusing on community events and the Tucson lifestyle while steering clear of divisive topics. More music and fewer interruptions meant playing at least fourteen songs per hour, according to Bailey.

Paying KDRI jocks a higher wage than what they might earn at other stations in town was another ingredient in Bobby's recipe for a winning station. "He took care of us, and we knew we were appreciated and able to be as creative as possible and have personalities, so people wanted to listen," Bailey said.

One of their biggest fans was a self-employed electrical contractor, Bob Blizzard the Electrical Wizard. He appreciated the good-natured banter and traffic reports while driving twenty thousand miles per year in his work truck. "I've always enjoyed a good laugh and a good smile in the morning, and I got both from any show that I ever listened to with Bobby behind the microphone," Blizzard said.

Songs you forgot you loved

Leslie Lois joined KDRI in 2021 as weekend DJ and office manager after twenty years at MIXfm. Jason Crane and Michael Morris got the call for occasional fill-in shifts. Billy Repka served as production director and music coordinator.

Helping establish what Bobby called the "stationality" of The Drive, Adrienne Walker voiced the recorded liners and promos inserted between songs and coming out of commercial breaks. "Radio for Tucson by Tucsonans" was one of the positioning statements that conveyed a strong local identity. "Songs you forgot you loved" was another message reinforcing the station's emotional appeal.

From a studio in Hollywood, recording engineer Tony Pepper produced most of The Drive's imaging, which he described as "friendly, approachable, and respectful of the audience." That meant none of the screaming voiceovers, explosions, or laser zaps heard on harder-edged stations.

"Bobby's playlist was so deep, and we'd talk for hours about segues and production elements that would work with the music," Pepper said.

Rob Sisco produced promos in Connecticut for The Drive's weekend programming, which included rebroadcasts of Casey Kasem's syndicated show *American Top 40*.

Sisco and Pepper provided their consulting and production services free of charge, doing it for the love of Bobby and personality radio.

Unlike competitor stations airing as many as seventeen commercials in a row, The Drive's spot load was limited to no more than two and a half minutes per break and a maximum seven and a half minutes of ads per hour. That formula yielded substantial ratings for time spent listening but not enough total listeners to turn a profit.

David and Goliath battle

On its one-year anniversary, The Drive tied for fourth place in the Nielsen ratings that measured the number of people 45 and older who listened to English-language music stations during morning drive, according to Jim Arnold. The GM reported a sixth-place finish in afternoon drive, and rankings between fourth and eighth place in the 45-plus age group throughout the day.[30]

After three years the station still wasn't generating a positive return on investment. "We did okay almost from the beginning but didn't get the big ratings that we could brag about," Bobby conceded.

"People here in Tucson are crazy in love with The Drive," he said. "They're all over fifty years old, so we hit our target. But not enough of them to keep us in the top five or top three for advertisers and commercials."

McCusker, Arnold, and Bobby found themselves in a David vs. Goliath battle. As small local operators, they were vulnerable to post-pandemic economic conditions and changes in broadcasting and music streaming that followed their 2019 purchase of the station.

"One big reason why we couldn't make it financially is because the radio business is now dominated by clusters of stations run by big companies like iHeart, Cumulus, and Lotus," Bobby explained.

"Whereas we were a stand-alone station playing only six minutes of commercials per hour, these groups with four, five, or six stations can

[30]*Arizona Daily Star, Sep 18, 2020* https://tucson.com/business/a-year-in-independent-tucson-radio-station-lands-in-nielsens-top-10/article_f41c622f-4c87-5ef1-9551-4209afa4949e.html

offer package deals to advertisers and still come out ahead on revenue. We just didn't have the ability to match the coverage that they could offer."

Detour for The Drive

The partners considered all possible options and determined there was no way to boost ad revenue without diminishing the pleasurable listening experience they had created.

Unwilling to play more commercials and less music, they concluded that the business model for an independent radio station was unsustainable. The trio agreed in March 2023 to sell The Drive and search for a buyer who would preserve the essence of their product.

The decision weighed heavily on Bobby. "I felt a personal responsibility because I developed the format, recruited all the talent, and got them to buy into a concept before I could even tell them what the format was going to be or where our studios were going to be. I just asked them to trust me, and they all did," he said.

"We were very successful in every area but one: revenue."

Majority owner McCusker commended all employees in a memo notifying them of the agreement to sell. "As much as we relish being the only locally owned radio station, it does not appear to matter to enough advertisers to pay the bills," he wrote.

Radio Tucson found a buyer in Amador Bustos, whose Portland-based broadcast group owned stations in Oregon, Washington, Wisconsin, Texas, California, and Arizona.

Bustos Media already had a strong presence in Tucson, with KTGV The Groove 106.3 FM (soul), KVOI The Voice 1030 AM (talk), KZLZ "La Poderosa" 105.3 FM (Spanish), and KZLZ-HD2 92.5 FM (urbana).

"Bustos will keep our studio, talent, and format," McCusker reassured The Drive staff. "They will begin immediately finding ways to bundle our station with the other Bustos stations and go head-to-head with iHeart, Lotus, and Cumulus."

According to published reports, $800,000 was the sale price.

Voluntary retirement plan

While the transfer of ownership was pending regulatory approval, Bobby remained on the air and contemplated his own future. In early April of 2023 he sounded uncertain about whether to stay with the station or step away. "Along with being a DJ, I've also been in management and programming for so long that I can't imagine not being on the radio," he mused.

During the FCC waiting period, he left town for a few days to visit Charlie Van Dyke, his friend since 1968. "It was a really great getaway, just talking with Charlie and his wife, Ingrid, telling stories, relaxing, appreciating my life and stuff." Returning from the road trip, Bobby decided it was time to hang up his mic and headphones.

On May 4 he announced on the air, "I have chosen to retire, and my last show will be a week from tomorrow." He played the Grateful Dead song "Truckin'" and it occurred to him what a long and wondrously strange trip it had been.

Bobby's first farewell message to the radio audience was also shared on his Facebook page:

Every plane must land eventually. After over 50 years behind a microphone, it's time to put my feet back on the ground. May 12th, 2023, will be my last day on the air at KDRI/The DRIVE Tucson.

I brought my family to Tucson where we could put our arms around the market, and we love it here. We raised our daughters here, and they are flourishing and will probably never leave. More than anything else, I've had the privilege to make radio integral to the fabric of the community.

My final gift is KDRI The Drive Tucson, where I created a unique new format playing curated timeless music, recruited a dream team of radio professionals, and made a market-centric success with our targeted 45+ demo.

I am choosing to retire.

From the time I first spoke into a microphone at the age of fifteen in Ephrata, Washington, my ride of a lifetime career took me to twenty-three radio stations in fourteen cities. Including Los Angeles, Philadelphia, New York City, Seattle, and my beloved cities of San Diego and Tucson.

Along the way, I had the honor of working with, performing with, and being mentored by a host of radio royalty. I am eternally grateful to those dear friends. As a bonus, I enjoyed numerous opportunities to be a mentor, and that gives me abundant gratification.

This career has been about turning on a microphone (usually located in a tiny room inside of a big building), connecting and communicating with listeners one-to-one. That's something that only happens on the radio. It never gets old, and it's rewarding beyond words.

I am truly blessed with a family that I love and a beautiful, smart, and caring wife who doesn't seem to mind the fact that I am a teenage disc jockey in an old man's body.

Radio was my first love.

It will be my last.

"Thanks for listening!"

Handing over keys to The Drive

Three weeks before his announcement, Bobby's partner revealed that she would be leaving the station. Bailey had already moved with her family to South Carolina. She co-hosted with Bobby from her home studio until the end of April. He then soloed for his last two weeks. That timing allowed them to say their respective goodbyes to each other and the audience.

Bobby and Bailey's final days together brought an outpouring of affection from listeners. Thousands of well-wishers reached out via social media, phone calls, and texts to express appreciation for four years of morning entertainment and companionship on The Drive.

A sample of messages posted on his Facebook page reflected the depth of Bobby's connection with Tucsonans:

- Ted C: "Very happy for you, Bobby! Congratulations on your retirement. I moved to Tucson in 1990, and you started your stint here shortly after that. I have been listening to you for 30+ years now. I consider you a dear friend though we have never met in person."
- Gary: "Bobby and Bailey helped lighten our struggles with the pandemic. Well done!"
- Cindy: "Thank you for being in my radio. You got me through a lot of rough times over the years, and you are very well deserving of retirement. Go dance with the stars and go sing with the sun. Congratulations and happy retirement, Bobby Rich!"
- David: "I cannot thank you enough for the years of listening pleasure you have given me and so many others. Your gift of KDRI to Tucson is the kind of legacy so many can only dream of, and you have done it. Enjoy taking it easy but please don't disappear."
- Leanne: "You don't know this, but you are family to me. Through the years you have been there for me. I'll never forget 9/11 and how I heard it from you on my way to work. Thank you for the memories and God bless you and Debbie."

Magic of radio

After Bailey's departure, she remained in long-distance communication with Bobby and even rescued him from dead air on the day he announced his retirement. From two thousand miles away, she was able to remotely bypass a power failure in his studio, allowing him to reconnect and resume his news bulletin.

"Is this a sign? Did somebody up there not want me to make this announcement?" Bobby wondered out loud.

"Once again, that's the magic of radio," he said, thanking Bailey for getting him back on the air so he could tell the audience that he would soon be going off the air.

A little traveling music please

Throughout his final week, he promoted a station-sponsored concert, Live and Let Die: The Music of Paul McCartney, featuring Tony Kishman, who starred in the Broadway musical *Beatlemania*. The event was a fundraiser for Hope of Deliverance, a nonprofit dog rescue organization. Bobby and Debbie adopted their pit bull from the group and made a $5,000 donation to support adoptions and veterinary care at rural animal shelters.

Before he introduced the concert at the Fox Tucson Theatre, his cofounders at The Drive and the station's new owner presented him with a plaque inscribed: "Bobby Rich—in recognition of your fifty-plus year distinguished broadcast career. The radio industry has benefited from your outstanding talent as an on-air personality and your programming genius. The audience has enjoyed your wit and great music selection. Your colleagues have benefited from you as a mentor and a friend. In grateful appreciation: Fletcher McCusker, Jim Arnold, and Amador Bustos."

On one of his final shows, Bobby fact-checked his own retirement news release, noting the career actually spanned more than sixty years. "It started when I was fifteen and I'm now seventy-seven. So, it's about time," he said before playing "Last Dance" by Donna Summer.

'Somebody call my mom!'

On Friday, May 12, 2023, Bobby wistfully told his audience, "My last day on the radio . . . I've never said that before." Once again updating his profile and age, he joked, "I'm retiring after a million years. I'm a million and seven."

Over the course of his four-hour shift, he composed a farewell and apologized for an industry beset by economic forces.

"I just absolutely love what I do," Bobby said. "Even when it wasn't so wonderful, I was loving it still. And that will never end. And I'm sorry for what's happened to radio overall. But it's still important, and it will always be there for you and for me. And I'll keep listening and The Drive will go on, with the music and the format and the people."

After naming each member of the air staff that he hired, including Matt Gentry, whom he recommended to succeed him as PD, Bobby professed, "I love everybody we have here at The Drive. Matt is among my eight favorites."

"When in doubt, play your all-time favorite classic songs. That's what I'm doing today," he advised, breaking format with Van Halen's version of "Happy Trails," which had never been played on The Drive.

"I haven't made any notes for this moment, believe it or not," Bobby said, segueing into his signature musical signoff, "Beginnings."

"The song that has begun and ended everything I've done since it came out in 1971," he roared over the opening of Chicago's driving jazz-rock anthem that marked his first and last air shifts in Davenport, then Miami, New Haven, San Diego, Los Angeles, Seattle, and Tucson.

"And I always say, it's only the beginning . . ." as the fanfare of horns, guitars, and drums punctuated his parting words. "There's only a beginning every time you want to have one. So, there doesn't need to be an ending, just another beginning."

Bobby's radio journey spanning eleven states, fifteen cities, and two dozen stations came down to a half-minute intro on a seven-and-a-half-minute song. Emotion filled the voice of a man who had started in broadcasting before he was old enough to drive.

Talking up the record before the vocals hit, he exclaimed, "I'm Bobby Rich! Somebody call my mom and tell her to come and pick me up, I'm through! And I love you!"

His time as program director and morning DJ was over. Turning off the microphone, Bobby cranked up the studio monitor, pushed his chair back from the control board, took a deep breath, and listened to his signoff music play out to precisely ten o'clock. He had no idea what would follow the top-of-the-hour station ID.

In yet another magical moment of Bobby's life, a song by the Beatles was next up on The Drive. He exited to an apropos aloha: "Hello, Goodbye."

World Boogie Headquarters, aka Bobby's home studio, Tucson, Feb. 9, 2013. (Photo by Pat Gaffey)

Clock by East Coast Eddie, featuring The Drive Tucson air staff. Clockwise from top: Bobby, Ken Carr, Leslie Lois, Hill Bailey, Mikey Esparza, Jim Arnold, Bobby, Brenda Catalina, Matt Gentry, Hill, Billy Repka, Maria Mendez.

Chapter 51

Say Goodnight, Gracie

At the culmination of his more than six-decade career, dozens of radio friends recorded voice messages for playback during Bobby's last week on the air at KDRI.

Brother-in-law, confidant, and longtime programming partner Rob Sisco collected greetings from broadcasters who had worked with and for Bobby in Los Angeles, New York, Philadelphia, San Diego, Seattle, Toledo, and Tucson.

A sample of their well wishes included these:

- Michael O'Shea (WJIM) – "Hello Bobby, congratulations on this next chapter in your life. Hope you and Debbie get a lot of enjoyment out of more spare time and I hope you take a baseball bat to that alarm clock. We have so many memories going back to the Happy Machine in Toledo, to when you and I were roomies in Los Angeles in Sherman Oaks, sitting in the spa dreaming up radio promotions, and we were both working at competing stations."
- Charlie Van Dyke (KSTT) – "Hi Bobby, just wanted to add my congratulations on your retirement. Fifty years in broadcasting, outstanding. You'll have some more free time now. I understand your parole agent says it won't be long before you can travel out of the state. So, something to look forward to."
- John Leader (R&R) – "Hey, Bobby, this is your older-than-you

broadcast buddy from Los Angeles. I kind of shudder to think how many times you must have played "You Light Up My Life." Enjoy sleeping in, staying up late, and not having to say what time it is every four minutes! I sincerely wish you the best."

- Gene Knight (B-100) – "Bobby Rich is the greatest innovator that I've ever worked with. He invented the B-100 brand that was copied all over the country. And could Bobby ever spot and develop talent. Bob R, best wishes for your retirement, from Green R, and I already know whatever you do, it's gonna be great."
- Steve Wexler (KMXZ) – "Hey, Bobby, first-time caller, longtime listener. My first general manager job was in Tucson in the late '90s. Here I was, moving across the country to join you and the team, and I remember your passion, your creativity, your mischief for sure. But what I most recall was your kindness and your big heart. You welcomed me and my family to the desert, and you helped make it feel like home for us."
- Ken Levine (B-100) – "Hi, Bobby, Beaver Cleaver, sending you congratulations on your long overdue retirement. It has been quite a career. I guess you began, as people know, as a booth announcer for the NBC Blue Network. What people don't know is that you coined the popular term "hitbound" since you were the very first person to play the brand-new record by George and Ira Gershwin, "Embraceable You." So now enjoy your retirement and maybe, finally, you can get a real job."
- Scott Shannon (Z-100) – "Hello friends and radio lovers all around the world. Congratulations to Bobby Rich on one of the greatest broadcast careers known to man. He could still be going if he wanted to, people still love him, and he still sounds great. Bobby, congratulations, man, you're one of the best who have ever cracked a microphone. Shannon out."

- Hill Bailey (KDRI) – "Hi Bobby, I learned so much from being your partner for four years. You have a truly kind heart, a ridiculous sense of humor, and I know you will be missed every single day. Now it's your chance to sit back, relax, and let somebody else do the work. No wait, that was our show! Ha ha ha. I love you. Congratulations."
- Charley Steiner (KSTT) – "You and I go back a very long time, KSTT in Davenport on the banks of the Mississippi River, WAVZ in New Haven, and at 99X where you paired me with the great Jay Thomas. Three different stations in the formative years of my career. And fifty something years later, they're still trotting me out there every day as the voice of the Dodgers. I would not be where I am had it not been for the time you and I spent together. I learned so much about radio, the ability to communicate with our listeners, from you. You're one of the great broadcasting talents I have ever worked with. I am not kidding. I can't thank you enough. Congratulations on a race so gracefully run."

Chapter 52

People in My Life

Bobby's retirement in 2023 did not bring an end to the joyful memories and melancholy tears that marked his parting at KDRI The Drive Tucson.

The silencing of his public microphone created time for personal reflection. Adjusting to a new daily routine without a dreaded morning alarm clock, he prepared a gratitude list.

"All the women in my life contributed greatly to whatever success I've enjoyed," Bobby said, "starting with my mom, Marge, and my sisters, Jan and Marcia. They were my first audience when I was just a kid with a hobby shop radio kit.

"My first wife, Judy, helped me get started professionally, and it wasn't easy on her and our boys, Bryan and Jeff. They were so supportive, especially moving around the country as often as I did in the early years."

After remarrying in 1984, Bobby made two more career moves before establishing a permanent home in Tucson with his wife, Debbie, and their daughters, Laine and Lesley. "Without Debbie's love and understanding, I never would have lasted all these years going to work at five in the morning," he confided. "She and the girls gave me the strength and stability to stay grounded and creative."

Contemplating his life and longevity in radio, Bobby added, "I have to express my deepest appreciation to the people whose kindness and guidance had the most profound impact on my career."

Those influential friends and family are listed below, in alphabetical order.

- Erica Farber – "Erica was an exceptional leader in the broadcasting industry and in my career. She hired me at 99X in New York and did everything to protect me from external consultants and a well-known radio researcher who thought he was a programmer but was out of his league telling client stations what they should do with the data he generated. Erica was in it to win and proved herself as a GM in the biggest radio market in America. We had some success at WXLO, but not enough for the corporate bosses who pressured her to make a format change. When she had to finally let me go, we had a pity party to see who could cry harder."
- Sam Holman – "As my first program director, Sam was fantastic and taught me stuff at WOHO in Toledo that I hadn't learned on my own yet. He had already conquered major market radio at WLS in Chicago and WABC in New York. When Sam shared some of the rules that big stations required their jocks to master, I was excited because he'd given me an advantage over my competitors who didn't have that information. He was real smart, fun, lovable, and a huge influence on me."
- Bwana Johnny – "I met Bwana when we were eighteen or nineteen and both of us had just made the leap to Corvallis. He'd grown up in Portland, hung out with jocks from KISN and absorbed tons of information, reading memos from their PD on what to do or not do on the air. Our friendship started with an elaborate practical joke, and he got me good. Bwana was a very funny jock, did all his own character voices, and people were drawn to him. The wardrobe I chose for the *B Morning Zoo* in San Diego was copied

from Bwana's pith helmet and safari outfit in Miami Beach. He also worked in New York and at KJR in Seattle. Long after we met, Bwana would send me programming ideas, always creative."

- Scott Kenyon – "As a high school intern in 1967, Scott was my phone screener on the night shift at WOHO in Toledo. Then I hired him in Davenport. Using his real name Ben, we almost paired up as the Rich Brothers, Bobby and Benjie. But on his second day in town, he got his draft notice and went back to Toledo for college and a student deferment. He had a solo career as a major market DJ and PD in Denver and San Francisco and worked in Kansas City and Salt Lake City. We teamed up again in 1984 at B-100 in San Diego. Scott inspired me with his creativity and willingness to push boundaries. He definitely liked being on the edge. Some of his wild ideas couldn't be used on the radio unless I cleaned them up. I'd tell him, 'Okay, we've got to get serious now,' and he'd say, 'I am being serious!' Scott was more of a brother than I could ever imagine. When he passed in 2011, I went weeks without words to share. I quite literally think about him every single day. Forever."
- Mike Kinosian – "We met in 1980 working at Drake-Chenault as national programming consultants. Mike's office was next door to mine. After work we'd drive around LA and just talk about radio. Sometimes I'd have to pull my car over to the side of the road because we'd be laughing so hard. Other times I'd be having a failure of confidence and Mike built me up. He's just a genuine guy with a quick wit and always has the right word or the right phrase. I made him an offer to be one of the Rich Brothers when I was first assembling *the B Morning Zoo*, but he didn't want to leave his dream job at Drake-Chenault where he stayed for five years. Since then, Mike's been a terrific writer and editor at *Radio & Records, Inside Radio, Talkers* magazine, and *RadioInfo*,

covering the AC and Hot AC formats that I specialized in. So, he didn't join me on the air at B-100, but he's always been there for me as a great friend."

- Ken Levine – "When KSEA in San Diego flipped formats and quit playing Top 40, Beaver Cleaver and their entire air staff got blown out the week before Christmas in '74. Beaver, whose real name is Ken Levine, went back to comedy writing in LA. As soon as we got B-100 up and running a few months later, I offered him a weekend jock shift whenever he wanted. Beaver would call me on a Thursday to be added to the DJ schedule and then catch a PSA flight from LAX down to San Diego to do a Saturday and Sunday show. I'd take him to dinner, we'd hang out, and he'd do his shift and stay at the Travolator motel a block from KFMB's studios at Fifth and Ash. Beaver was funny as hell, had a one-liner for every song he played, and never repeated them. If he played a hit song three times on a seven to midnight shift, he'd have a different line each time."
- John Long – "My friendship with John started in Iowa when I was working in Davenport at KSTT and John was in Cedar Rapids, doing a similar style of radio. Then he went off to New Haven and I moved to Miami, but I wasn't happy there. John bailed me out and brought me to New Haven in 1972. The whole time I was at WAVZ with John, he was sharing my tapes and production with Paul Drew, his boss in Los Angeles. That led to my hiring at KHJ. A couple years later, John was a big help to me when I put the original B-100 on the air."
- Pat O'Day – "The one person it all goes back to for me is Pat O'Day in Seattle. I got inspired listening to him on KJR and that became the one and only station where I wanted to work. A brilliant entertainer, his voice was captivating, his characters were

funny, and he dominated radio ratings in Seattle. To this day, I think back on how much I enjoyed listening to KJR in the '60s, when he was DJ, PD, and ultimately GM. Pat's influence was so huge that he shaped the station's overall identity and listening experience. His on-air style became the personality, or 'stationality' of KJR."

- Michael O'Shea – "Our friendship started in 1966 at WJIM in Lansing, based on our mutual love of radio. Michael left for a job at WOHO and recommended me when they were looking for another jock. So that's how I got to Toledo. We've remained close even through an awkward and difficult time when we ran competing stations in Seattle. We battled for listeners, and his station beat the shit out of mine. Outside of that professional rivalry, Michael would always drop everything and dive into making suggestions and coaching me in areas I didn't know as much about like station management and ownership."
- Paul Palmer – "Paul was the first GM who understood the sound I wanted to create and trusted me to make it happen. He'd reel me in as needed but let me program the radio station. The first time Paul called me into his office to discuss ratings, he pointed to the book and said, 'Well, looks like our numbers are a little bit soft in this particular demo.' I tried to reassure him, 'Yeah, I think we're going to come out of it.' To my surprise, he asked, 'Would it help if we ran a big contest with a $10,000 prize?' Without hesitation, I replied, 'Yes, I'm quite positive it would.' Two years later, we got a great ratings book, and Paul told me, 'Hey, we kicked ass. Why don't you take ten grand for a new contest to keep the momentum going.' I realized he budgeted that promotional money but never told me until he felt the timing was right. I was not accustomed to that kind of big thinking. B-100 is where I had the most

fun ever—first in the '70s and again in the '80s. Both times, it was Paul who gave me the freedom, and I loved him for it."

- Debbie Rich – "Debbie is my sweetheart and partner for life. We've gotten married to each other three different times. It's a true love story. The theme of our first wedding was 'Partners for Life.' We took a little break a couple of times but couldn't let go. We divorced, got back together, and remarried. After a second separation we didn't divorce but reconciled and got married again. I've always said Debbie had most of the best ideas I ever claimed. She has taught me more about my target audience than any other source. When we had financial problems at KTZN, she came in and served as office manager, working for no pay as we tried to keep it together and stay in business. Whenever I felt challenged by all the bullshit from management and consultants, which was fairly constant, Debbie was my sounding board and helped me make better decisions."
- Rob Sisco – "I've enjoyed a very close friendship with Rob, personally and professionally, even before I married his twin sister, Debbie. He's more like a brother to me than a brother-in-law. I hired Rob to be my assistant PD in New York, and he was my only choice for PD when I became a GM in Seattle. In between, he was a PD in Pittsburgh and San Francisco, and a top executive at *Radio & Records* and Nielsen. We've just always worked well together. I taught him everything I know about radio, and when I ran out of stuff to teach, I started learning things from him. Some of the stuff he picked up from me he liked enough to use at other stations. A best friend and programming partner who encouraged me when I was struggling, Rob understands and shares my philosophy, corrects me when I'm wrong, and helped me refine my radio playbook."

Chapter 53

But Wait, There's More . . .

Bobby was in good company, choosing to retire in 2023. He joined a list of entertainment legends who decided to quit working that year or at least announced that they would no longer be touring.

During his radio career, Bobby played songs recorded by all of them.

The class of 2023 retirees and their final concert tours included:

- Elton John (Farewell Yellow Brick Road Tour)
- The Eagles (The Long Goodbye Farewell Tour)
- Kenny Loggins (This is It Farewell Tour)
- Foreigner (The Historic Farewell Tour)

Sleeping in

The early days of his retirement took some getting used to. Bobby vowed not to take up golf, pickleball, fishing, hiking, birdwatching, or gardening.

Rewiring his body clock was high on the to-do list. "I figure I've got about forty years of lost sleep to catch up on," the former morning man quipped.

Three months after his final show aired, Bobby posted a Facebook message to celebrate the fourth anniversary of The Drive and express his feelings about his coworkers, their legacy, and the audience.

"Successful radio stations have great people supporting them, fulfill community needs, and are FUN for the staff and the listeners. The Drive has that. Never mind a pandemic (many said we helped you get through it) and a recession.

"We gave you songs you forgot you loved, local and friendly DJs who are companions sharing what's going on, weather alerts, and road reports for your drive. It's been a privilege for me. Here's to many more years of the Drive Tucson."

Bittersweet and magic dust

Six months into retirement, Bobby described what it was like to leave his dream station at the end of a lifelong broadcast journey across America.

"Of course, I was disappointed. I had high hopes that this would be my final hurrah in the radio industry, and I'd go out being a guy who at age seventy-three put a new radio station on the air and took it right to the top.

"The Drive did extremely well, but not as well as many had hoped, much less me, and it's greatly bittersweet. But still a pleasure for me to listen because it's the best sounding thing in Tucson, even though I'm not there to add the magic dust."

Invited to a New Year's Eve broadcast with all the jocks, Bobby returned to the station for the first time as a guest rather than a host. In a festive studio interview, he admitted that sleeping in every morning was nice, but he had not yet adjusted to his new reality as a retiree.

The vibe abides

Matt Gentry, his successor as PD and morning man at The Drive, complimented Bobby for letting his hair grow long and commented, "I always pictured you in the '60s as kind of hippie-ish . . ."

"When I look back at those days," Bobby said, "I realize that I was playing that role, the hip guy or the hippie guy. And I never did drugs. But the people I worked with, especially the record promotion people, they all lived that way, you know, rock'n'roll, sex, drugs, and all that. So, to fit in, I borrowed some of their vibe.

"That's where I got it. I would write the promotional announcements for station contests and stuff, and I would find out from all my friends who were druggies or hippie types what the hip terms were and then I'd use them on the air."

He told his former colleagues, "One of the great things about being a disc jockey, as everyone in this room knows because you do it every day, is you can be anybody you want to be on the radio."

Bobby's voice was heard again on The Drive when Gentry paid tribute to a select group of groundbreaking air personalities in Tucson. The "Summer of Legends" program also honored "Sunny Jim" Arnold and Adrienne Walker. Bobby's segment included a tape from his high school DJ days and other recorded relics of a life in radio.

Eighteen months after stepping away from the broadcast booth, Bobby's biggest challenge was finding his new identity without a microphone or morning show.

Reconnecting with friends in and out of the business, he and Debbie took road trips to beach towns in Mexico and central California, vacationed in San Diego, and attended two radio reunions.

He created an atmosphere

At one of the DJ get-togethers, Bobby met up with industry legend Dave "Your Duke" Sholin, Top 40 jock and music director at KFRC San Francisco during its glory years. They worked together when Bobby was program director of 99X in New York and Sholin was national music director of the RKO Radio chain.

"He's fearless and honest," Sholin said in 2024. "And that comes across on the air. I think that's what connected him to listeners. In San Diego, what Bobby brought to the Hot AC format was that incredible group at B-100 and the personality of the station. He created an atmosphere, and the people around him would be doing the same thing because he was the leader."

Joel Denver, former DJ, PD, and Contemporary Hit Radio editor at *Radio & Records* commented, "Bobby was just so positive and so creative." After publishing his own radio industry news site for nearly thirty years, Denver said of Bobby, "A brilliant air talent and programmer . . . always with a realistic edge. Not a guy just pumping smoke up your ass."

Keeping radio alive

Nearly two years removed from his last air shift, Bobby acknowledged making some minor modifications to his daily routine.

"I keep working on releasing my need to listen to the radio all day long," he said. "The Drive is still the station I love to listen to, though I do check out other formats.

"I've developed an appreciation for modern country because the new music is more mass appeal than country used to be and some of it has a pretty strong rock flavor to it." Citing the crossover appeal of Chris Stapleton, he also gave a shoutout to pop star Dua Lipa. "I watched her concert with Elton John at Royal Albert Hall. She knocked me out; I was so impressed."

In late 2024, Bobby found enjoyment as an unpaid adviser for two former employees who followed in his footsteps as program directors. He also offered guidance for a startup oldies station and established a website to promote his book.

The pro bono programming assistance kept him quasi-involved in a lifelong obsession, he explained. "Keeping radio alive. Sharing some wisdom. And specializing in the over-50 age group that's being ignored.

"It's too much work for me to run anything, but I'm willing to help out others who appreciate my consulting advice," Bobby said.

"I don't want to take credit. I just want to not be forgotten."

Additional facts, photos and airchecks from Bobby's career can be found on his website bobbyrichradio.com, where you can also send questions, comments, complaints and compliments.

Bobby Rich and Pat Gaffey at radio reunion in San Diego, Nov. 16, 2024.

Acknowledgments

The magic of radio requires a band of unseen helpers who make it possible for the voice of a DJ to appear out of thin air. Likewise, an invisible circle of people was essential in helping to make this book of a DJ's life in radio appear in print. I am thankful to longtime friends and newfound acquaintances who kindly offered encouragement, ideas, and know-how that contributed to a better biography of the boogiemaster Bobby Rich. My foremost appreciation goes to David Gleason, broadcaster, historian, and webmaster extraordinaire who digitized millions of pages of radio magazines and newspapers including *Broadcasting, Billboard, The Gavin Report, Radio & Records, Cashbox,* and *Record World.* His online archive was extremely valuable in my research, allowing examination of these industry publications for music and programming news from past decades. Gleason earned the inaugural "Excellence in Broadcast Preservation Award" from the Library of American Broadcasting Foundation for establishing his free online library at www.worldradiohistory.com. Dave Coopman's comprehensive history *Someplace Special—KSTT* was another excellent resource for information on that station and its staff from 1968–1972. Airheads Radio Survey Archive, also dedicated to preserving broadcast history, contained useful data on DJs, hit songs, and stations across the country. Reference librarian Hang Nguyen and her colleague Cynthia Dietz at the State Historical Society of Iowa located out-of-print research materials. Reference archivist Elaine Price helped me access the Washington State Historical Society's photo collection. Frank Anthony, keeper of *B Morning Zoo* airchecks, loaned original cassette tapes stored in his garage since the 1980s. Mark Gleason and Wild Bill Calhoun unearthed articles, interviews, surveys, and memos from the 1970s. Additional tips and recordings were provided by Rob Sisco and Tony Pepper. Broadcast engineer Gary Stigall provided technical consultation. My editor John Cannon and graphic designer Tim Brittain delivered professional guidance and expertise. Historian and teacher Richard Demeter volunteered his proofreading skill. My family gave me moral support. Taking classes with writing teacher Judy Reeves strengthened my craft and resolve. Published authors Joyce Gatta, John Freeman, Bill Tuli, and Karl Arthur generously shared their experience. I took inspiration from eminent writers Candice Millard, William Finnegan, TJ Newman, and Bernie Taupin. To all the above, thank you very much indeed.

About the Author

Pat Gaffey is a former broadcast journalist who wrote and reported more than 30,000 radio newscasts on seven stations in California. Born in San Francisco, he grew up in Los Angeles County and in Hong Kong.

Starting at KPCS Pasadena, KCSN Northridge, and KPOL/KZLA in Hollywood, he first worked with Bobby Rich at KHTZ in Los Angeles. At *American Top 40*, he was a production assistant for Casey Kasem, reading long-distance dedication requests and other fan mail.

His career as a newscaster took him to KKDJ Fresno in 1981 and continued in San Diego for the next twenty years. He rejoined Bobby on the B-100 *B Morning Zoo* in 1984 and later anchored the news on KFMB-AM before moving to KFMB-TV as a government reporter until 2001.

Pat covered the San Diego Padres' 1984 World Series season, the 1987 America's Cup finals in Australia, and the 1995 OJ Simpson criminal trial.

After a second career in corporate communications, nineteen winters in New England and thirteen trips to Japan, he returned to California. Pat enjoys taking road trips, swimming in the Pacific Ocean, and being ignored by white sharks.

Index

G

H

I

J

K

L

M

W

X

Y

Z

Made in the USA
Coppell, TX
03 March 2026